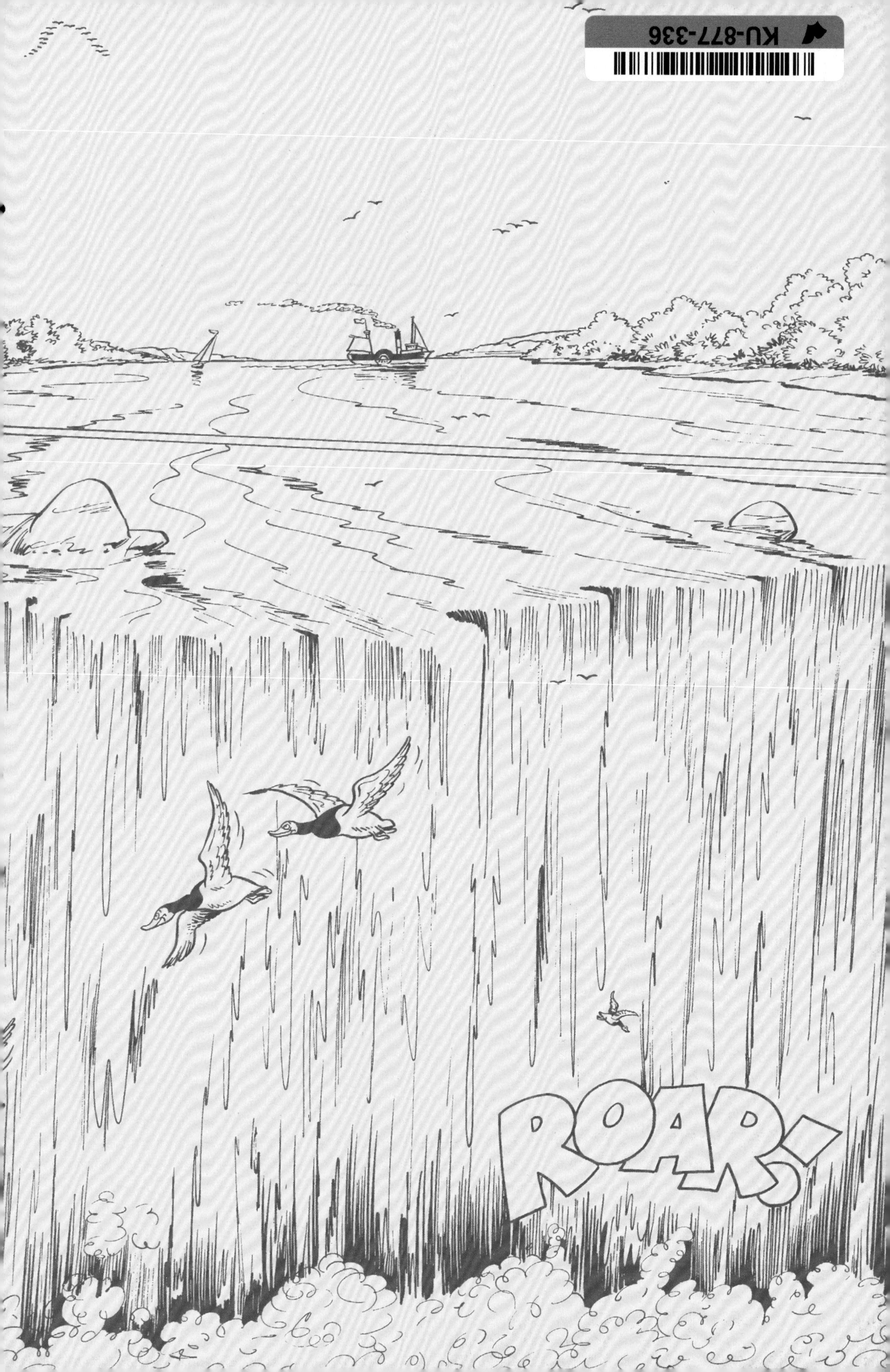
ROAR!

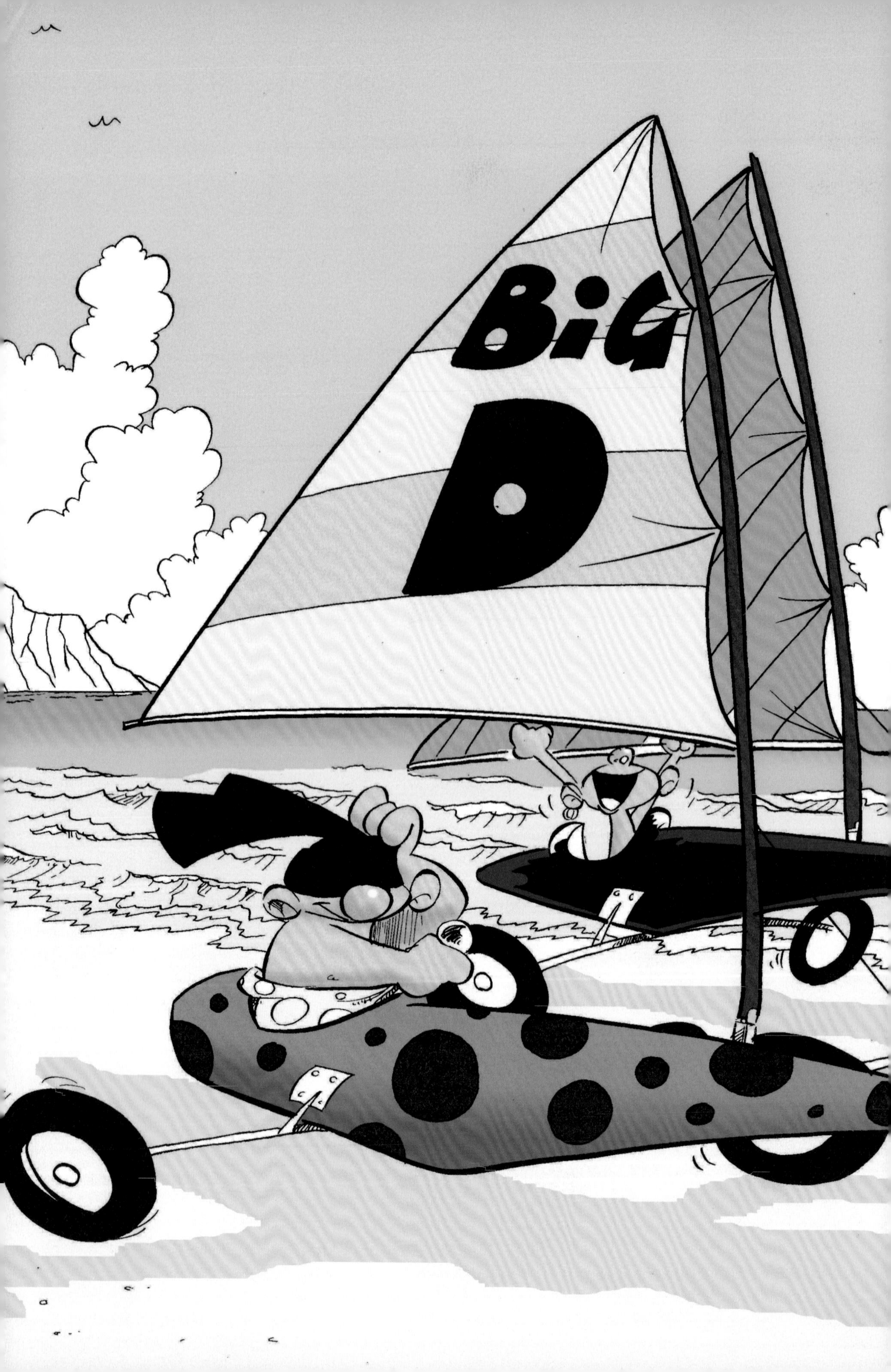
BiG
D

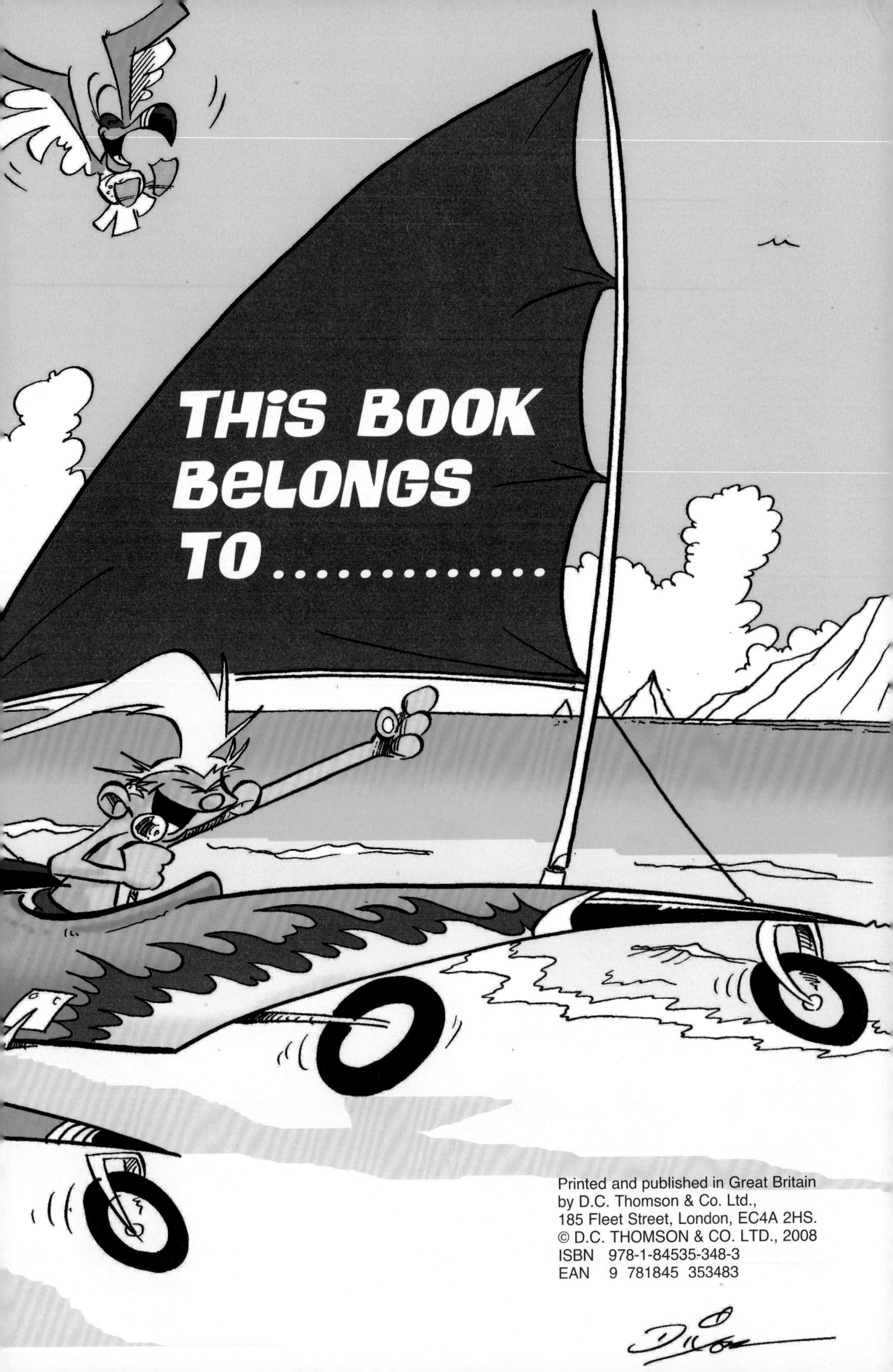
THIS BOOK
BELONGS
TO..............

Printed and published in Great Britain
by D.C. Thomson & Co. Ltd.,
185 Fleet Street, London, EC4A 2HS.

ISBN 978-1-84535-348-3
EAN 9 781845 353483

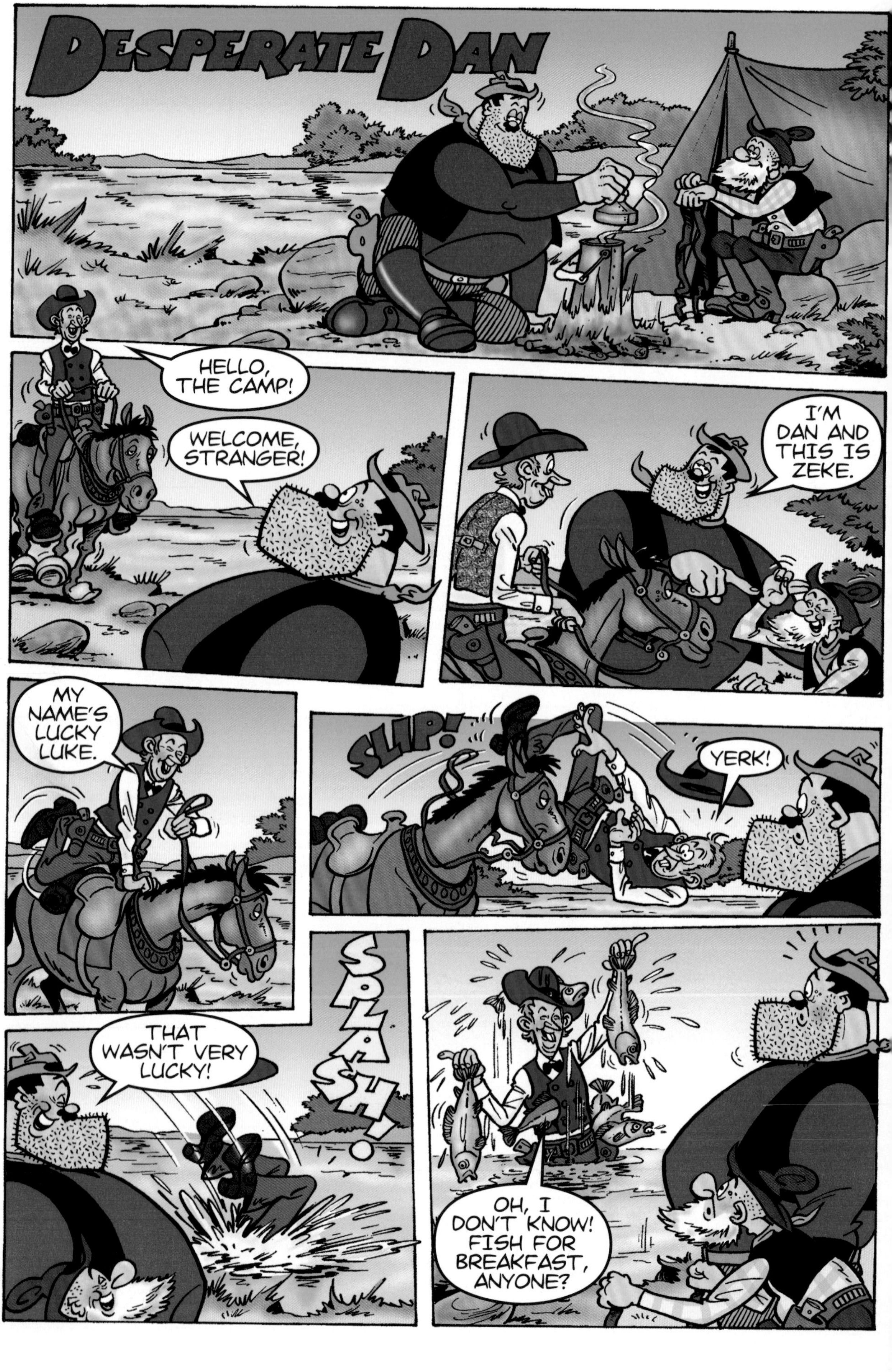
DESPERATE DAN
HELLO, THE CAMP!
WELCOME, STRANGER!
I'M DAN AND THIS IS ZEKE.
MY NAME'S LUCKY LUKE.
SLIP!
YERK!
SPLASH!
THAT WASN'T VERY LUCKY!
OH, I DON'T KNOW! FISH FOR BREAKFAST, ANYONE?

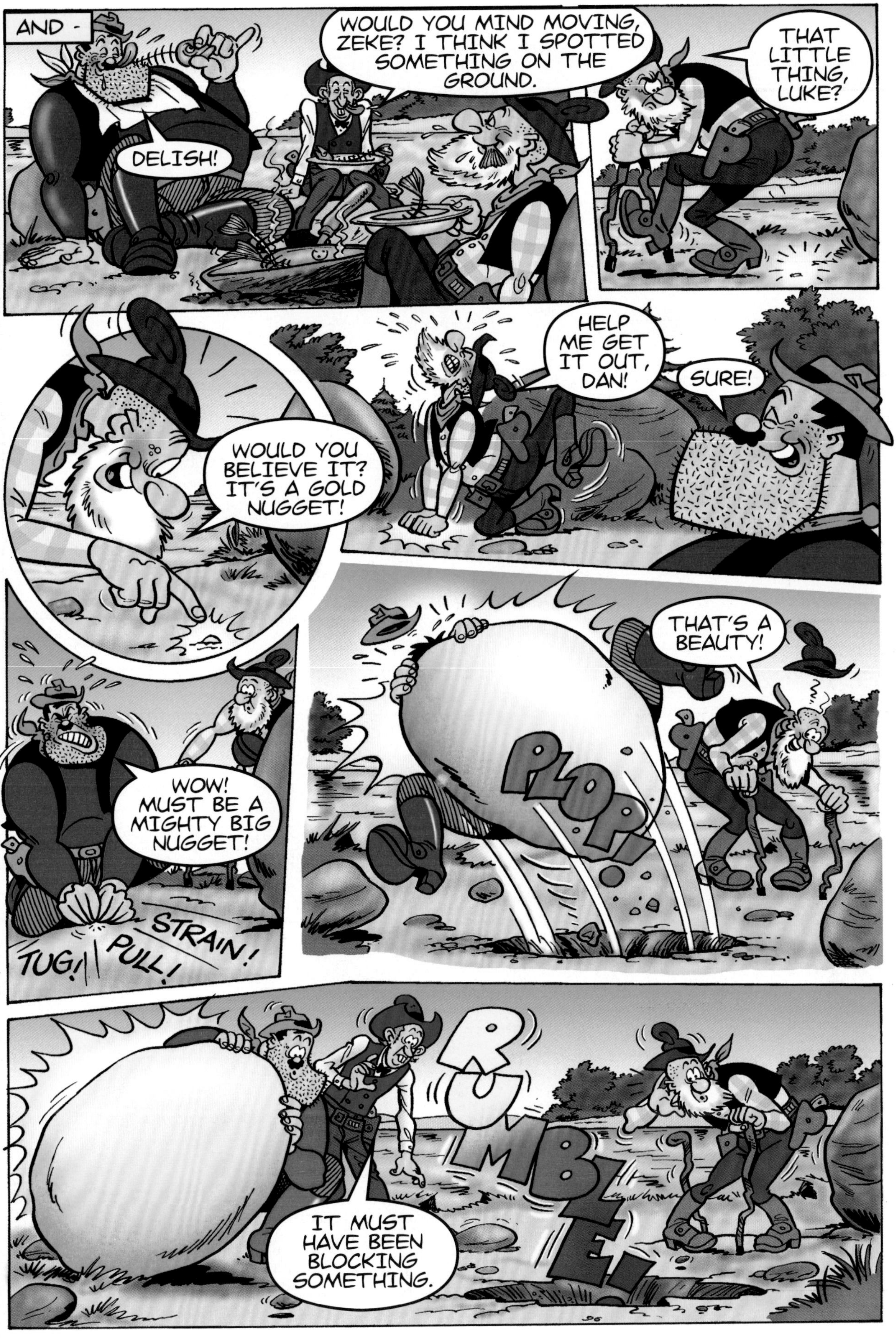
AND -
WOULD YOU MIND MOVING, ZEKE? I THINK I SPOTTED SOMETHING ON THE GROUND.
DELISH!
THAT LITTLE THING, LUKE?
WOULD YOU BELIEVE IT? IT'S A GOLD NUGGET!
HELP ME GET IT OUT, DAN!
SURE!
WOW! MUST BE A MIGHTY BIG NUGGET!
STRAIN!
TUG!
PULL!
PLOP!
THAT'S A BEAUTY!
RUMBLE!
IT MUST HAVE BEEN BLOCKING SOMETHING.

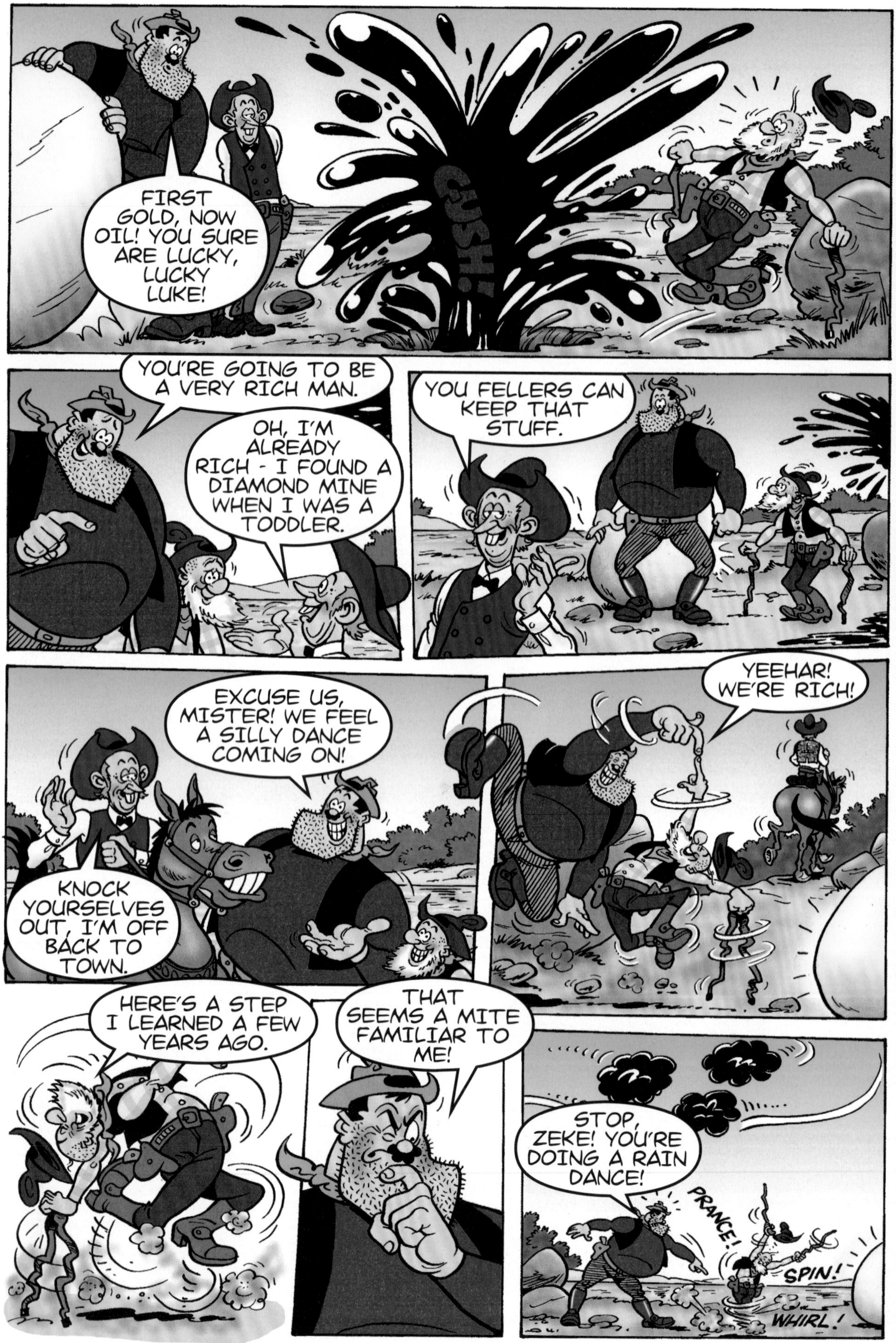
FIRST GOLD, NOW OIL! YOU SURE ARE LUCKY, LUCKY LUKE!
GUSH!
YOU'RE GOING TO BE A VERY RICH MAN.
OH, I'M ALREADY RICH - I FOUND A DIAMOND MINE WHEN I WAS A TODDLER.
YOU FELLERS CAN KEEP THAT STUFF.
EXCUSE US, MISTER! WE FEEL A SILLY DANCE COMING ON!
KNOCK YOURSELVES OUT, I'M OFF BACK TO TOWN.
YEEHAR! WE'RE RICH!
HERE'S A STEP I LEARNED A FEW YEARS AGO.
THAT SEEMS A MITE FAMILIAR TO ME!
STOP, ZEKE! YOU'RE DOING A RAIN DANCE!
PRANCE!
SPIN!
WHIRL!

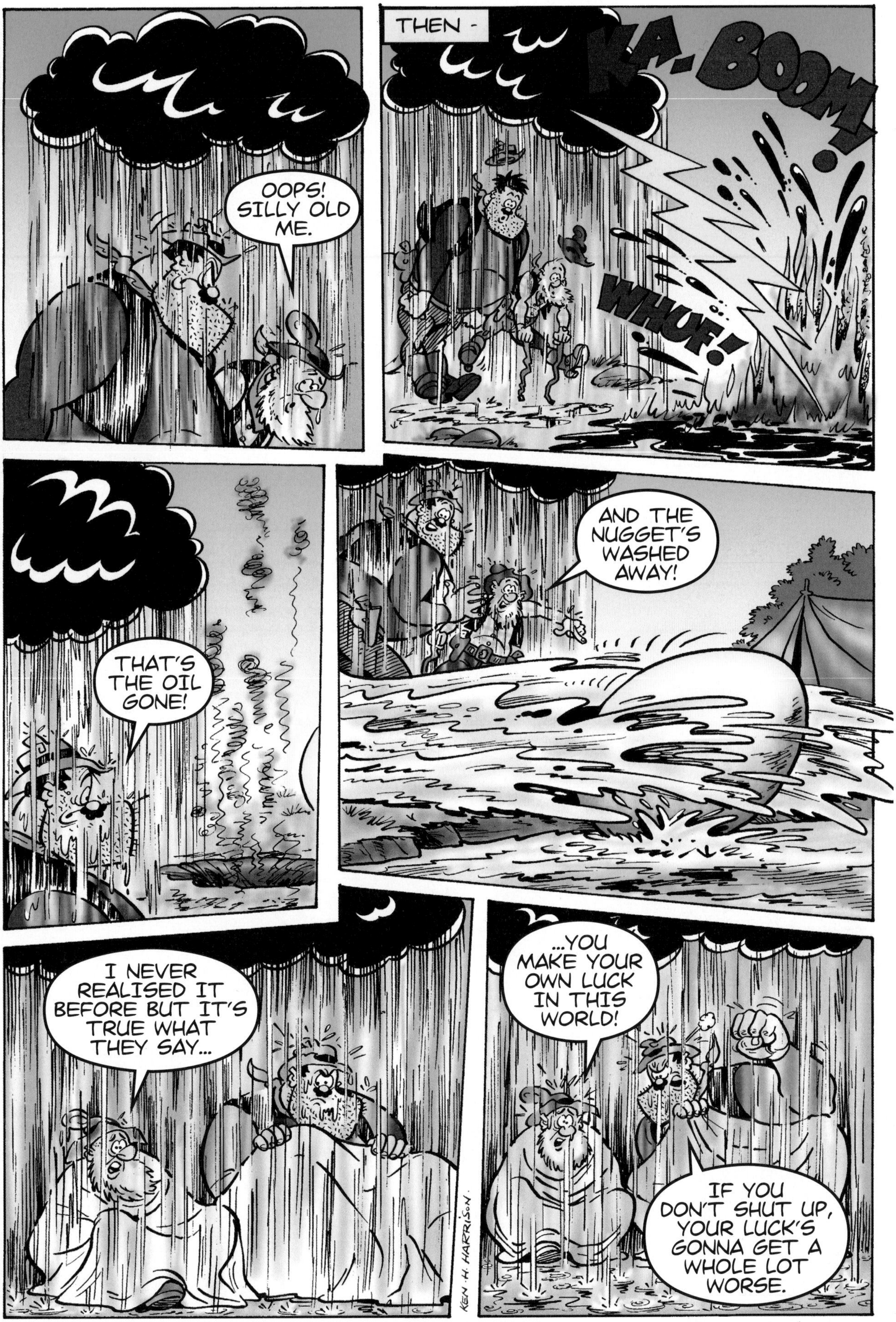
OOPS! SILLY OLD ME.
THEN -
KA-BOOM!
WHUF!
THAT'S THE OIL GONE!
AND THE NUGGET'S WASHED AWAY!
I NEVER REALISED IT BEFORE BUT IT'S TRUE WHAT THEY SAY...
KEN H. HARRISON
...YOU MAKE YOUR OWN LUCK IN THIS WORLD!
IF YOU DON'T SHUT UP, YOUR LUCK'S GONNA GET A WHOLE LOT WORSE.

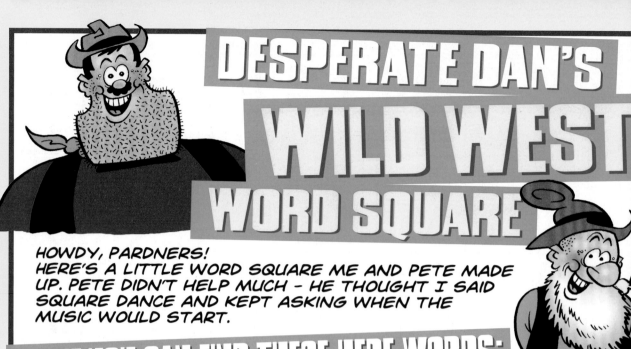

DESPERATE DAN'S WILD WEST WORD SQUARE

HOWDY, PARDNERS!
HERE'S A LITTLE WORD SQUARE ME AND PETE MADE UP. PETE DIDN'T HELP MUCH – HE THOUGHT I SAID SQUARE DANCE AND KEPT ASKING WHEN THE MUSIC WOULD START.

SEE IF YOU CAN FIND THESE HERE WORDS:

SADDLE | LASSO | HORSE
CACTUS | DESERT | DAN
PETE | AGGIE | CREEK
CRITTER | SALOON | DAWG
CACTUSVILLE
BRANDINGIRON

AND IF YER REAL CLEVER, REAL SNEAKY CLEVER, THERE'S AN EXTRA NINE-LETTER WORD HIDDEN FER YOU TO FIND.

WANT A CLUE? IT STARTS WITH AN A.

GOOD LUCK!

N	E	O	E	R	I	E	D	I	E	V	Z
O	L	O	S	A	L	O	O	N	G	L	P
R	L	A	A	D	R	R	T	R	C	D	R
I	I	S	D	I	G	T	T	I	T	A	O
G	V	A	C	R	P	R	R	E	G	D	T
N	S	L	C	R	E	E	K	G	I	D	A
I	U	U	G	L	T	S	I	O	T	A	G
D	T	C	T	T	E	E	R	E	A	R	I
N	C	T	I	C	G	D	B	O	R	R	L
A	A	R	S	L	A	S	S	O	H	D	L
R	C	D	D	W	K	C	A	S	G	T	A
B	D	O	G	S	R	E	E	W	T	R	P

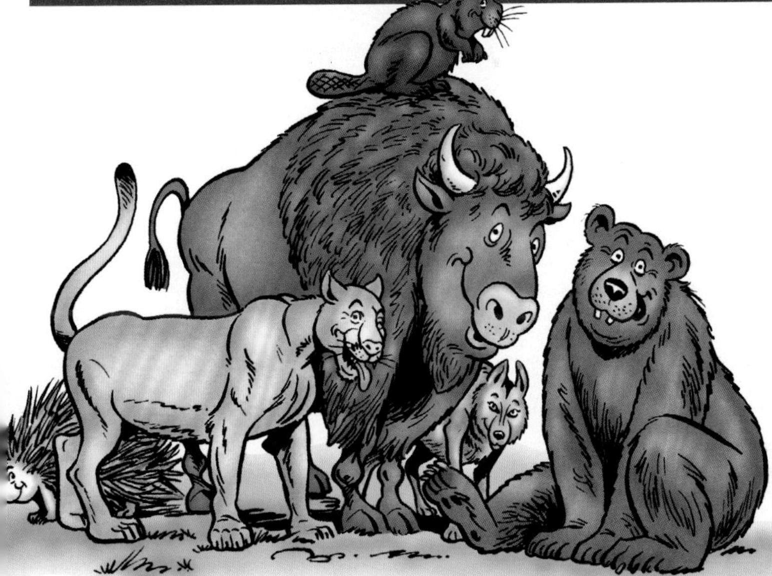

ANSWERS

N	E	O	E	R	I	E	D	I	E	V	Z
O	L	O	S	A	L	O	O	N	G	L	P
R	L	A	A	D	R	R	T	R	C	D	R
I	I	S	D	I	G	T	T	I	T	A	O
G	V	A	C	R	P	R	R	E	G	D	T
N	S	L	C	R	E	E	K	G	I	D	A
I	U	U	G	L	T	S	I	O	T	A	G
D	T	C	T	T	E	E	R	E	A	R	I
N	C	T	I	C	G	D	B	O	R	R	L
A	A	R	S	L	A	S	S	O	H	D	L
R	C	D	D	W	K	C	A	S	G	T	A
B	D	O	G	S	R	E	E	W	T	R	P

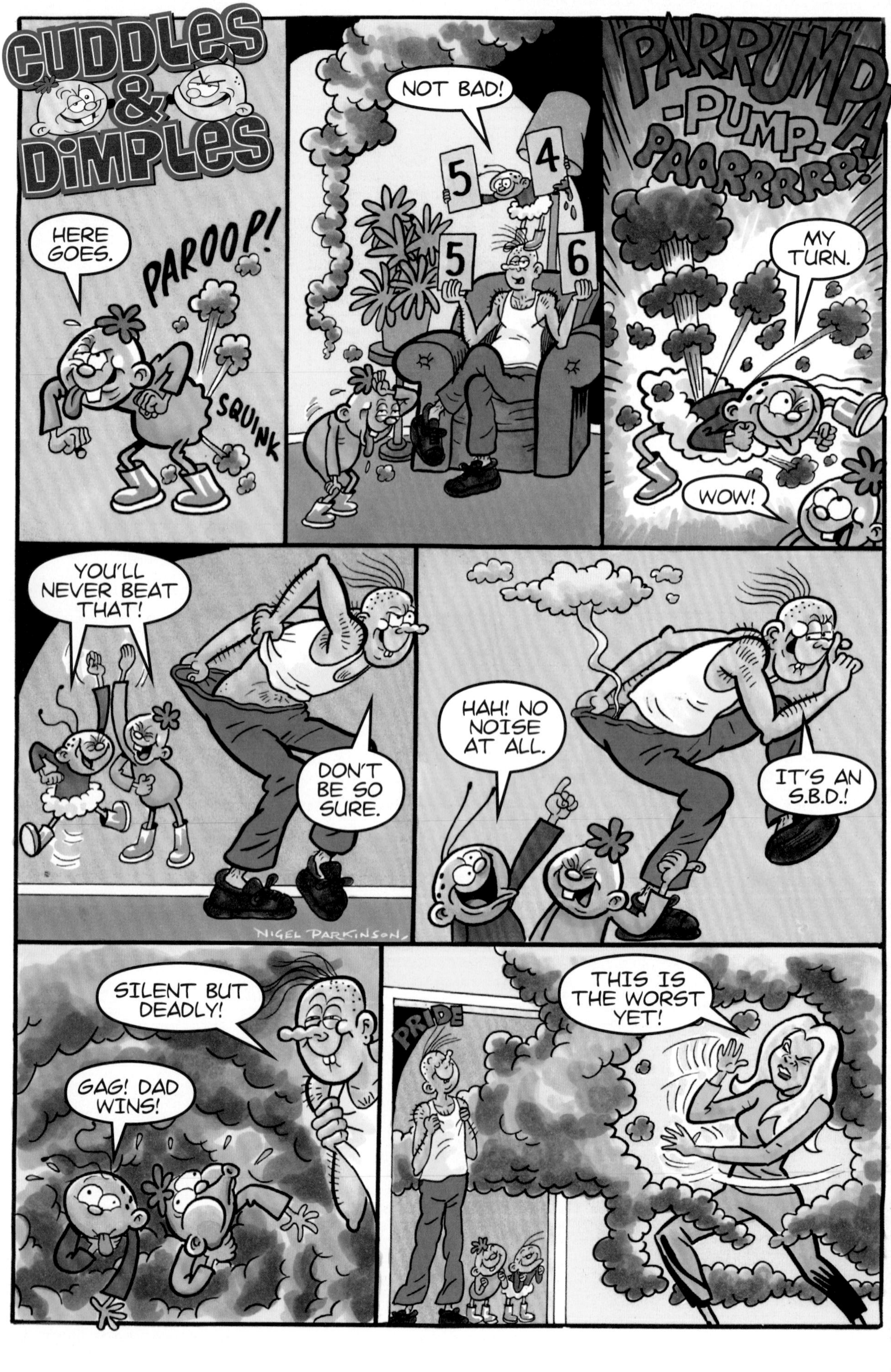
CUDDLES & DIMPLES
HERE GOES.
PAROOP!
SQUINK
NOT BAD!
5
4
5
6
PARRUMPA -PUMP- PAARRRRRP!
MY TURN.
WOW!
YOU'LL NEVER BEAT THAT!
DON'T BE SO SURE.
NIGEL PARKINSON
HAH! NO NOISE AT ALL.
IT'S AN S.B.D.!
SILENT BUT DEADLY!
GAG! DAD WINS!
PRIDE
THIS IS THE WORST YET!

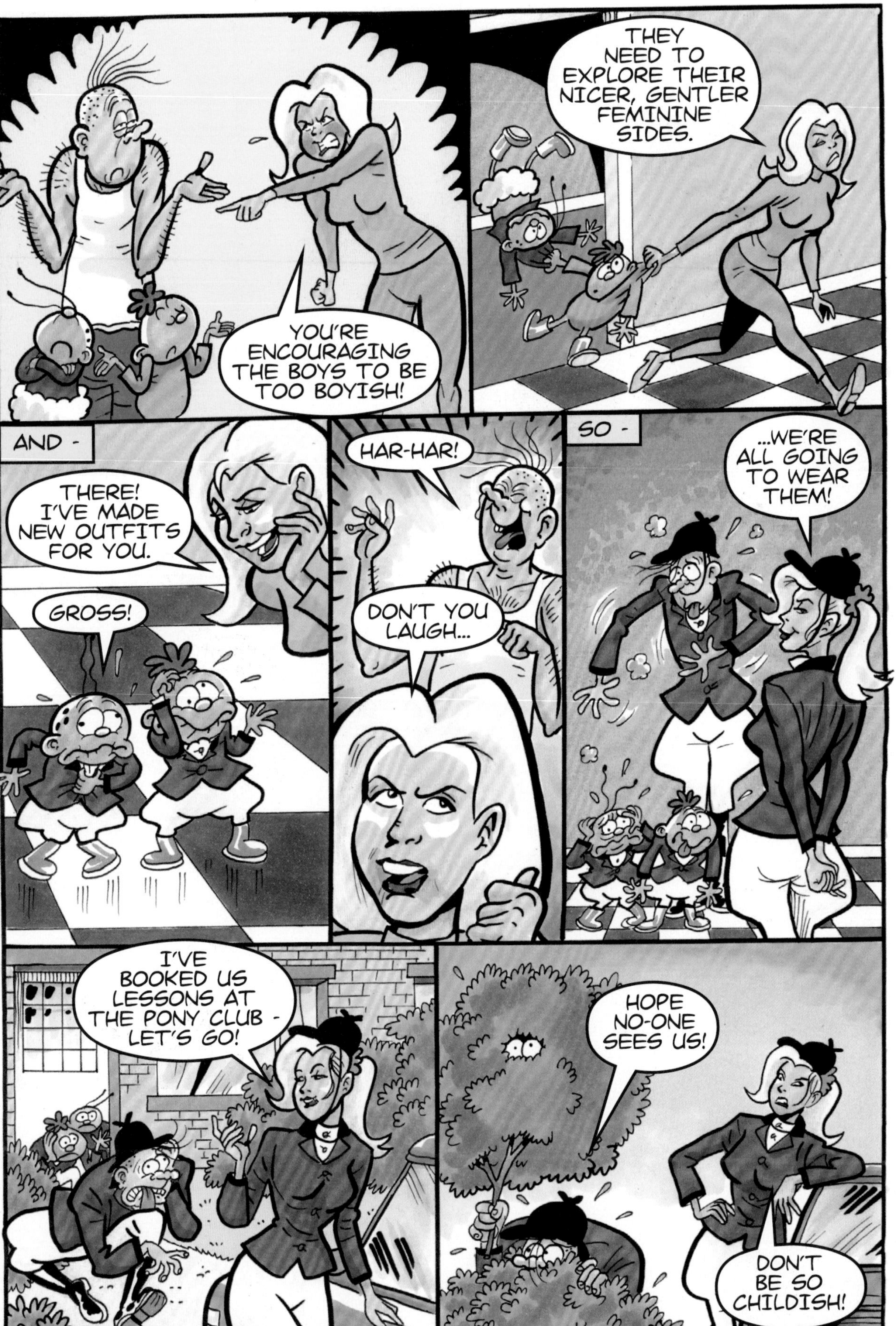
YOU'RE ENCOURAGING THE BOYS TO BE TOO BOYISH!
THEY NEED TO EXPLORE THEIR NICER, GENTLER FEMININE SIDES.
AND -
THERE! I'VE MADE NEW OUTFITS FOR YOU.
GROSS!
HAR-HAR!
DON'T YOU LAUGH...
SO -
...WE'RE ALL GOING TO WEAR THEM!
I'VE BOOKED US LESSONS AT THE PONY CLUB - LET'S GO!
HOPE NO-ONE SEES US!
DON'T BE SO CHILDISH!

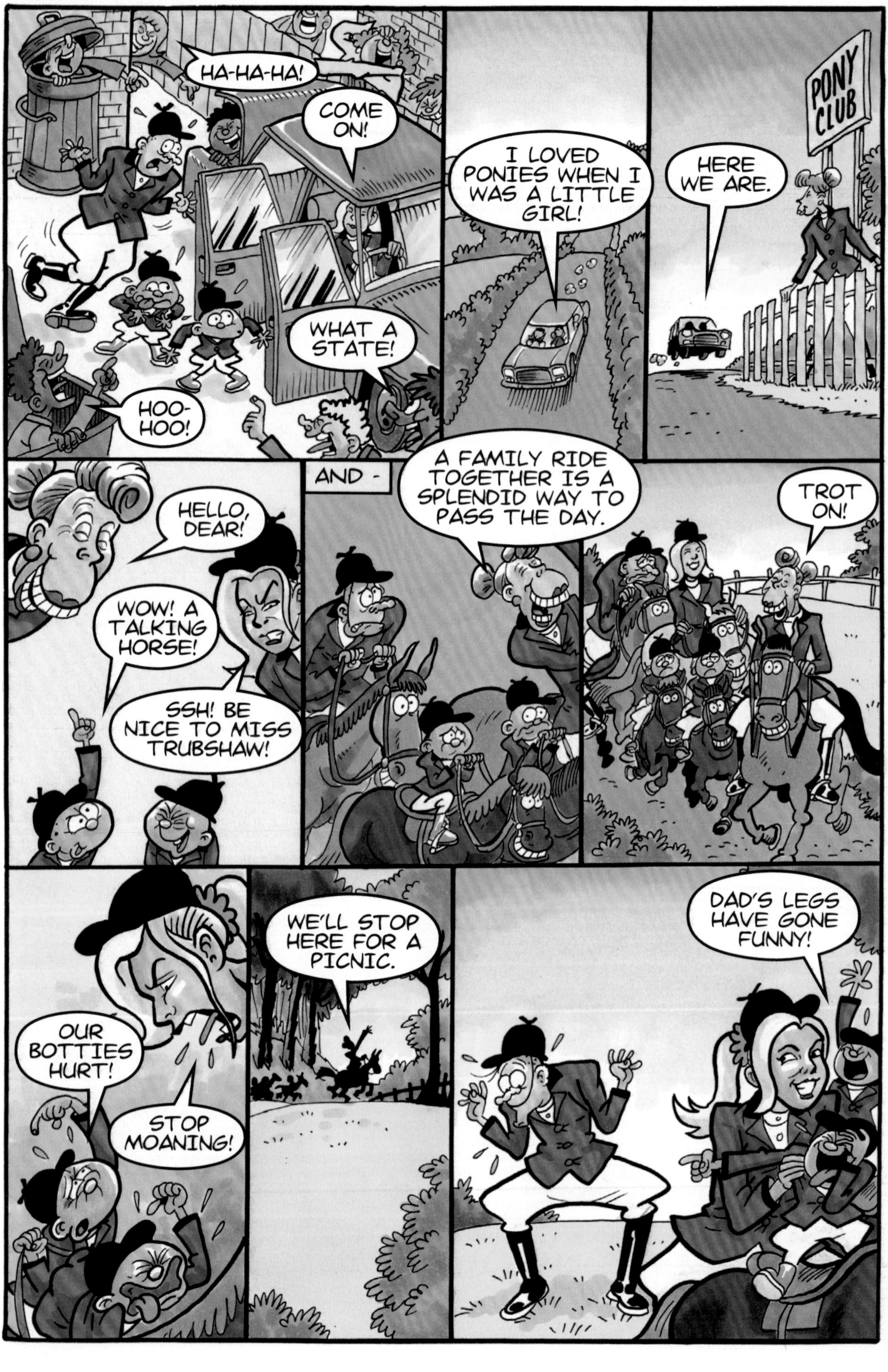
HA-HA-HA!
COME ON!
WHAT A STATE!
HOO-HOO!
I LOVED PONIES WHEN I WAS A LITTLE GIRL!
PONY CLUB
HERE WE ARE.
HELLO, DEAR!
WOW! A TALKING HORSE!
SSH! BE NICE TO MISS TRUBSHAW!
AND -
A FAMILY RIDE TOGETHER IS A SPLENDID WAY TO PASS THE DAY.
TROT ON!
OUR BOTTIES HURT!
STOP MOANING!
WE'LL STOP HERE FOR A PICNIC.
DAD'S LEGS HAVE GONE FUNNY!

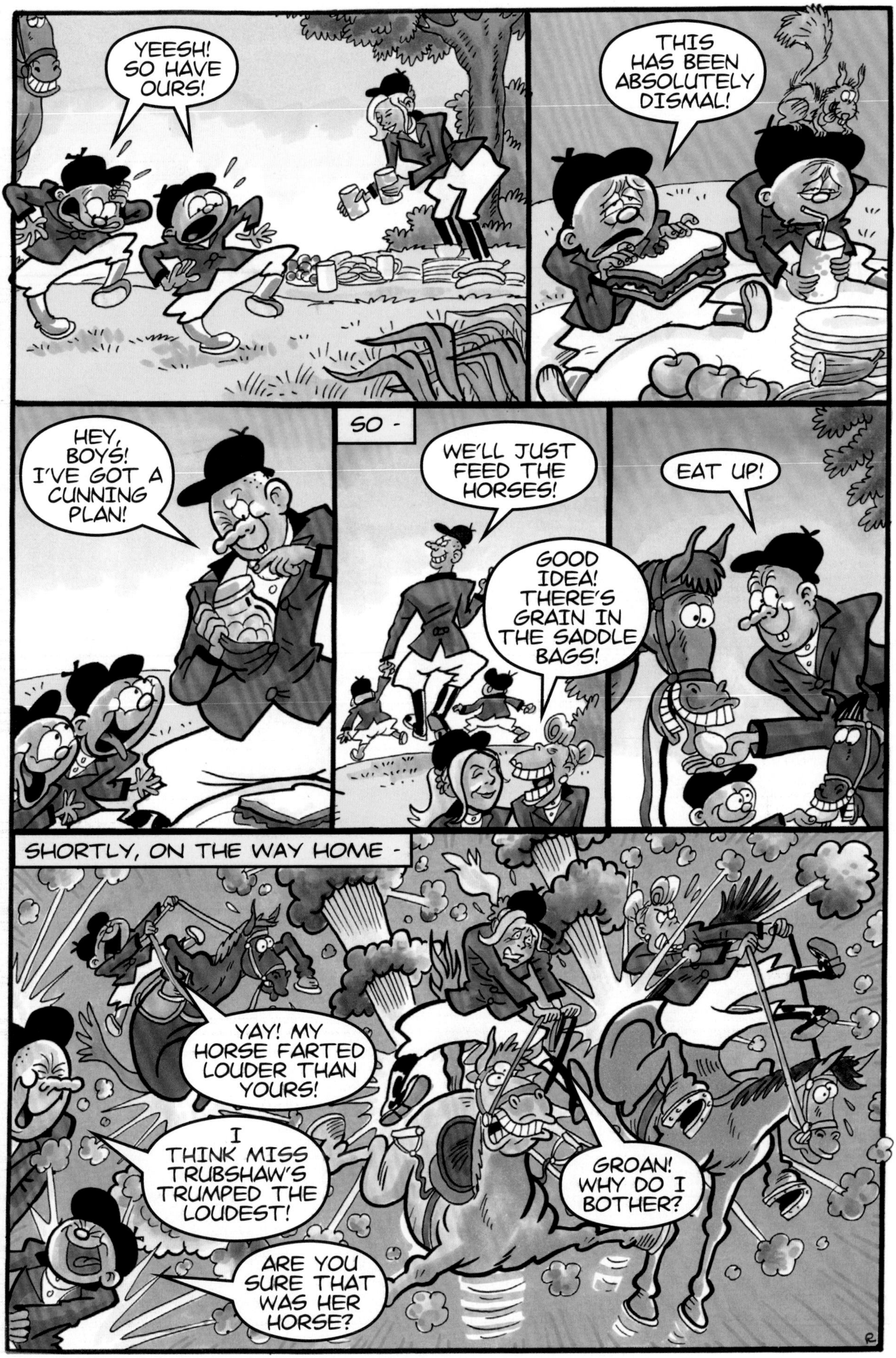
YEESH! SO HAVE OURS!
THIS HAS BEEN ABSOLUTELY DISMAL!
HEY, BOYS! I'VE GOT A CUNNING PLAN!
SO -
WE'LL JUST FEED THE HORSES!
GOOD IDEA! THERE'S GRAIN IN THE SADDLE BAGS!
EAT UP!
SHORTLY, ON THE WAY HOME -
YAY! MY HORSE FARTED LOUDER THAN YOURS!
I THINK MISS TRUBSHAW'S TRUMPED THE LOUDEST!
ARE YOU SURE THAT WAS HER HORSE?
GROAN! WHY DO I BOTHER?

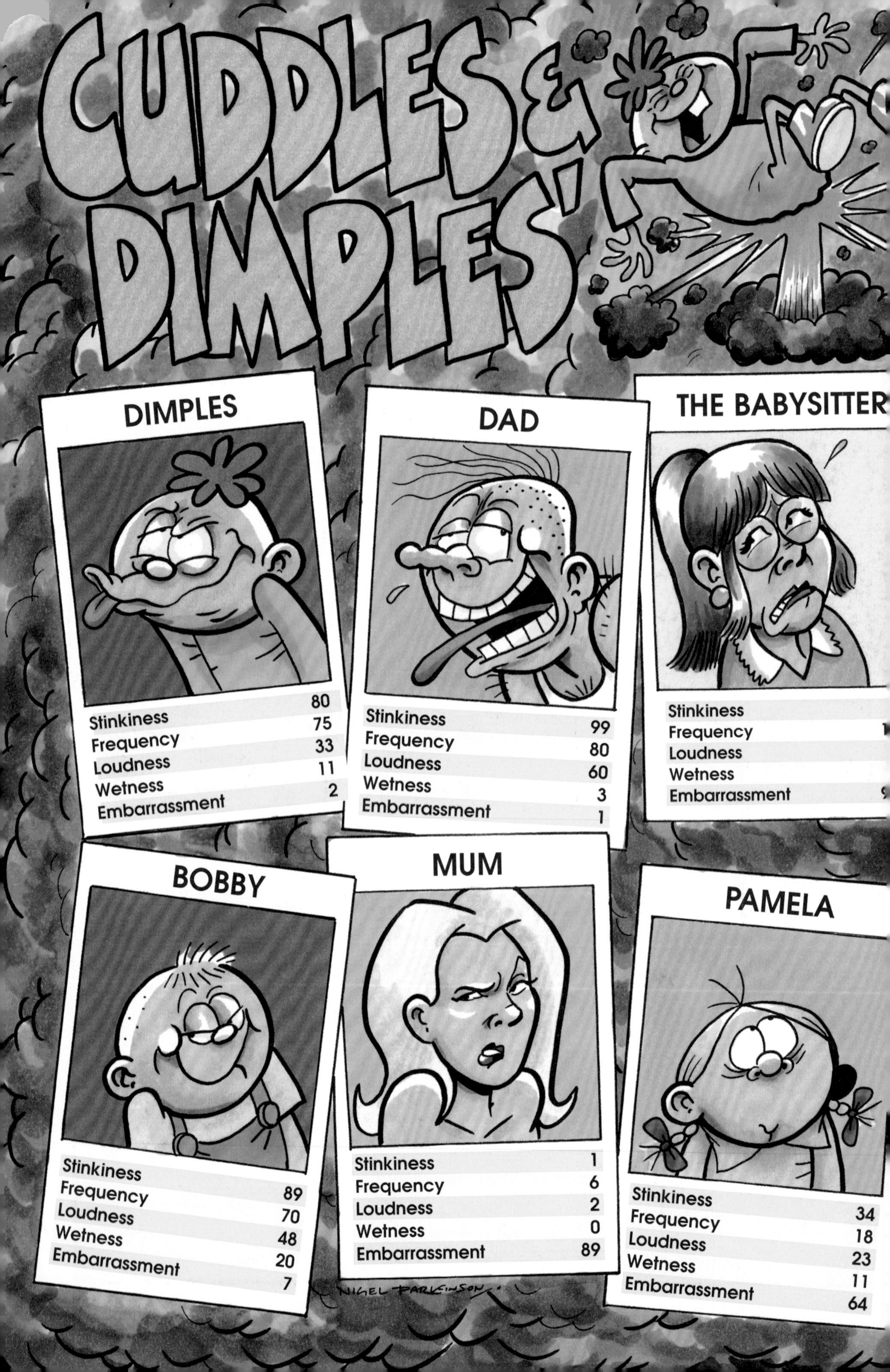
CUDDLES &
DIMPLES'
DIMPLES
80
Stinkiness
75
Frequency
33
Loudness
11
Wetness
2
Embarrassment
DAD
Stinkiness
99
Frequency
80
Loudness
60
Wetness
3
Embarrassment
1
THE BABYSITTER
Stinkiness
Frequency
Loudness
Wetness
Embarrassment
BOBBY
Stinkiness
Frequency
89
Loudness
70
Wetness
48
Embarrassment
20
7
MUM
Stinkiness
1
Frequency
6
Loudness
2
Wetness
0
Embarrassment
89
PAMELA
Stinkiness
Frequency
34
Loudness
18
Wetness
23
Embarrassment
11
64
NIGEL PARKINSON

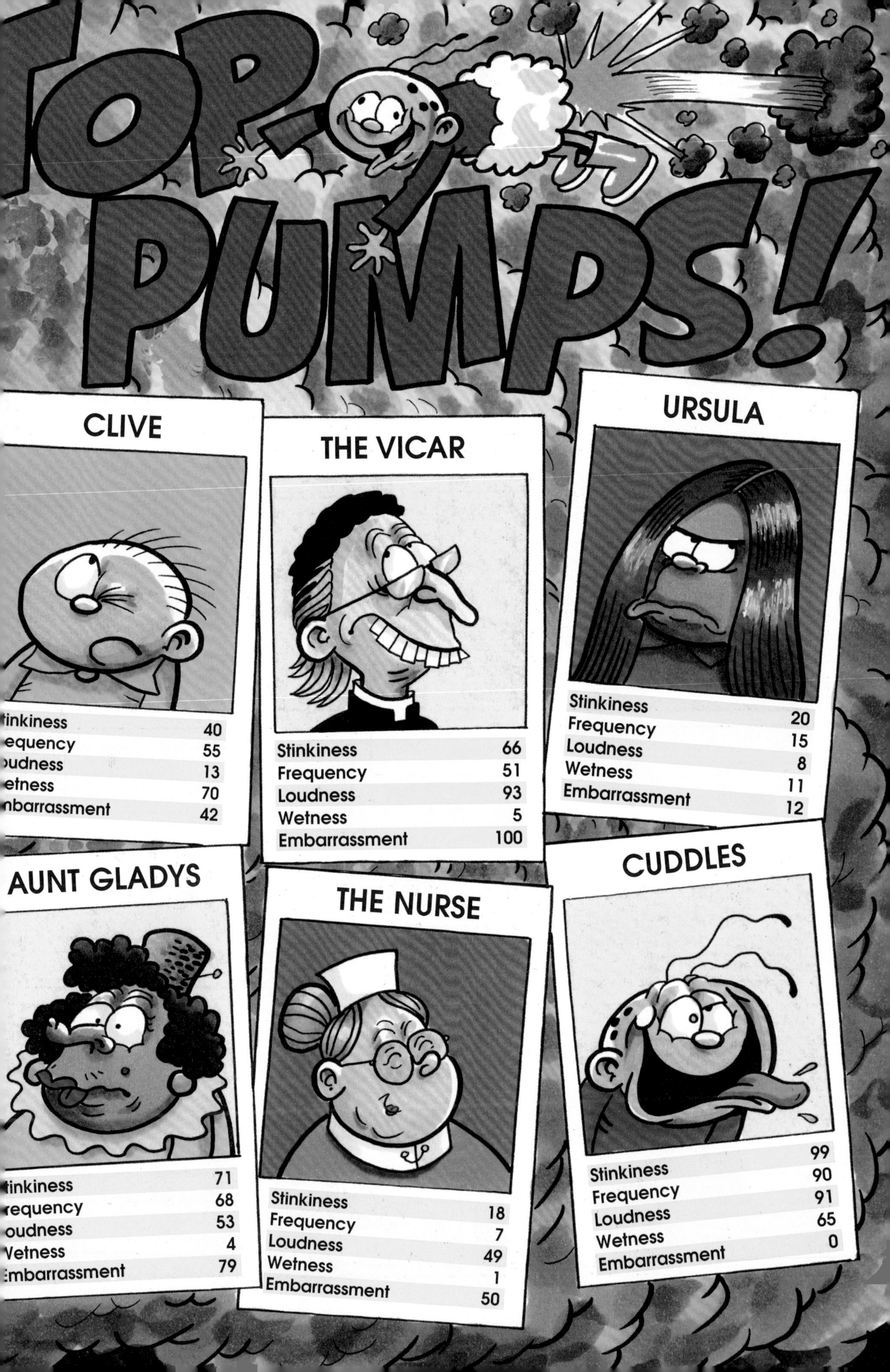
TOP PUMPS!
CLIVE
tinkiness 40
equency 55
udness 13
etness 70
nbarrassment 42
THE VICAR
Stinkiness 66
Frequency 51
Loudness 93
Wetness 5
Embarrassment 100
URSULA
Stinkiness 20
Frequency 15
Loudness 8
Wetness 11
Embarrassment 12
AUNT GLADYS
tinkiness 71
requency 68
oudness 53
Vetness 4
mbarrassment 79
THE NURSE
Stinkiness 18
Frequency 7
Loudness 49
Wetness 1
Embarrassment 50
CUDDLES
Stinkiness 99
Frequency 90
Loudness 91
Wetness 65
Embarrassment 0

JAK & TODD

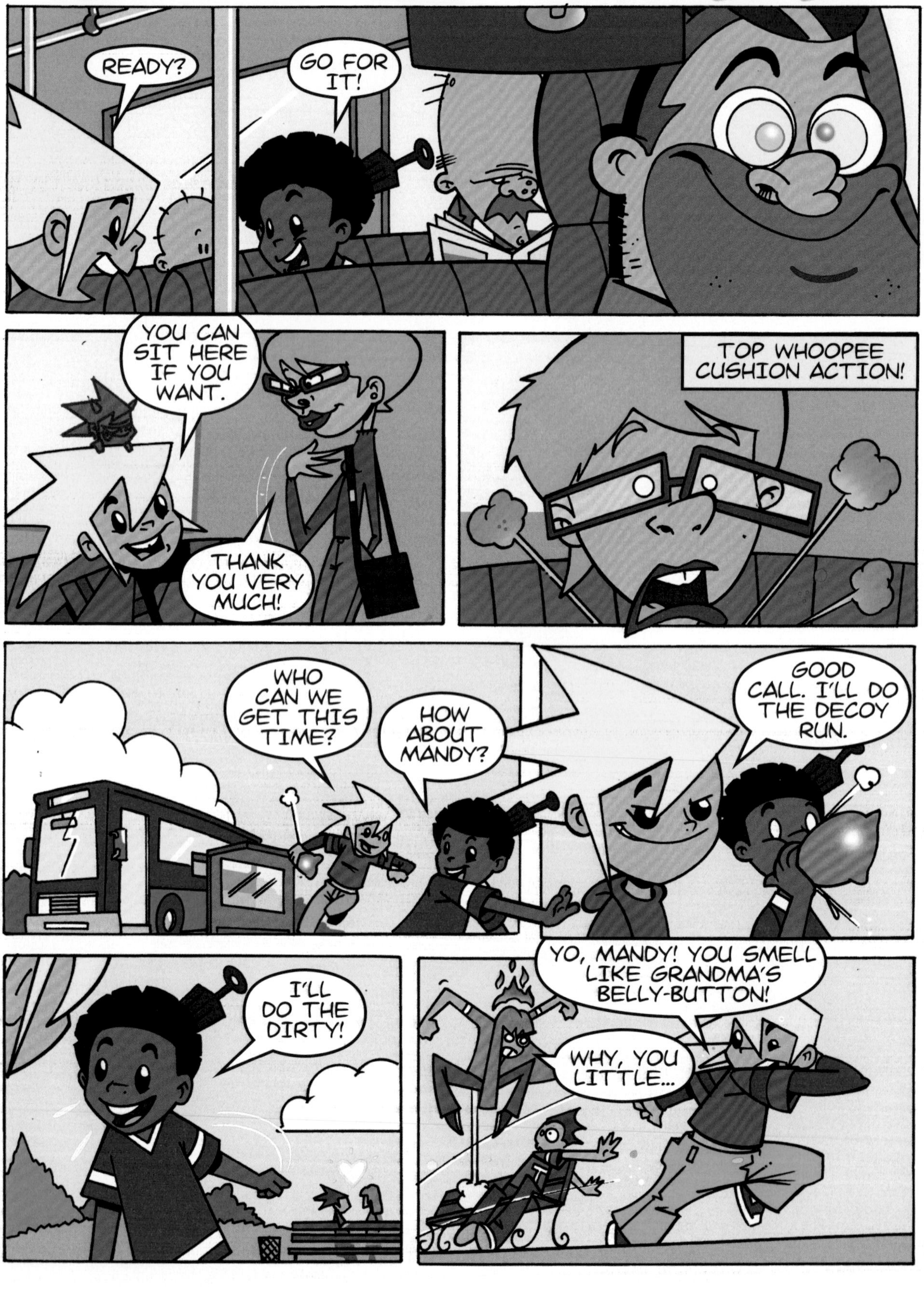
READY?
GO FOR IT!
YOU CAN SIT HERE IF YOU WANT.
THANK YOU VERY MUCH!
TOP WHOOPEE CUSHION ACTION!
WHO CAN WE GET THIS TIME?
HOW ABOUT MANDY?
GOOD CALL. I'LL DO THE DECOY RUN.
I'LL DO THE DIRTY!
YO, MANDY! YOU SMELL LIKE GRANDMA'S BELLY-BUTTON!
WHY, YOU LITTLE...

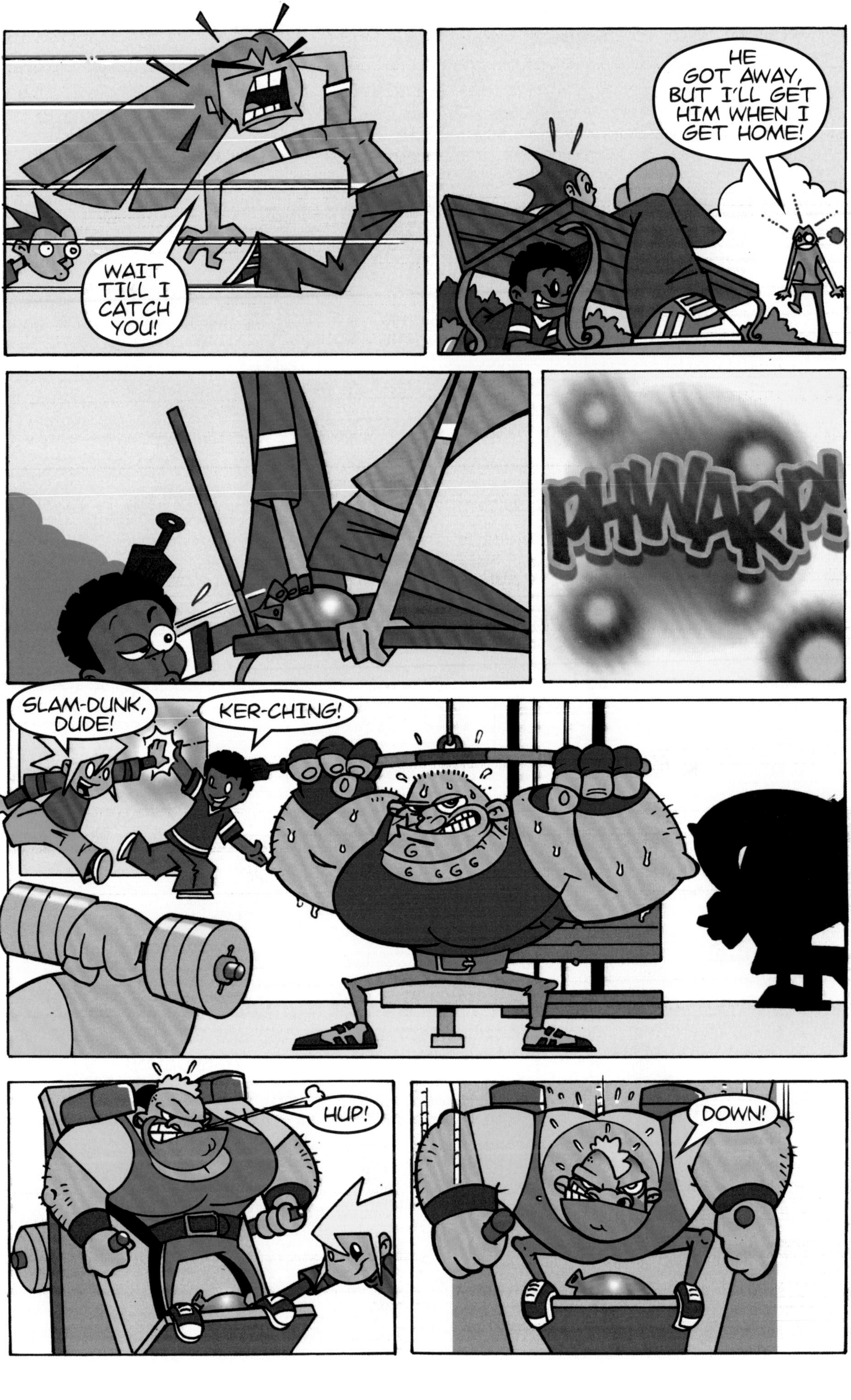
WAIT TILL I CATCH YOU!
HE GOT AWAY, BUT I'LL GET HIM WHEN I GET HOME!
PHWARP!
SLAM-DUNK, DUDE!
KER-CHING!
HUP!
DOWN!

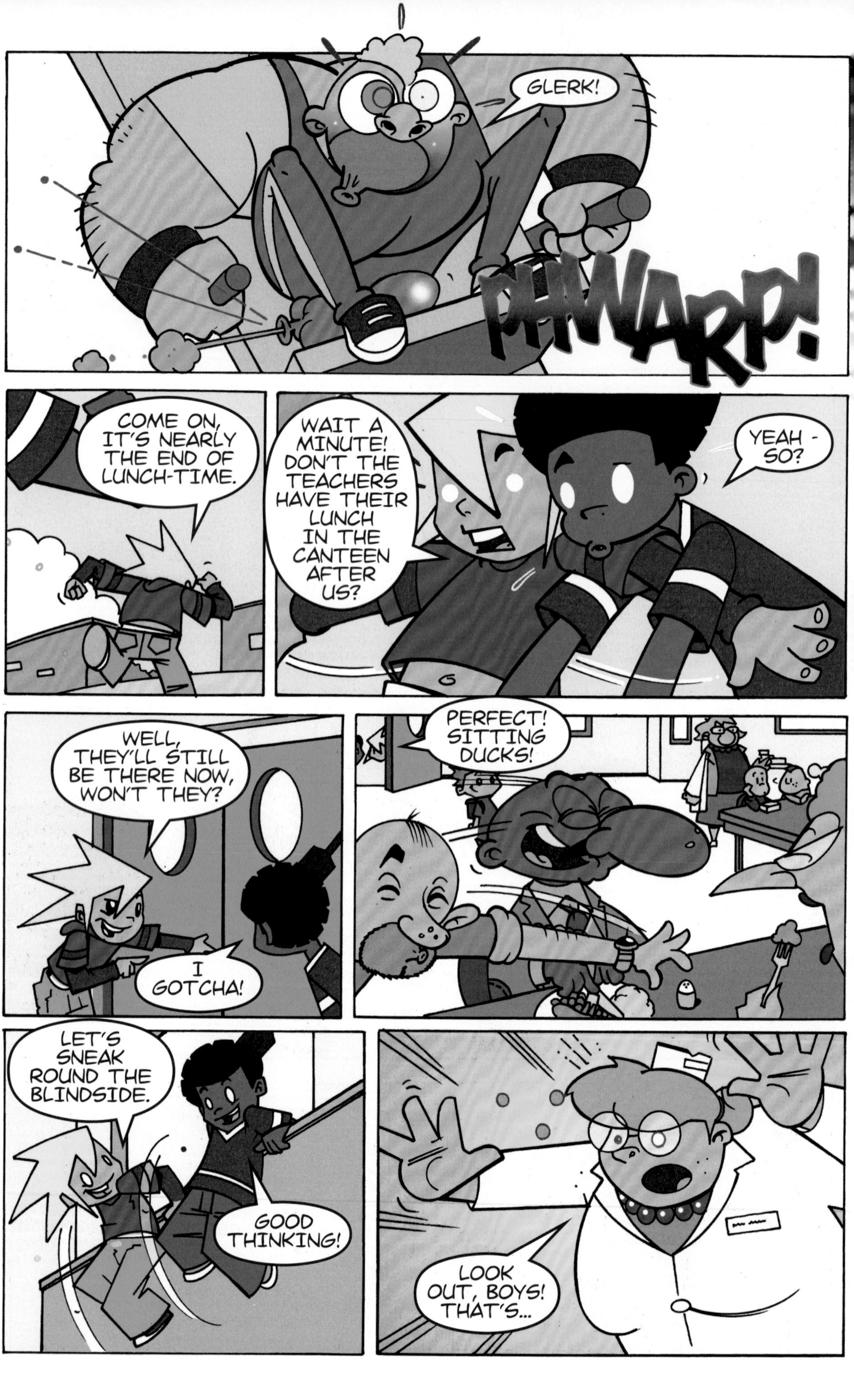
GLERK!
PHWARP!
COME ON, IT'S NEARLY THE END OF LUNCH-TIME.
WAIT A MINUTE! DON'T THE TEACHERS HAVE THEIR LUNCH IN THE CANTEEN AFTER US?
YEAH - SO?
WELL, THEY'LL STILL BE THERE NOW, WON'T THEY?
I GOTCHA!
PERFECT! SITTING DUCKS!
LET'S SNEAK ROUND THE BLINDSIDE.
GOOD THINKING!
LOOK OUT, BOYS! THAT'S...

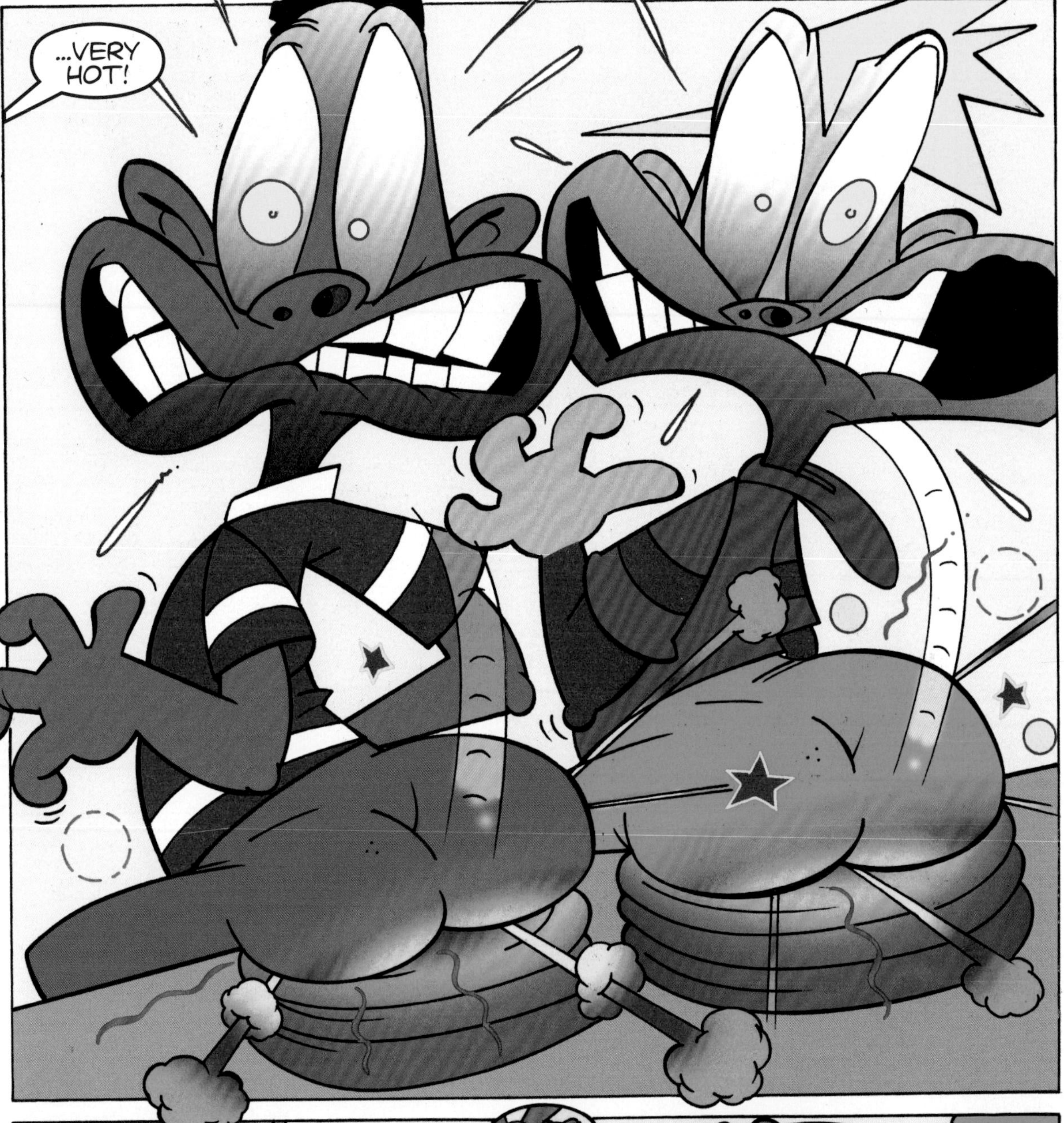
...VERY HOT!

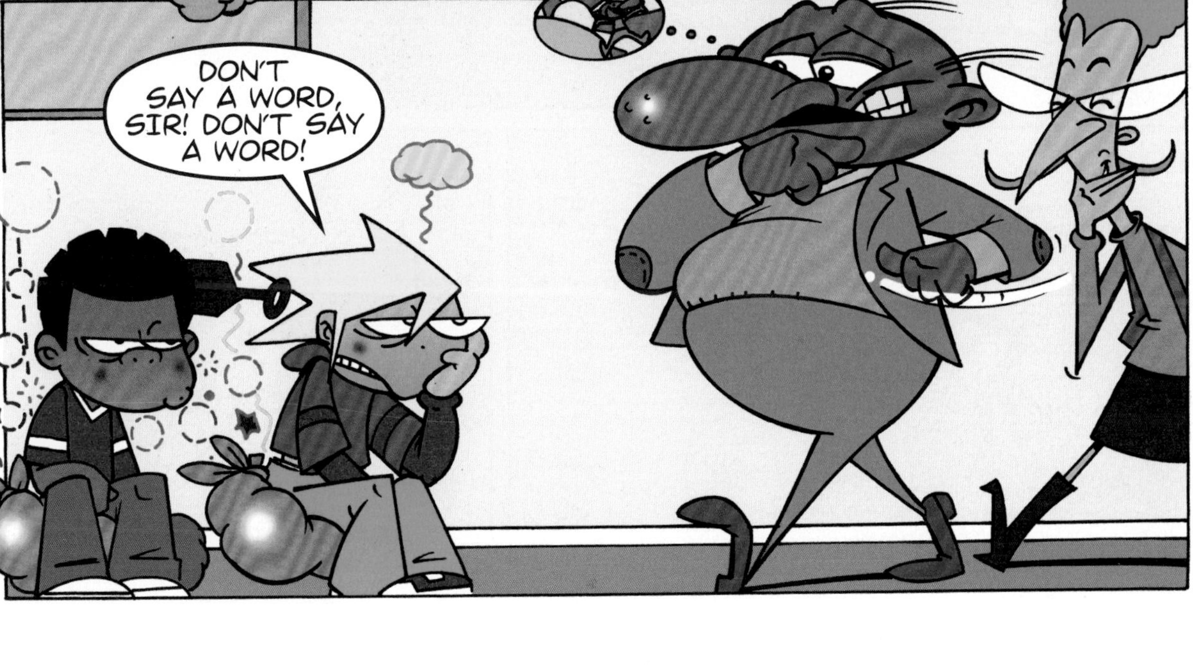
DON'T SAY A WORD, SIR! DON'T SAY A WORD!

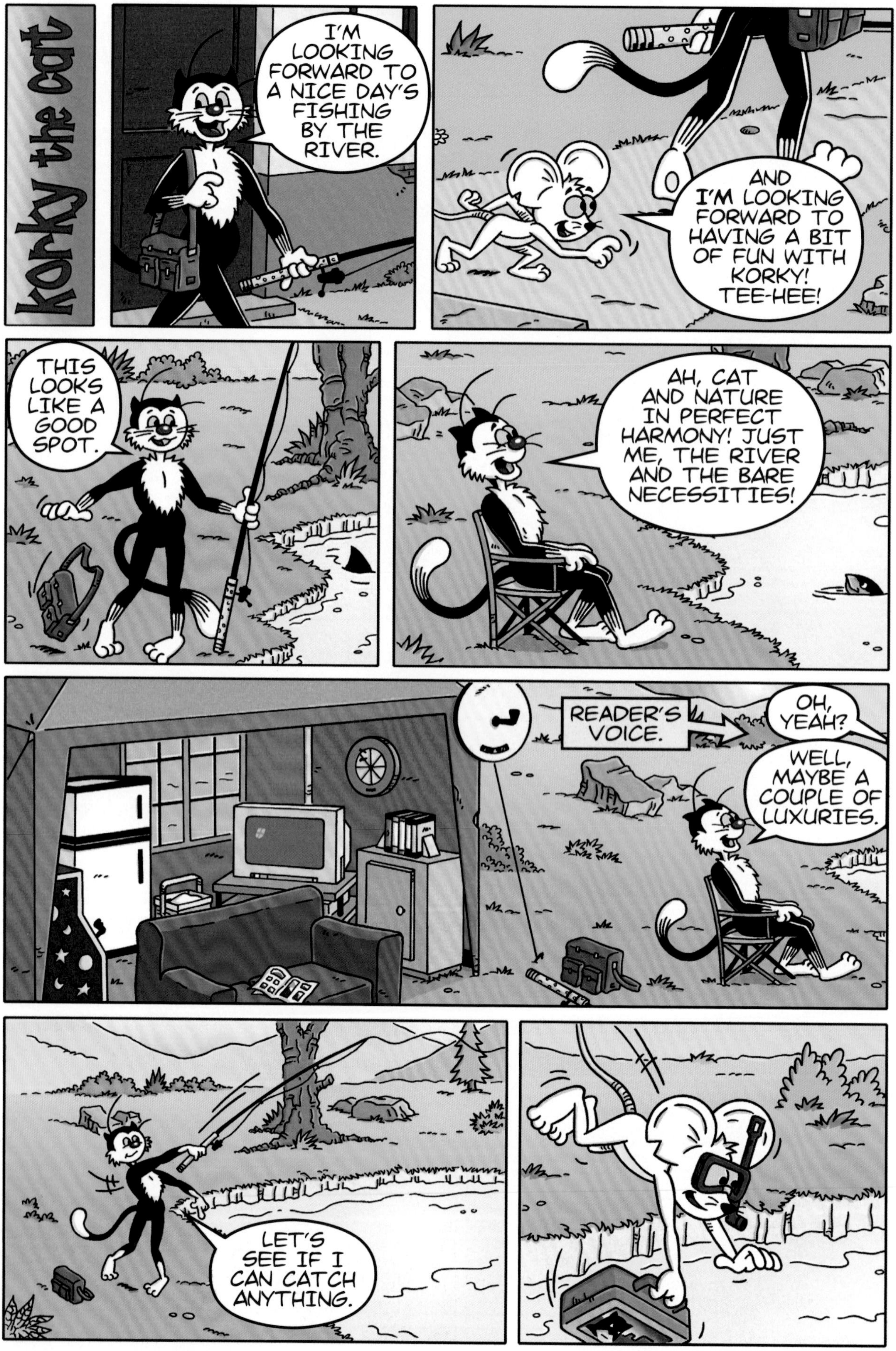
Korky the Cat
I'M LOOKING FORWARD TO A NICE DAY'S FISHING BY THE RIVER.
AND I'M LOOKING FORWARD TO HAVING A BIT OF FUN WITH KORKY! TEE-HEE!
THIS LOOKS LIKE A GOOD SPOT.
AH, CAT AND NATURE IN PERFECT HARMONY! JUST ME, THE RIVER AND THE BARE NECESSITIES!
READER'S VOICE.
OH, YEAH?
WELL, MAYBE A COUPLE OF LUXURIES.
LET'S SEE IF I CAN CATCH ANYTHING.

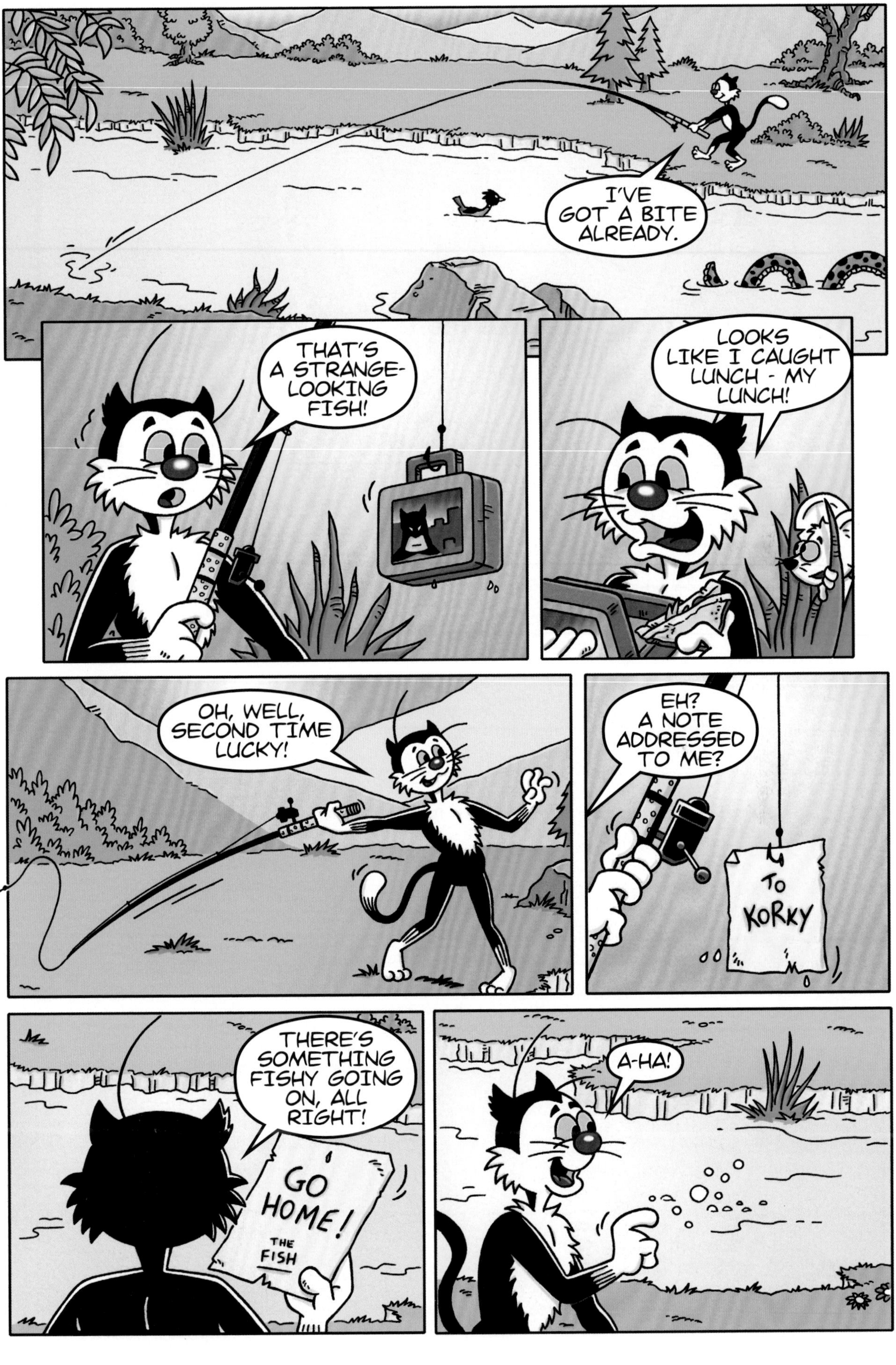
I'VE GOT A BITE ALREADY.
THAT'S A STRANGE-LOOKING FISH!
LOOKS LIKE I CAUGHT LUNCH - MY LUNCH!
OH, WELL, SECOND TIME LUCKY!
EH? A NOTE ADDRESSED TO ME?
TO KORKY
THERE'S SOMETHING FISHY GOING ON, ALL RIGHT!
GO HOME!
THE FISH
A-HA!

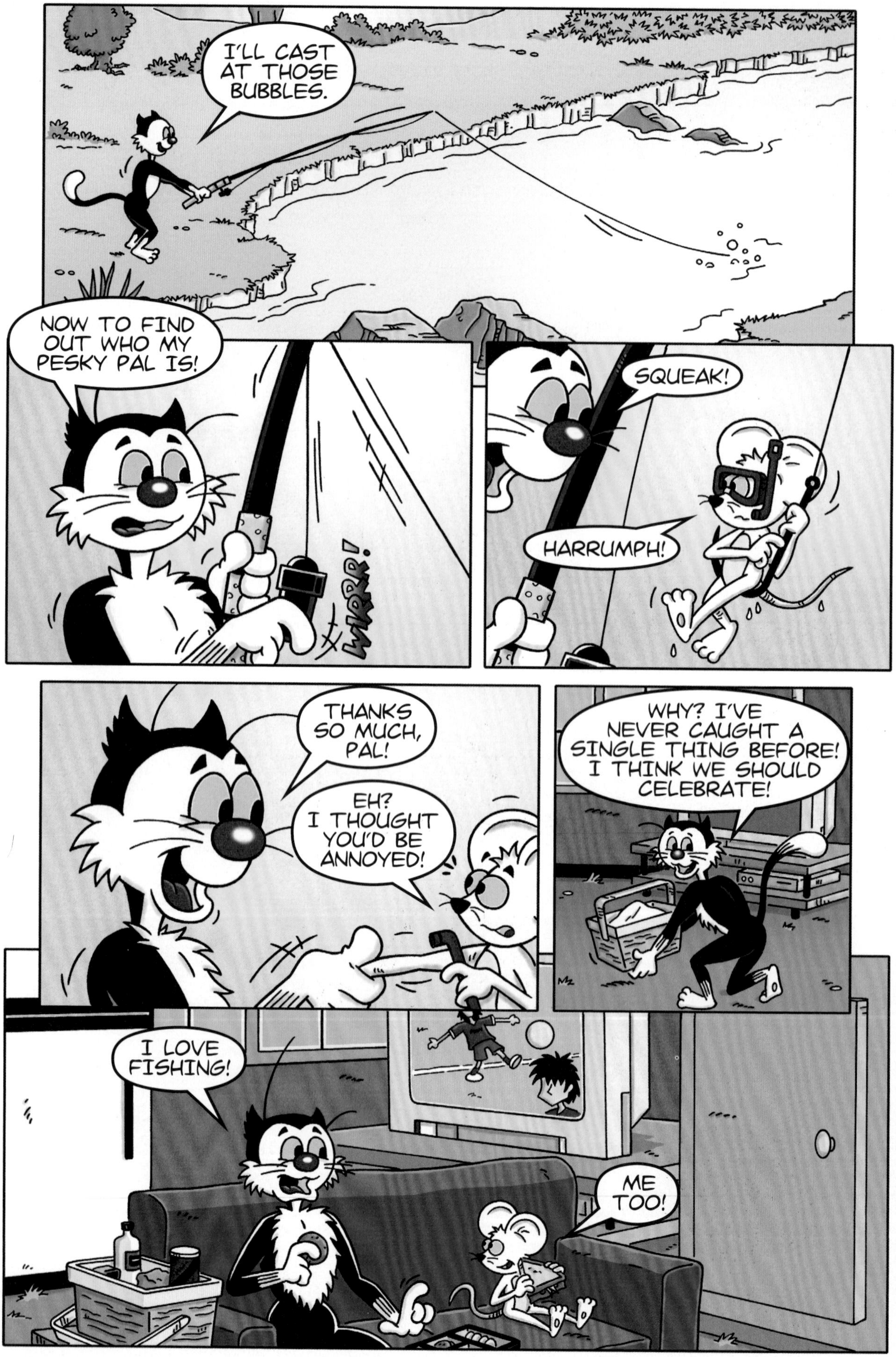
I'LL CAST AT THOSE BUBBLES.
NOW TO FIND OUT WHO MY PESKY PAL IS!
WIRRR!
SQUEAK!
HARRUMPH!
THANKS SO MUCH, PAL!
EH? I THOUGHT YOU'D BE ANNOYED!
WHY? I'VE NEVER CAUGHT A SINGLE THING BEFORE! I THINK WE SHOULD CELEBRATE!
I LOVE FISHING!
ME TOO!

LEARN TO DRAW–
KORKY THE CAT

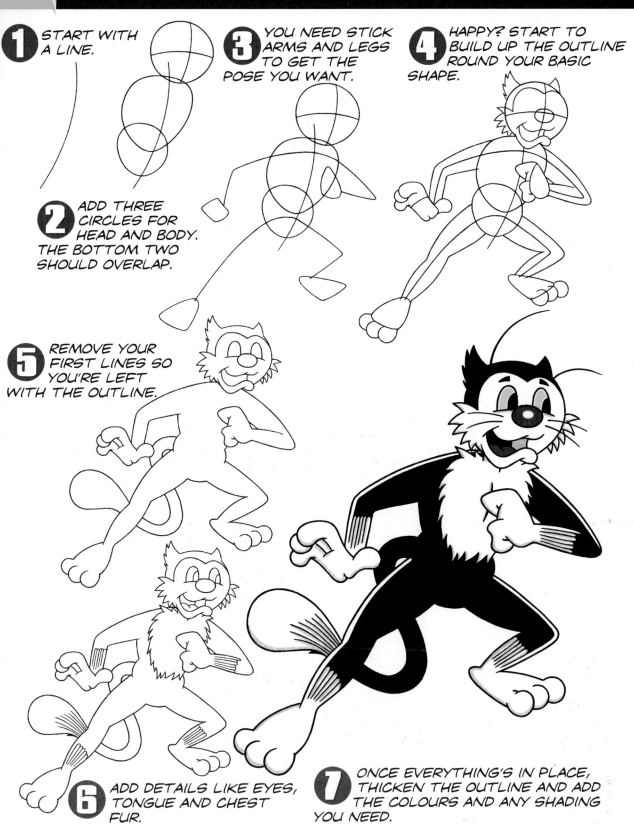

1 START WITH A LINE.

2 ADD THREE CIRCLES FOR HEAD AND BODY. THE BOTTOM TWO SHOULD OVERLAP.

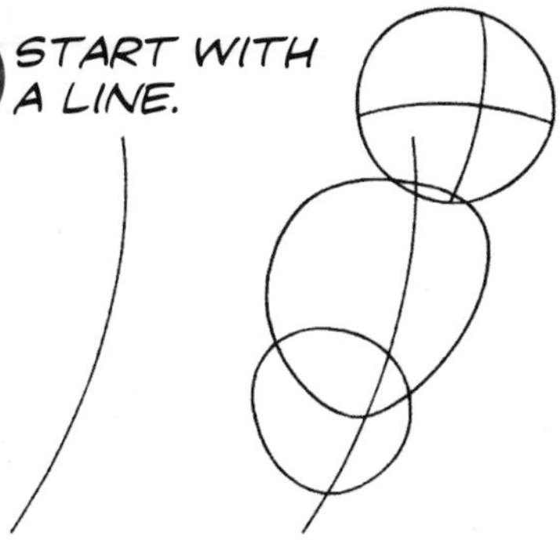

3 YOU NEED STICK ARMS AND LEGS TO GET THE POSE YOU WANT.

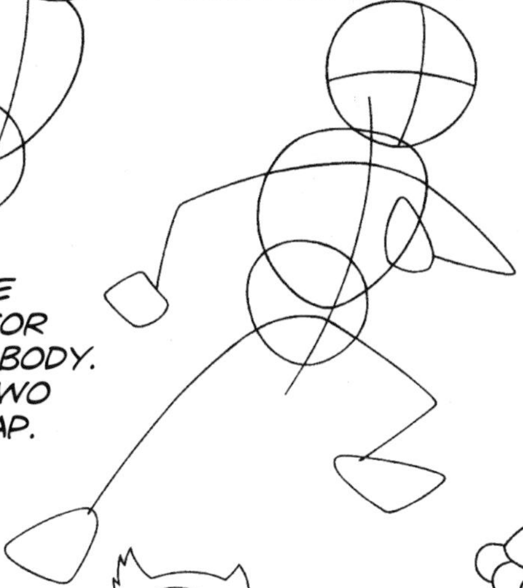

4 HAPPY? START TO BUILD UP THE OUTLINE ROUND YOUR BASIC SHAPE.

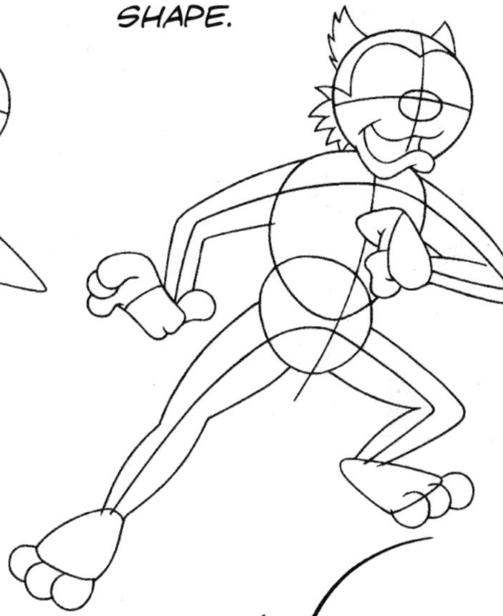

5 REMOVE YOUR FIRST LINES SO YOU'RE LEFT WITH THE OUTLINE.

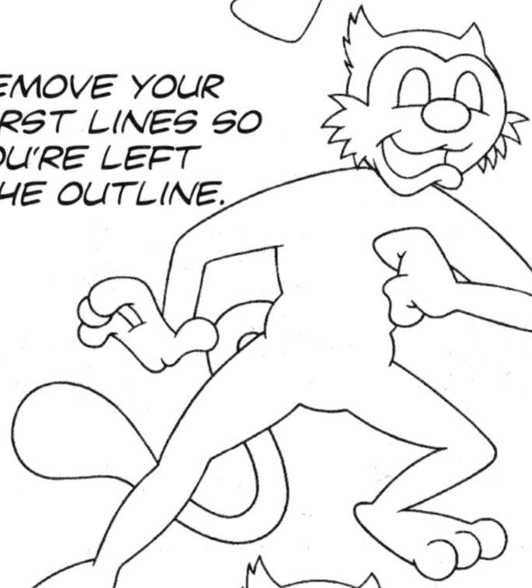

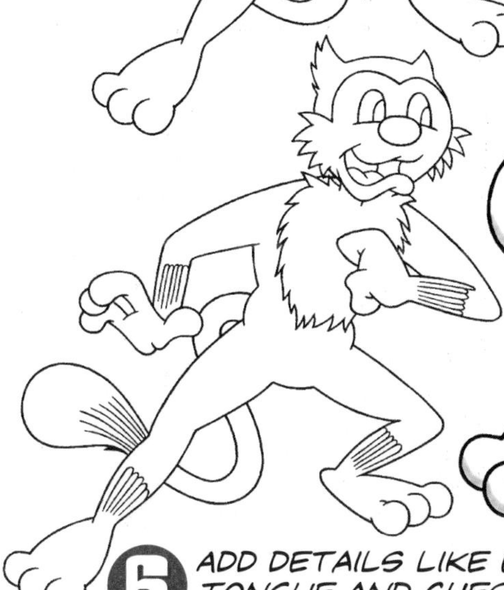

6 ADD DETAILS LIKE EYES, TONGUE AND CHEST FUR.

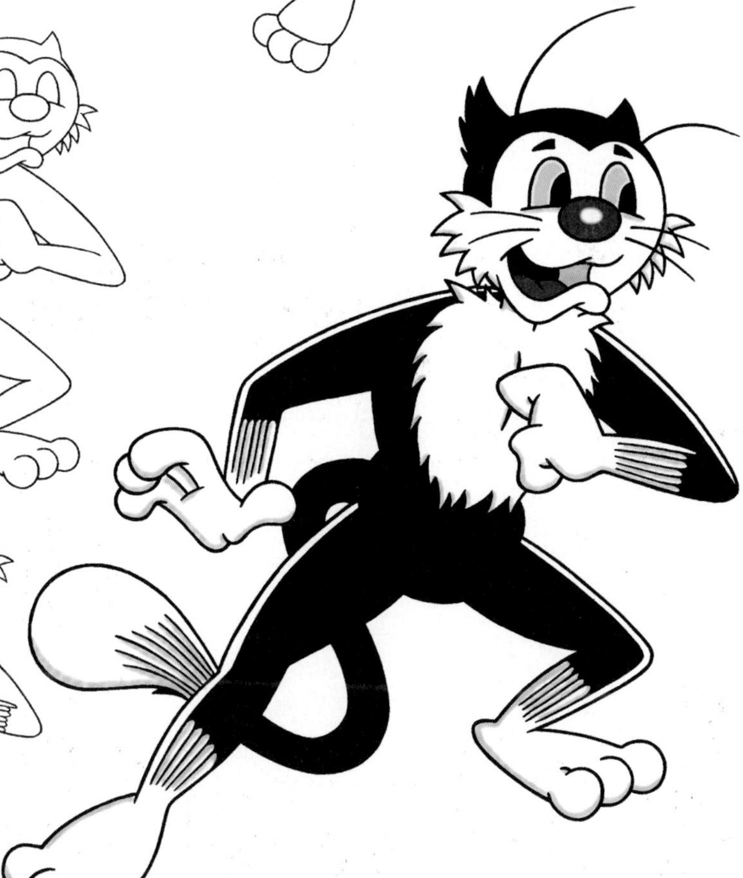

7 ONCE EVERYTHING'S IN PLACE, THICKEN THE OUTLINE AND ADD THE COLOURS AND ANY SHADING YOU NEED.

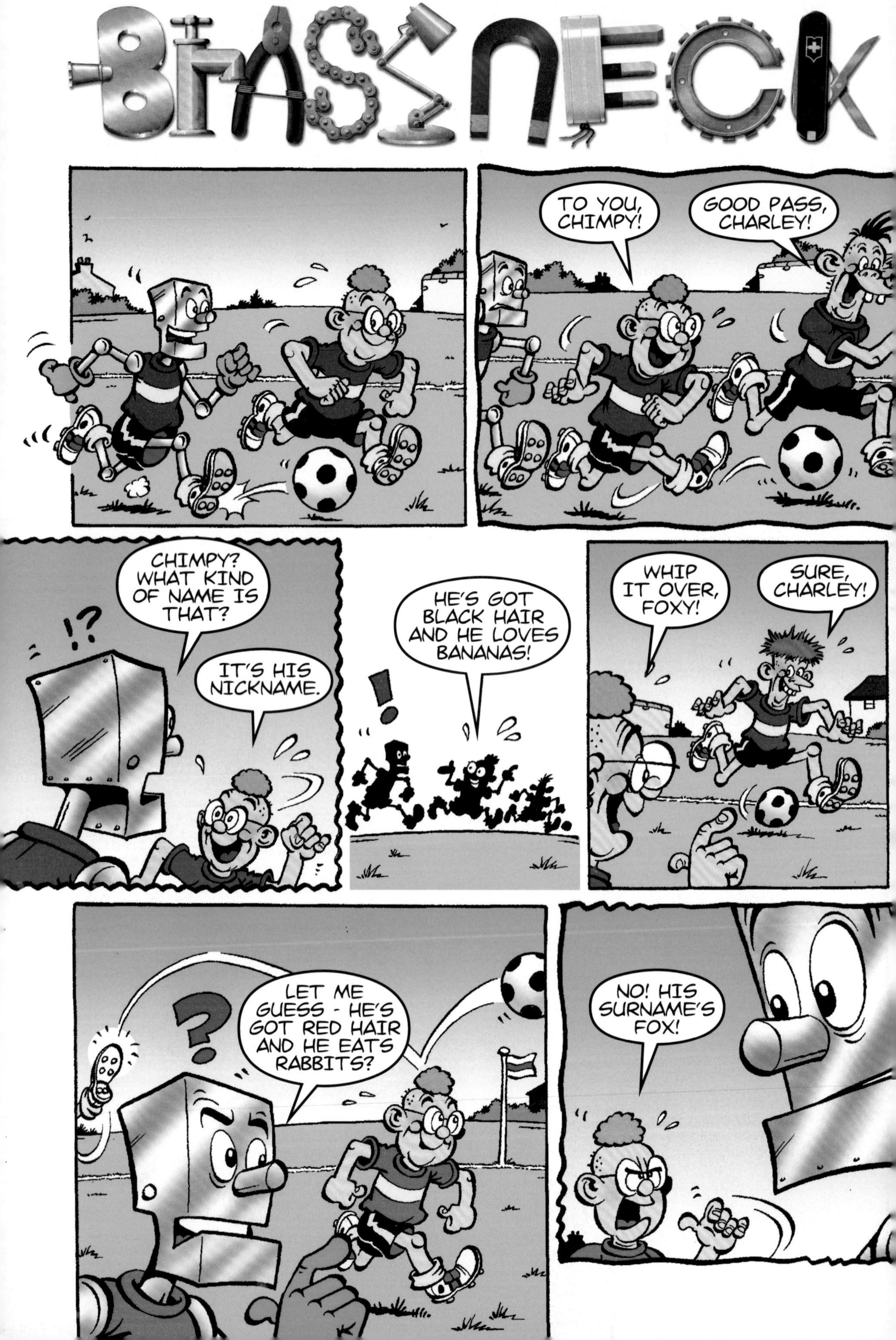
BRASSNECK
TO YOU, CHIMPY!
GOOD PASS, CHARLEY!
CHIMPY? WHAT KIND OF NAME IS THAT?
IT'S HIS NICKNAME.
!?
HE'S GOT BLACK HAIR AND HE LOVES BANANAS!
WHIP IT OVER, FOXY!
SURE, CHARLEY!
LET ME GUESS - HE'S GOT RED HAIR AND HE EATS RABBITS?
NO! HIS SURNAME'S FOX!

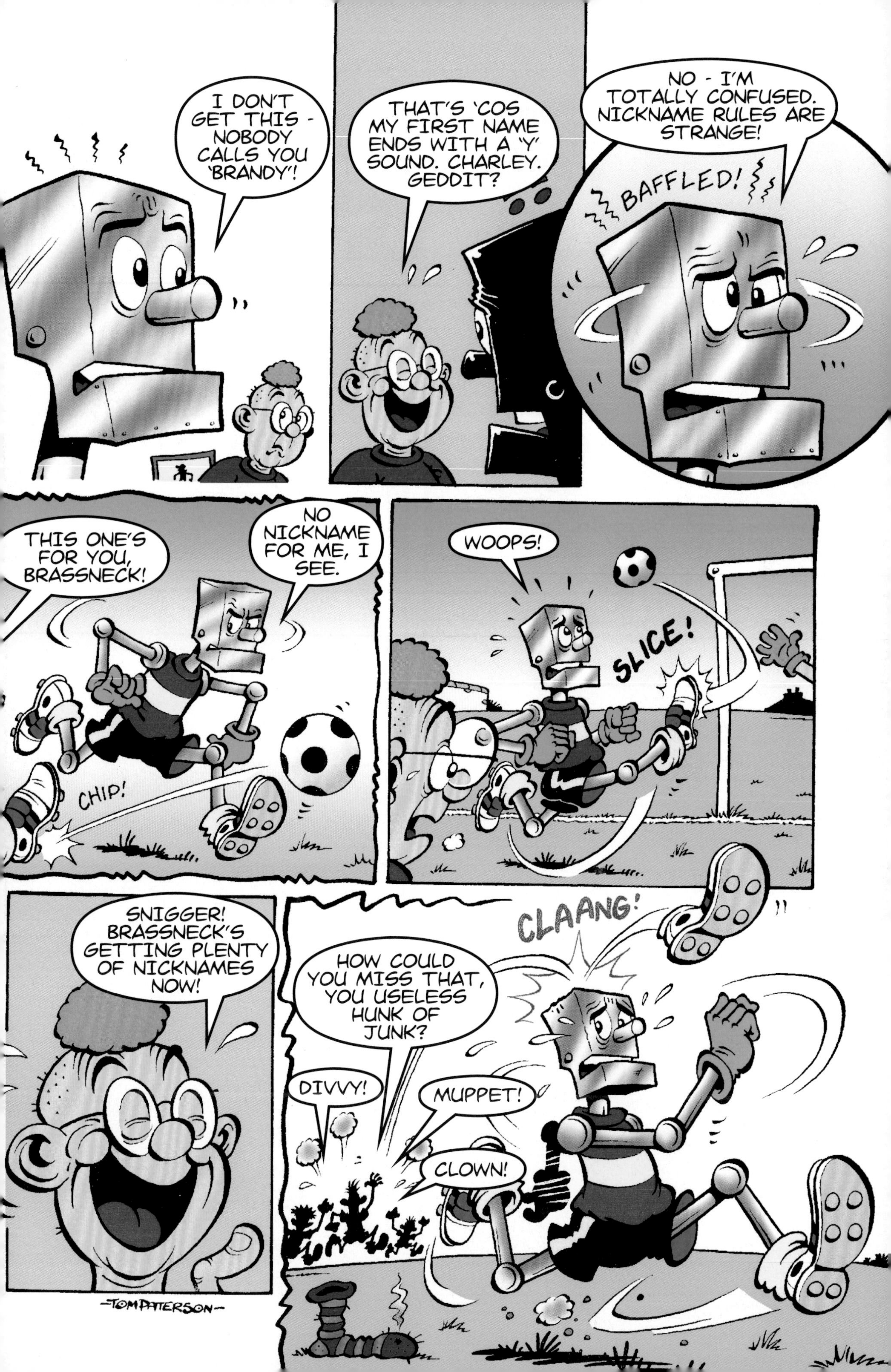

I DON'T GET THIS - NOBODY CALLS YOU 'BRANDY'!
THAT'S 'COS MY FIRST NAME ENDS WITH A 'Y' SOUND. CHARLEY. GEDDIT?
NO - I'M TOTALLY CONFUSED. NICKNAME RULES ARE STRANGE!
BAFFLED!
THIS ONE'S FOR YOU, BRASSNECK!
NO NICKNAME FOR ME, I SEE.
CHIP!
WOOPS!
SLICE!
SNIGGER! BRASSNECK'S GETTING PLENTY OF NICKNAMES NOW!
CLAANG!
HOW COULD YOU MISS THAT, YOU USELESS HUNK OF JUNK?
DIVVY!
MUPPET!
CLOWN!
TOM PATERSON

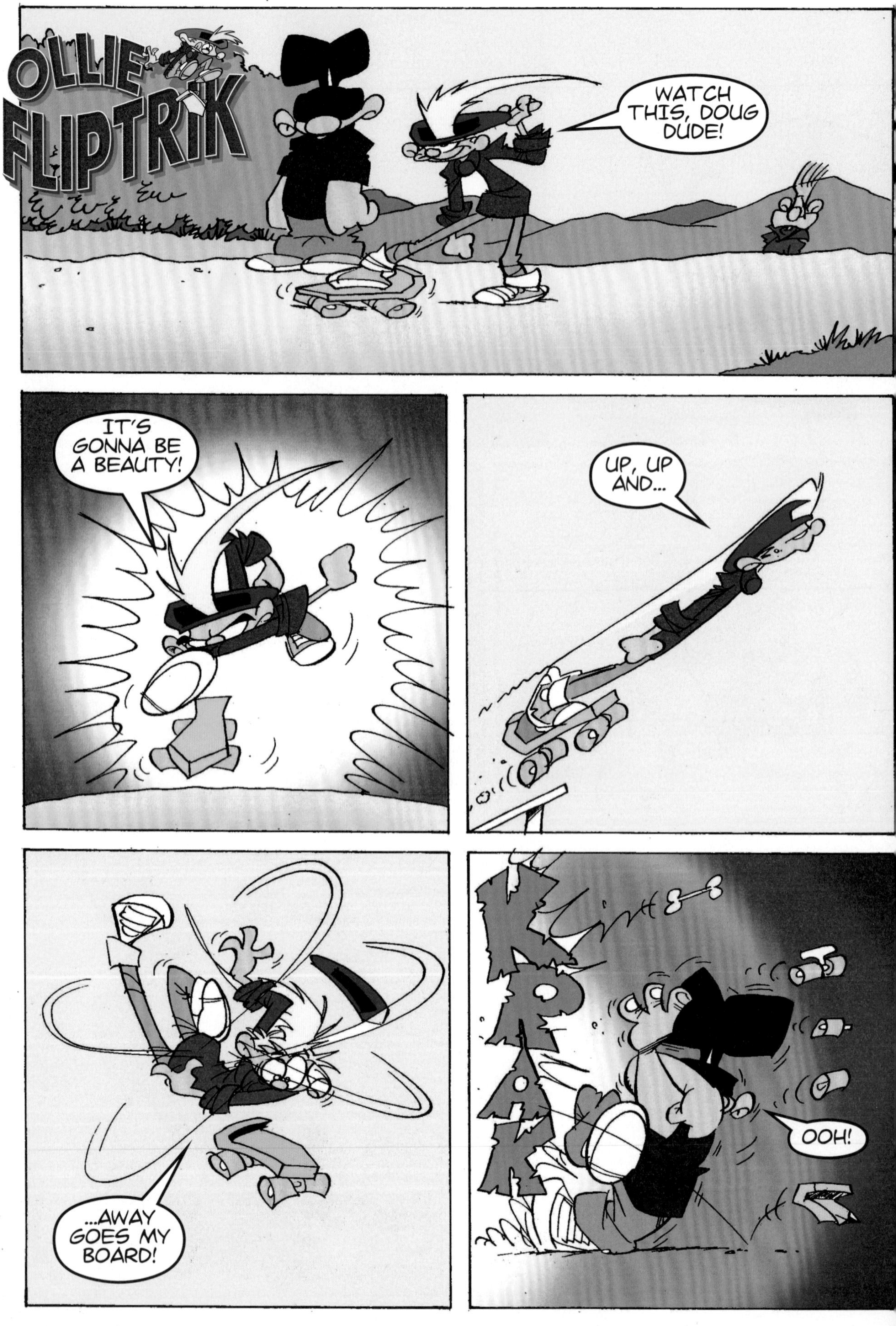
OLLIE FLIPTRIK
WATCH THIS, DOUG DUDE!
IT'S GONNA BE A BEAUTY!
UP, UP AND...
...AWAY GOES MY BOARD!
KRAK
OOH!

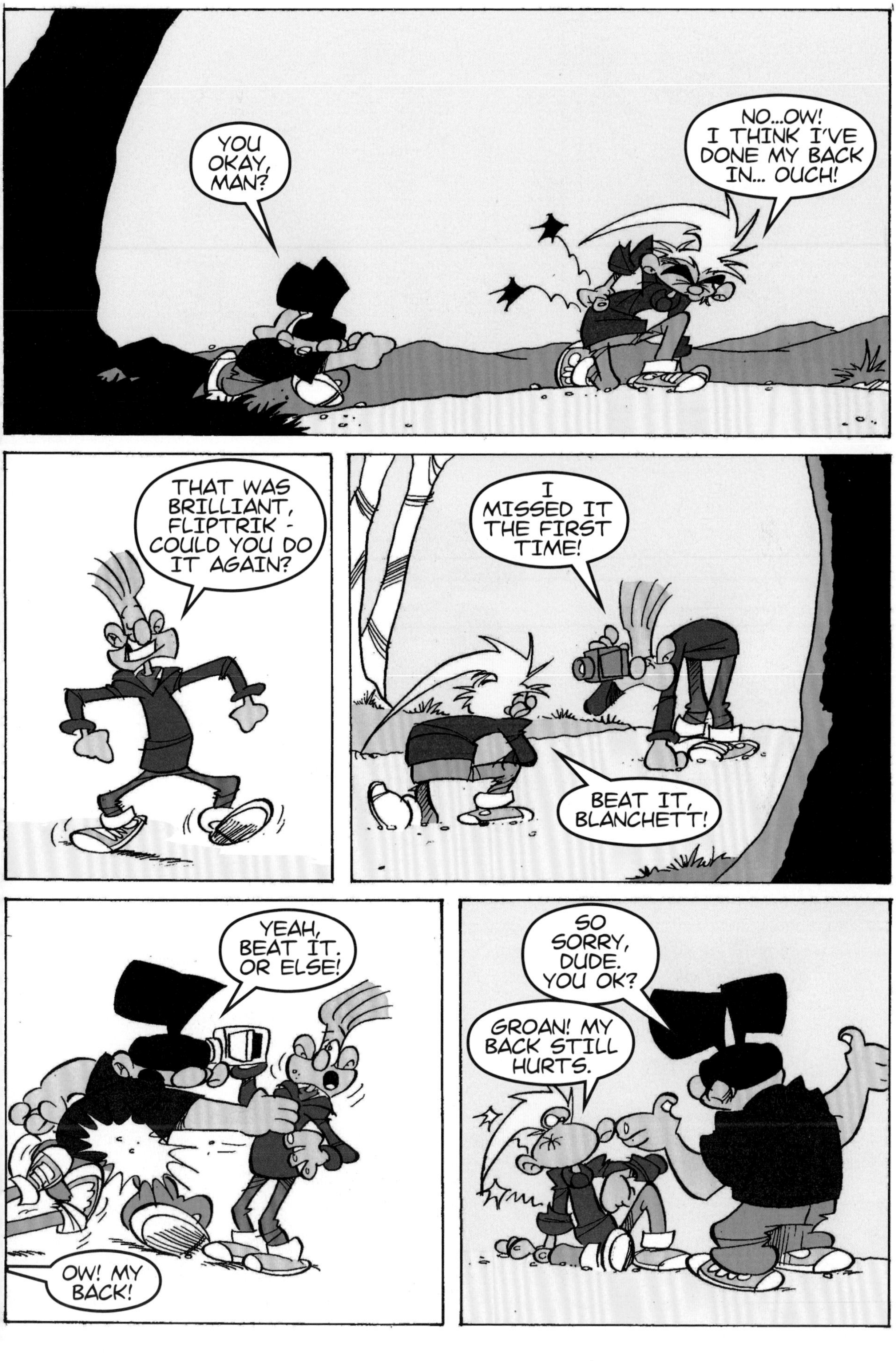
YOU OKAY, MAN?
NO...OW! I THINK I'VE DONE MY BACK IN... OUCH!
THAT WAS BRILLIANT, FLIPTRIK - COULD YOU DO IT AGAIN?
I MISSED IT THE FIRST TIME!
BEAT IT, BLANCHETT!
YEAH, BEAT IT. OR ELSE!
OW! MY BACK!
SO SORRY, DUDE. YOU OK?
GROAN! MY BACK STILL HURTS.

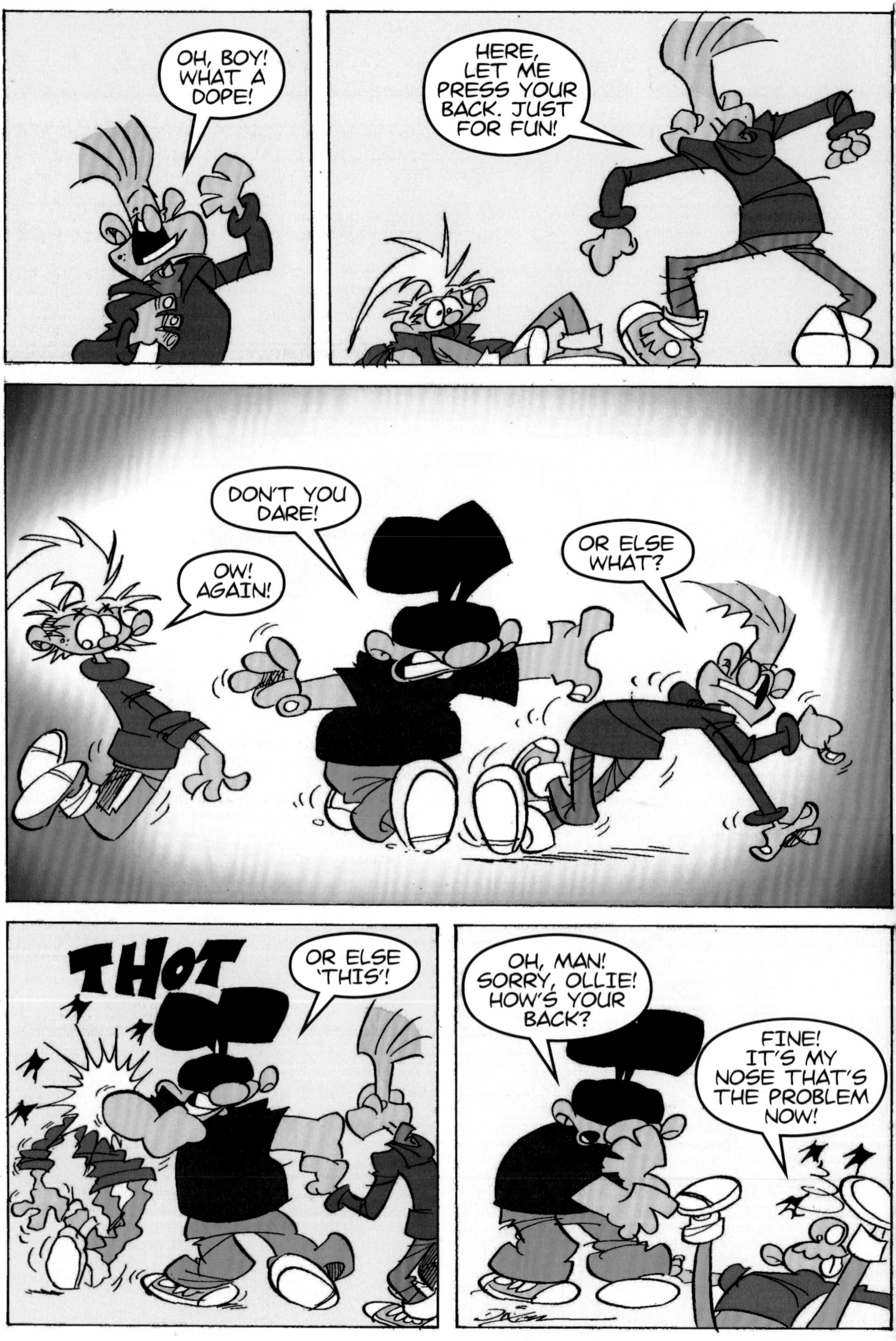
OH, BOY! WHAT A DOPE!
HERE, LET ME PRESS YOUR BACK. JUST FOR FUN!
DON'T YOU DARE!
OW! AGAIN!
OR ELSE WHAT?
THOT
OR ELSE 'THIS'!
OH, MAN! SORRY, OLLIE! HOW'S YOUR BACK?
FINE! IT'S MY NOSE THAT'S THE PROBLEM NOW!

HYDE 'N' SHRIEK

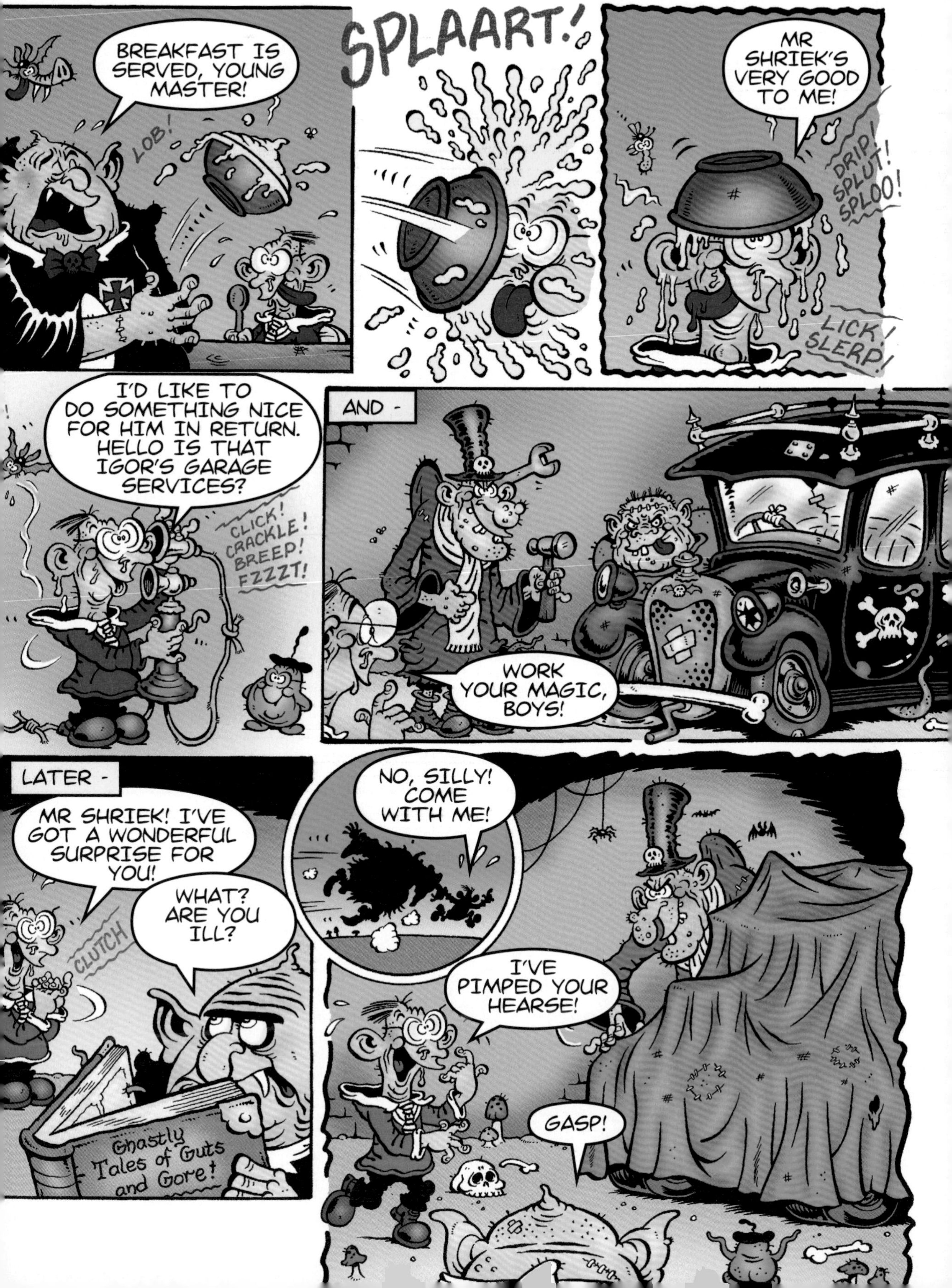
BREAKFAST IS SERVED, YOUNG MASTER!
LOB!
SPLAART!
MR SHRIEK'S VERY GOOD TO ME!
DRIP! SPLUT! SPLOO!
LICK! SLERP!
I'D LIKE TO DO SOMETHING NICE FOR HIM IN RETURN. HELLO IS THAT IGOR'S GARAGE SERVICES?
CLICK! CRACKLE! BREEP! FZZZT!
AND -
WORK YOUR MAGIC, BOYS!
LATER -
MR SHRIEK! I'VE GOT A WONDERFUL SURPRISE FOR YOU!
CLUTCH
WHAT? ARE YOU ILL?
Ghastly Tales of Guts and Gore!
NO, SILLY! COME WITH ME!
I'VE PIMPED YOUR HEARSE!
GASP!

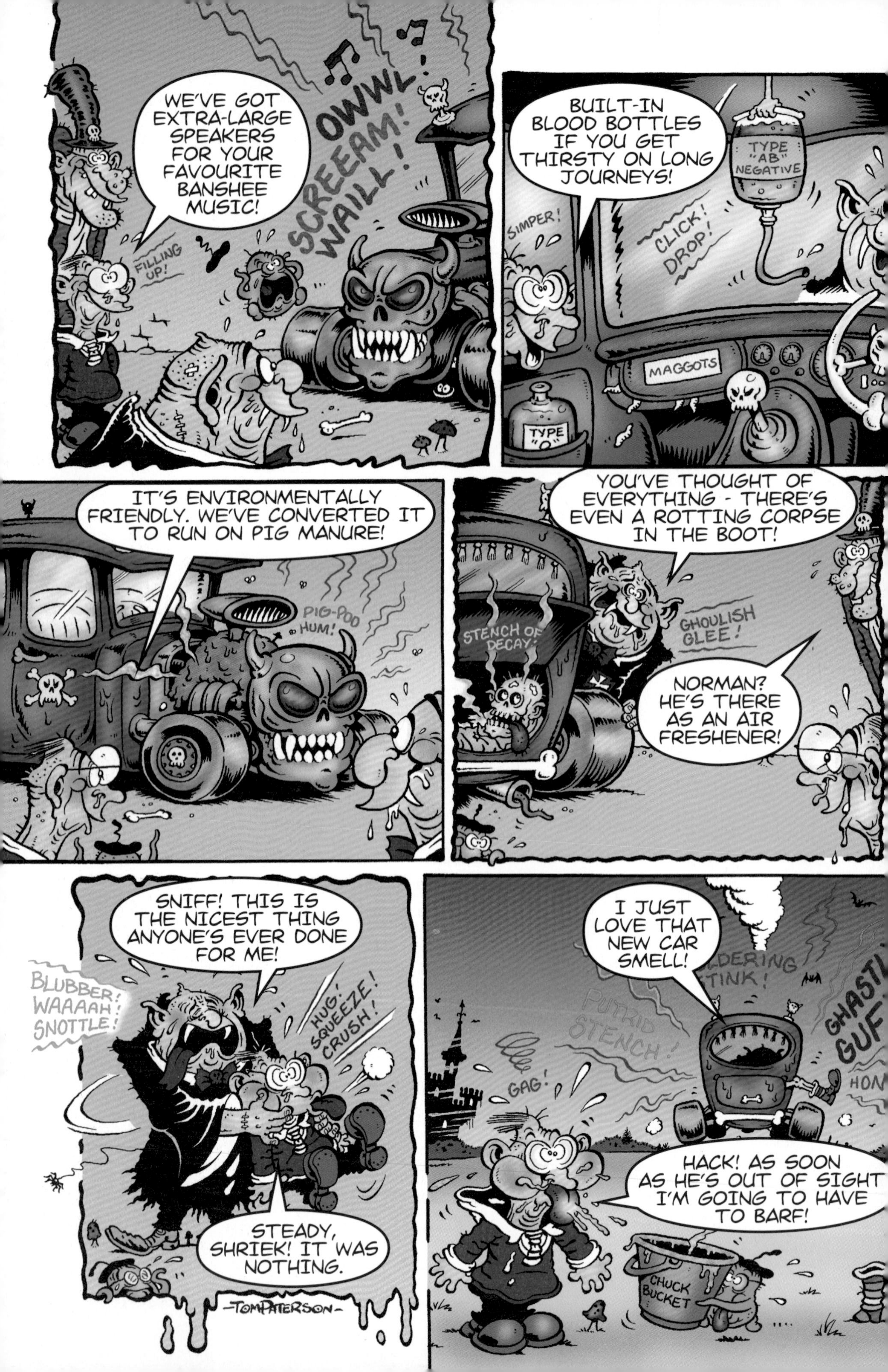
WE'VE GOT EXTRA-LARGE SPEAKERS FOR YOUR FAVOURITE BANSHEE MUSIC!
OWWL SCREEAM! WAILL!
FILLING UP!
BUILT-IN BLOOD BOTTLES IF YOU GET THIRSTY ON LONG JOURNEYS!
TYPE "AB" NEGATIVE
SIMPER!
CLICK! DROP!
MAGGOTS
TYPE "O"
IT'S ENVIRONMENTALLY FRIENDLY. WE'VE CONVERTED IT TO RUN ON PIG MANURE!
PIG-POO HUM!
YOU'VE THOUGHT OF EVERYTHING - THERE'S EVEN A ROTTING CORPSE IN THE BOOT!
STENCH OF DECAY!
GHOULISH GLEE!
NORMAN? HE'S THERE AS AN AIR FRESHENER!
SNIFF! THIS IS THE NICEST THING ANYONE'S EVER DONE FOR ME!
BLUBBER! WAAAAH! SNOTTLE!
HUG! SQUEEZE! CRUSH!
STEADY, SHRIEK! IT WAS NOTHING.
-TOM PATERSON-
I JUST LOVE THAT NEW CAR SMELL!
PUTRID STENCH!
GAG!
HACK! AS SOON AS HE'S OUT OF SIGHT I'M GOING TO HAVE TO BARF!
CHUCK BUCKET

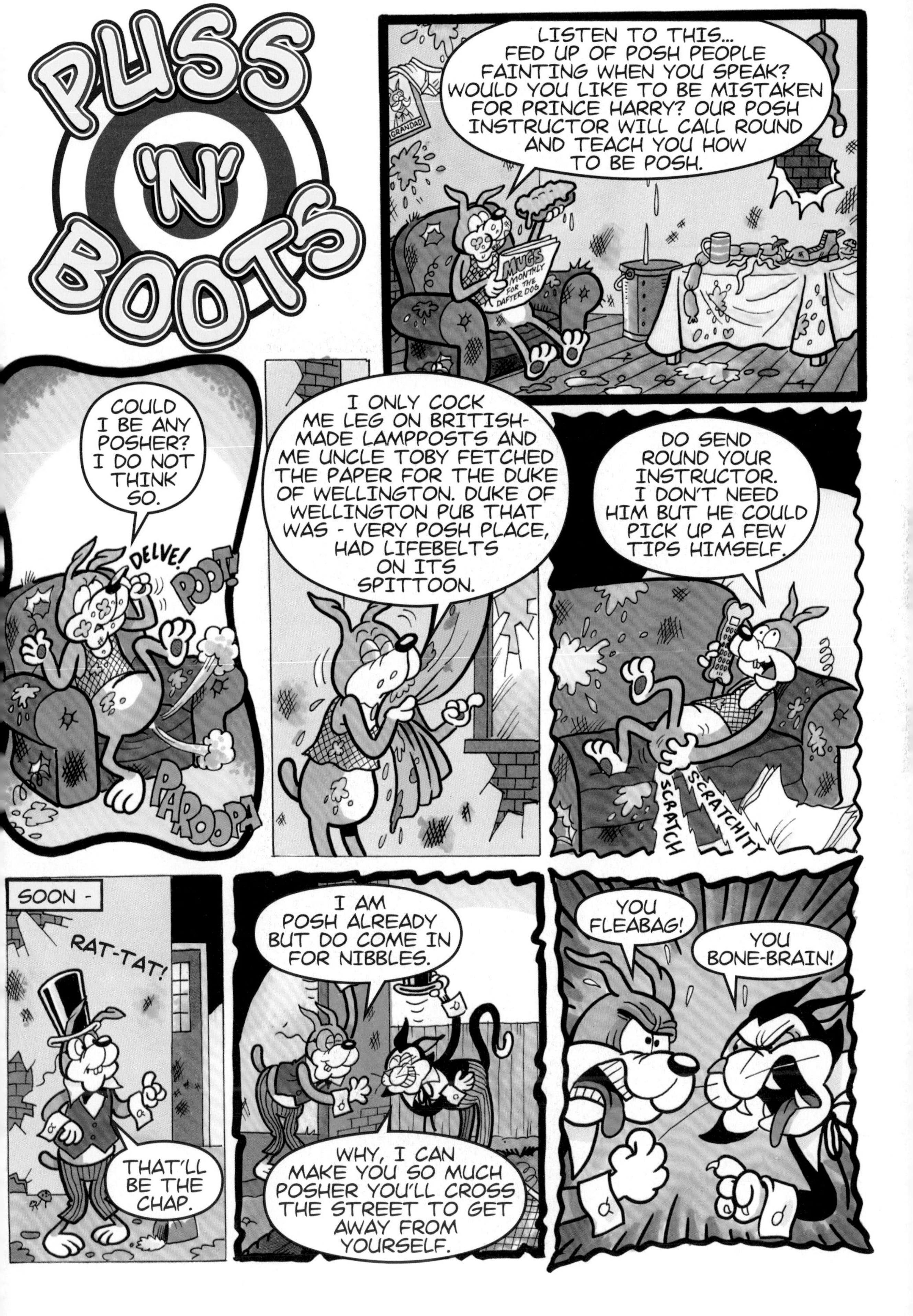
PUSS 'N' BOOTS
LISTEN TO THIS... FED UP OF POSH PEOPLE FAINTING WHEN YOU SPEAK? WOULD YOU LIKE TO BE MISTAKEN FOR PRINCE HARRY? OUR POSH INSTRUCTOR WILL CALL ROUND AND TEACH YOU HOW TO BE POSH.
GRANDAD
MUGS MONTHLY FOR THE DAFTER DOG
COULD I BE ANY POSHER? I DO NOT THINK SO.
DELVE!
POOT!
PAROOPA!
I ONLY COCK ME LEG ON BRITISH-MADE LAMPPOSTS AND ME UNCLE TOBY FETCHED THE PAPER FOR THE DUKE OF WELLINGTON. DUKE OF WELLINGTON PUB THAT WAS - VERY POSH PLACE, HAD LIFEBELTS ON ITS SPITTOON.
DO SEND ROUND YOUR INSTRUCTOR. I DON'T NEED HIM BUT HE COULD PICK UP A FEW TIPS HIMSELF.
SCRATCH
SCRATCHITY
SOON -
RAT-TAT!
THAT'LL BE THE CHAP.
I AM POSH ALREADY BUT DO COME IN FOR NIBBLES.
WHY, I CAN MAKE YOU SO MUCH POSHER YOU'LL CROSS THE STREET TO GET AWAY FROM YOURSELF.
YOU FLEABAG!
YOU BONE-BRAIN!

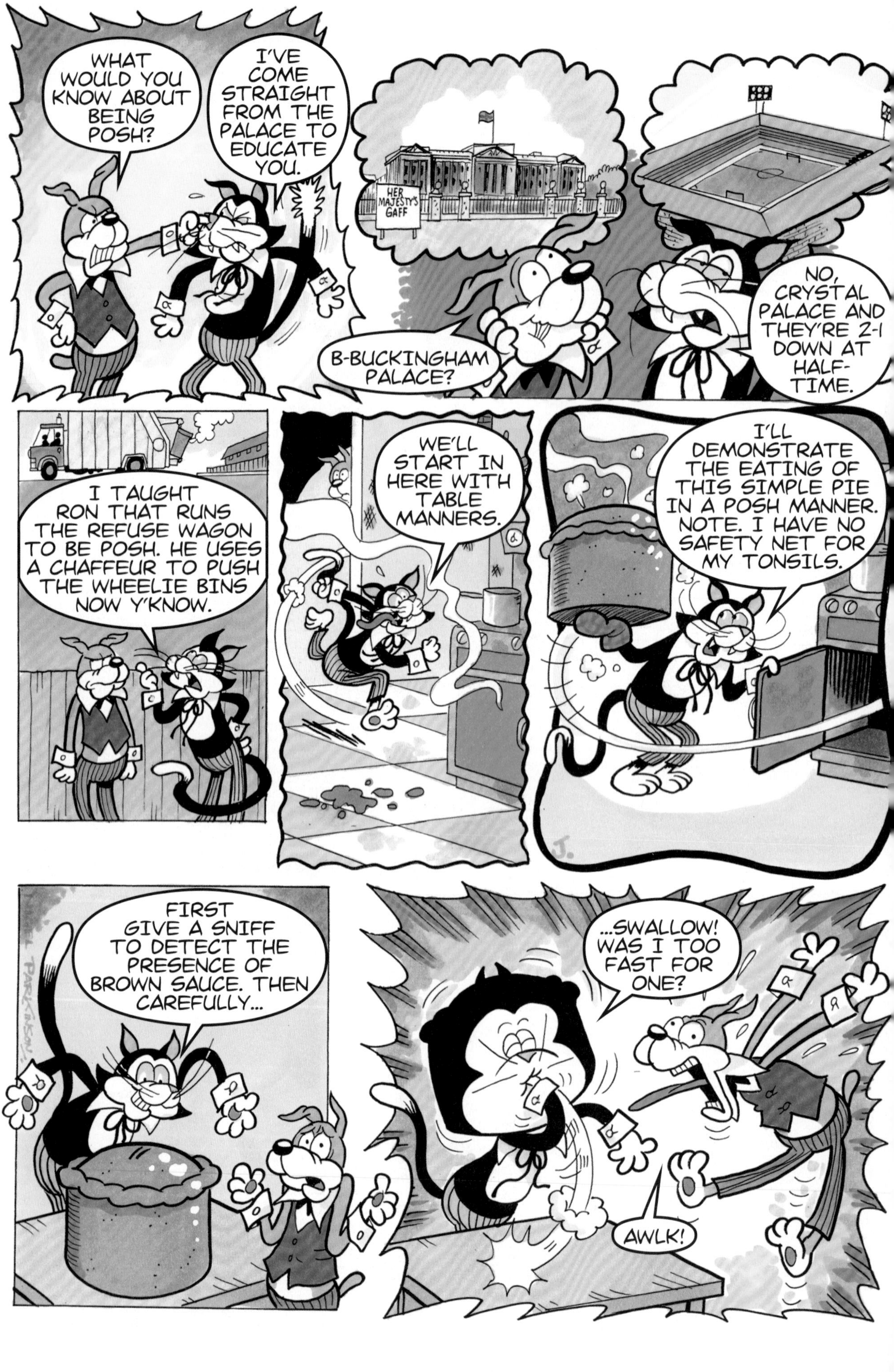
WHAT WOULD YOU KNOW ABOUT BEING POSH?
I'VE COME STRAIGHT FROM THE PALACE TO EDUCATE YOU.
HER MAJESTY'S GAFF
B-BUCKINGHAM PALACE?
NO, CRYSTAL PALACE AND THEY'RE 2-1 DOWN AT HALF-TIME.
I TAUGHT RON THAT RUNS THE REFUSE WAGON TO BE POSH. HE USES A CHAFFEUR TO PUSH THE WHEELIE BINS NOW Y'KNOW.
WE'LL START IN HERE WITH TABLE MANNERS.
I'LL DEMONSTRATE THE EATING OF THIS SIMPLE PIE IN A POSH MANNER. NOTE. I HAVE NO SAFETY NET FOR MY TONSILS.
J.
FIRST GIVE A SNIFF TO DETECT THE PRESENCE OF BROWN SAUCE. THEN CAREFULLY...
...SWALLOW! WAS I TOO FAST FOR ONE?
AWLK!

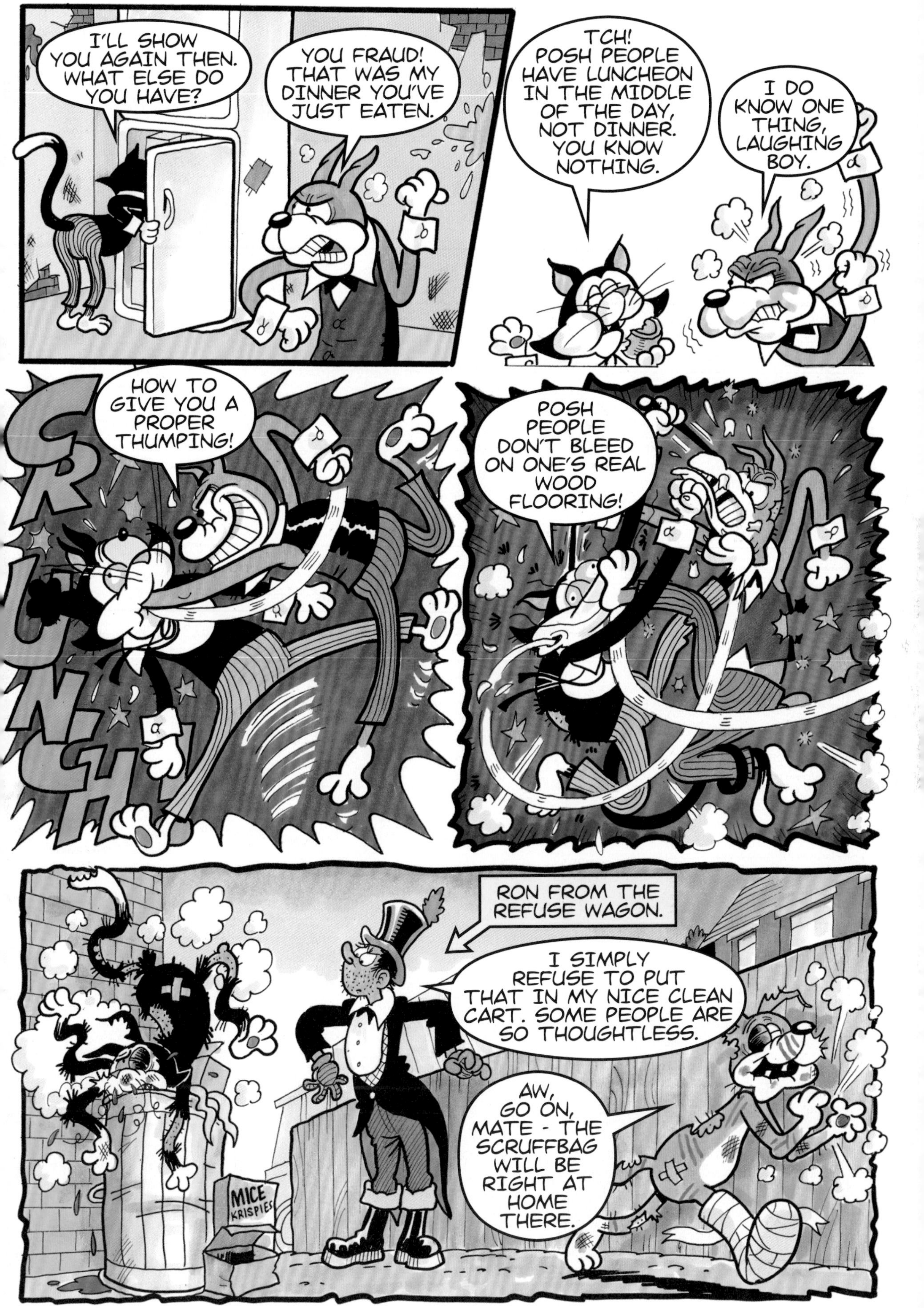
I'LL SHOW YOU AGAIN THEN. WHAT ELSE DO YOU HAVE?
YOU FRAUD! THAT WAS MY DINNER YOU'VE JUST EATEN.
TCH! POSH PEOPLE HAVE LUNCHEON IN THE MIDDLE OF THE DAY, NOT DINNER. YOU KNOW NOTHING.
I DO KNOW ONE THING, LAUGHING BOY.
SCRUNCH
HOW TO GIVE YOU A PROPER THUMPING!
POSH PEOPLE DON'T BLEED ON ONE'S REAL WOOD FLOORING!
RON FROM THE REFUSE WAGON.
I SIMPLY REFUSE TO PUT THAT IN MY NICE CLEAN CART. SOME PEOPLE ARE SO THOUGHTLESS.
AW, GO ON, MATE - THE SCRUFFBAG WILL BE RIGHT AT HOME THERE.
MICE KRISPIES

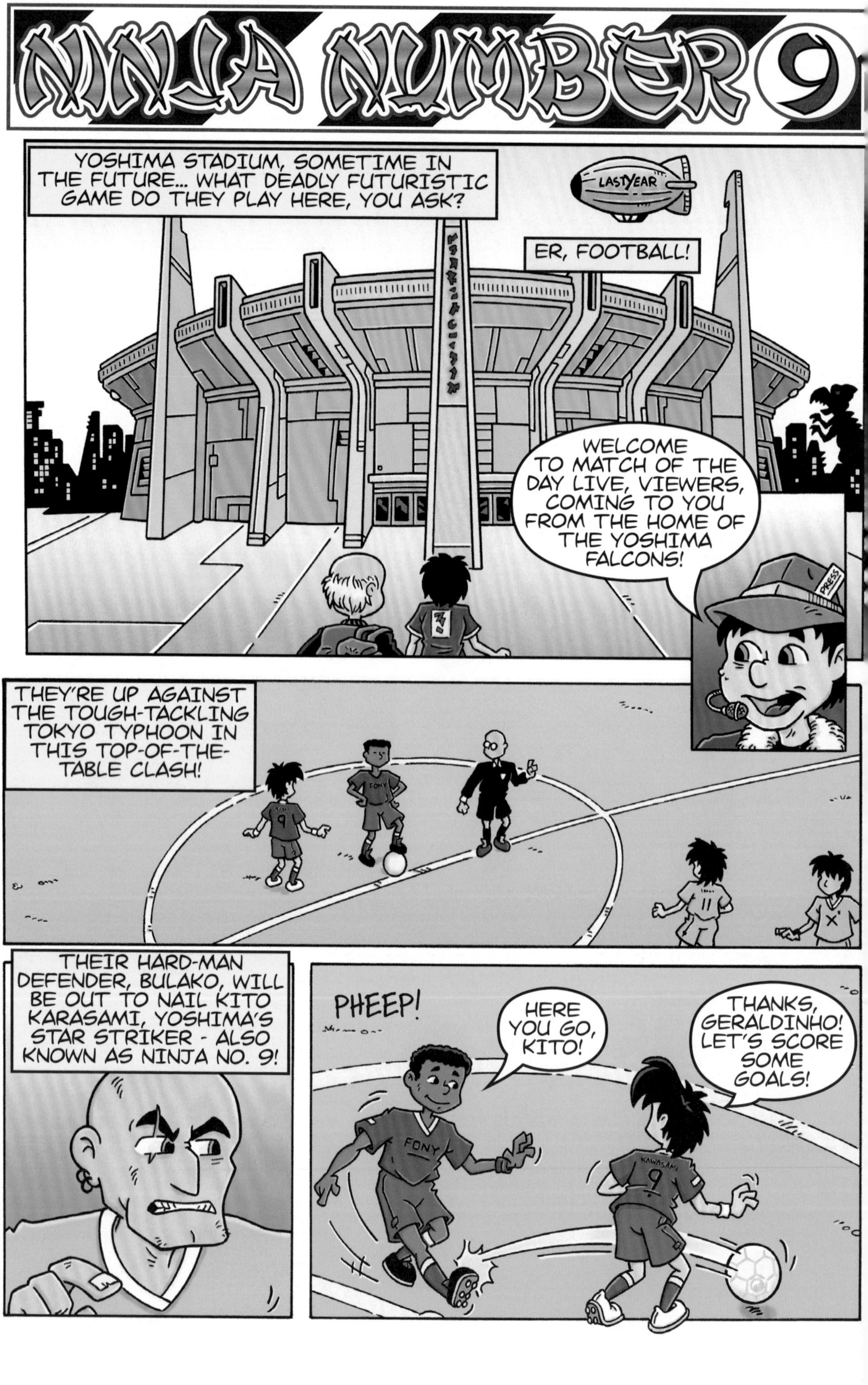
NINJA NUMBER 9
YOSHIMA STADIUM, SOMETIME IN THE FUTURE... WHAT DEADLY FUTURISTIC GAME DO THEY PLAY HERE, YOU ASK?
LASTYEAR
ER, FOOTBALL!
WELCOME TO MATCH OF THE DAY LIVE, VIEWERS, COMING TO YOU FROM THE HOME OF THE YOSHIMA FALCONS!
PRESS
THEY'RE UP AGAINST THE TOUGH-TACKLING TOKYO TYPHOON IN THIS TOP-OF-THE-TABLE CLASH!
THEIR HARD-MAN DEFENDER, BULAKO, WILL BE OUT TO NAIL KITO KARASAMI, YOSHIMA'S STAR STRIKER - ALSO KNOWN AS NINJA NO. 9!
PHEEP!
HERE YOU GO, KITO!
THANKS, GERALDINHO! LET'S SCORE SOME GOALS!
FONY
KAWASAMI

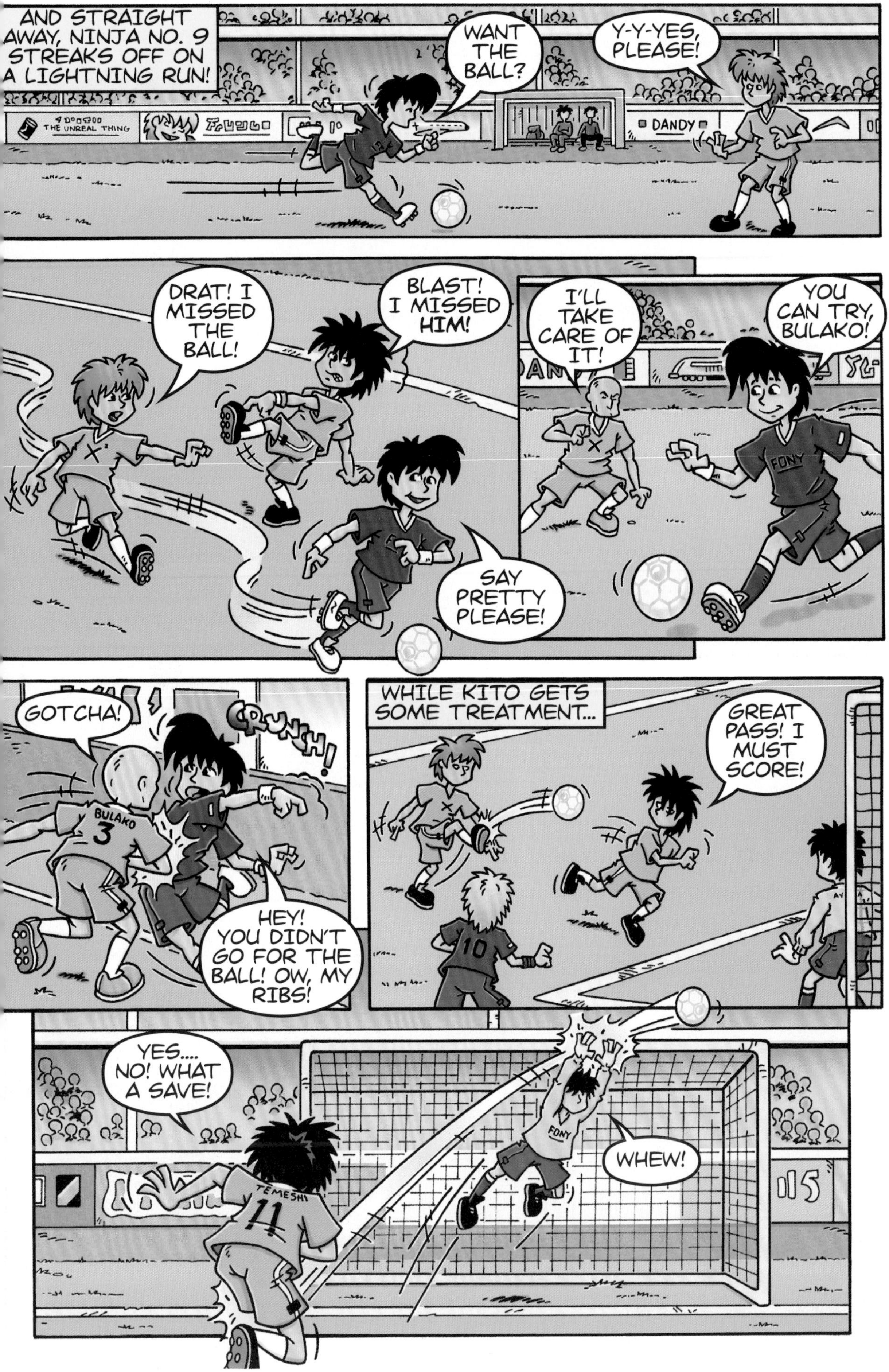
AND STRAIGHT AWAY, NINJA NO. 9 STREAKS OFF ON A LIGHTNING RUN!
THE UNREAL THING
DANDY
WANT THE BALL?
Y-Y-YES, PLEASE!
DRAT! I MISSED THE BALL!
BLAST! I MISSED HIM!
SAY PRETTY PLEASE!
I'LL TAKE CARE OF IT!
YOU CAN TRY, BULAKO!
FONY
GOTCHA!
CRUNSH!
BULAKO
3
HEY! YOU DIDN'T GO FOR THE BALL! OW, MY RIBS!
WHILE KITO GETS SOME TREATMENT...
GREAT PASS! I MUST SCORE!
10
YES.... NO! WHAT A SAVE!
FONY
WHEW!
TEMESHI
11

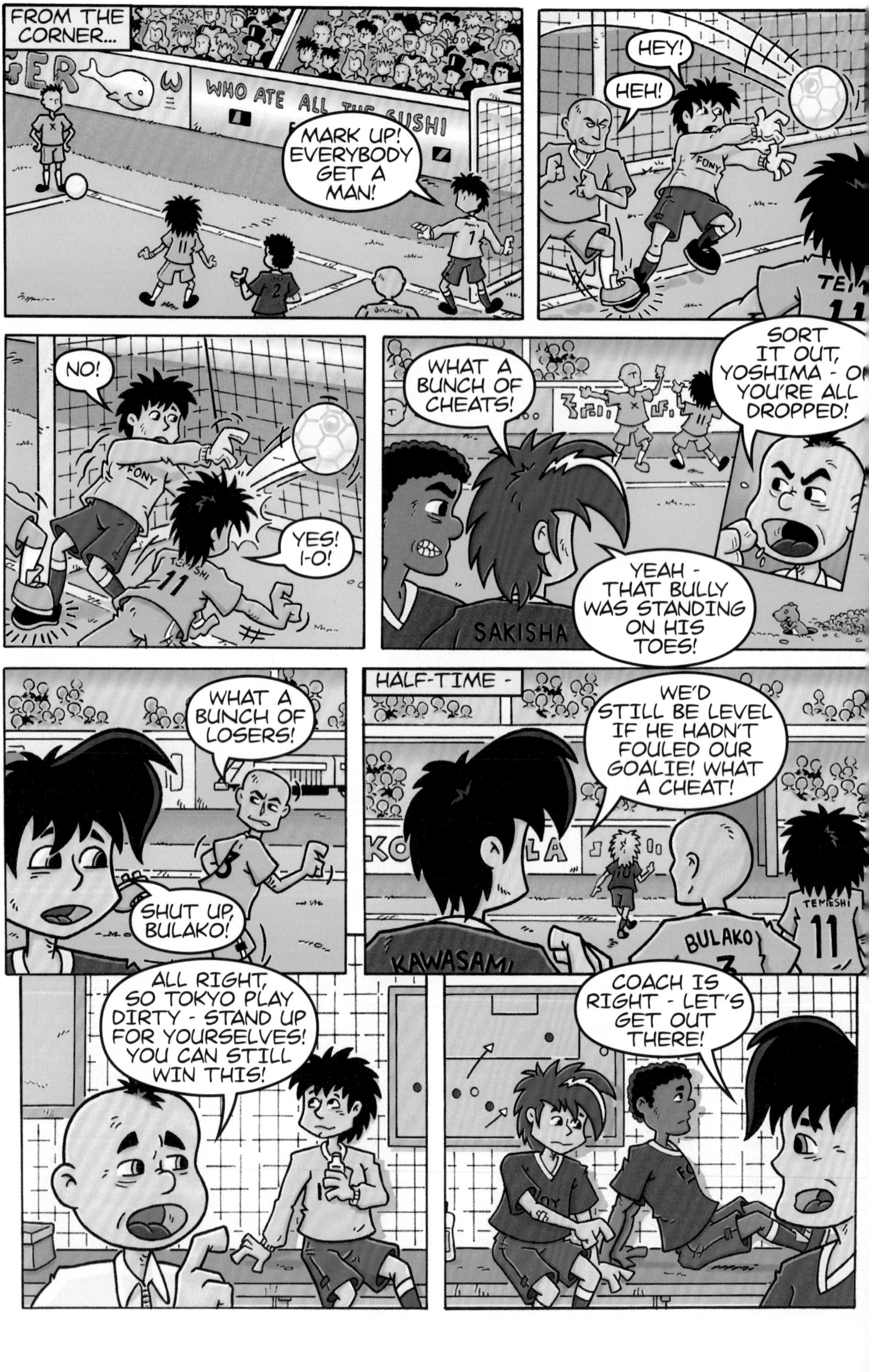

FROM THE CORNER...
MARK UP! EVERYBODY GET A MAN!
HEY!
HEH!
NO!
YES! 1-0!
WHAT A BUNCH OF CHEATS!
SORT IT OUT, YOSHIMA - O
YOU'RE ALL DROPPED!
YEAH - THAT BULLY WAS STANDING ON HIS TOES!
WHAT A BUNCH OF LOSERS!
SHUT UP, BULAKO!
HALF-TIME -
WE'D STILL BE LEVEL IF HE HADN'T FOULED OUR GOALIE! WHAT A CHEAT!
ALL RIGHT, SO TOKYO PLAY DIRTY - STAND UP FOR YOURSELVES! YOU CAN STILL WIN THIS!
COACH IS RIGHT - LET'S GET OUT THERE!

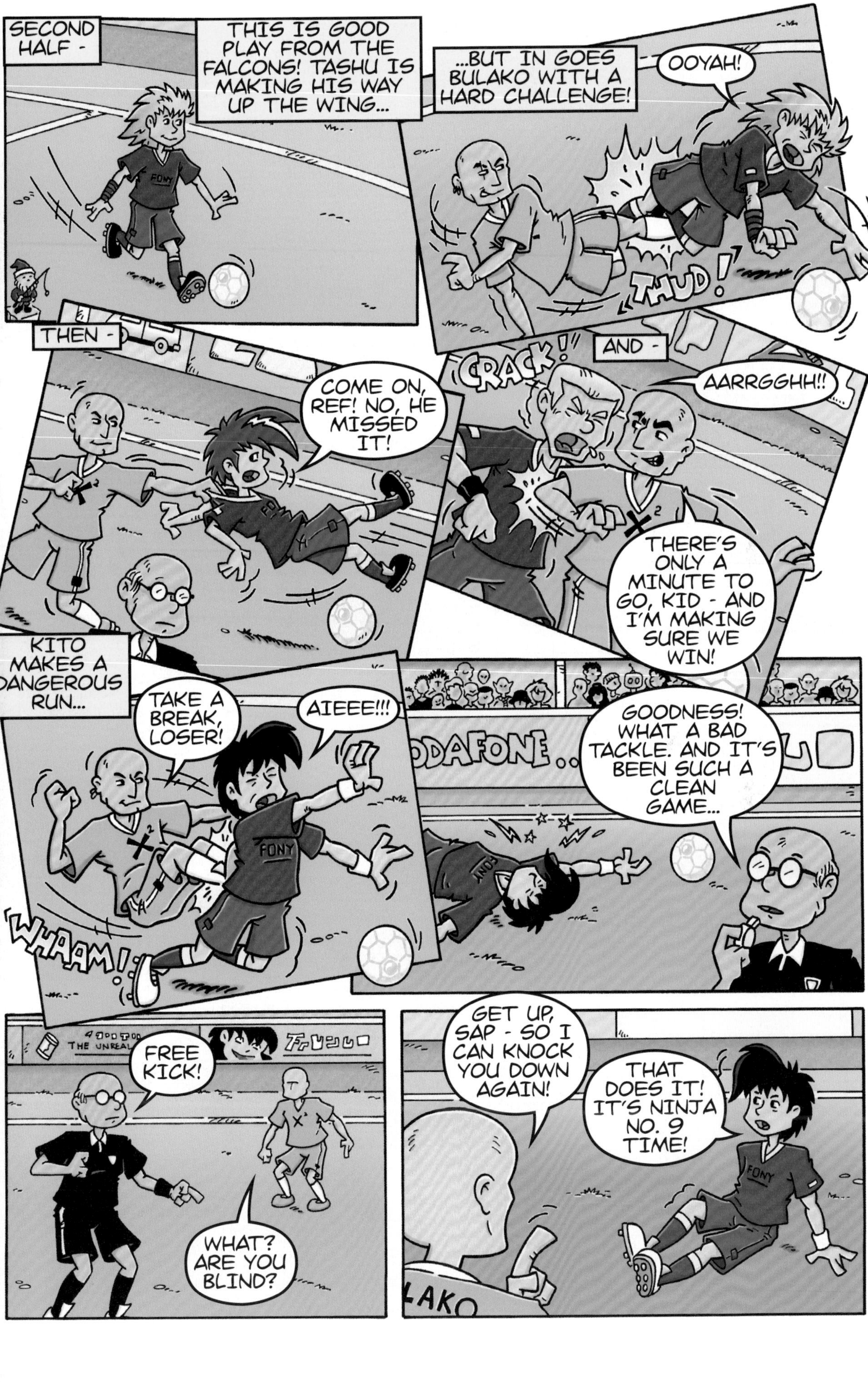
SECOND HALF -
THIS IS GOOD PLAY FROM THE FALCONS! TASHU IS MAKING HIS WAY UP THE WING...
...BUT IN GOES BULAKO WITH A HARD CHALLENGE!
OOYAH!
THUD!
THEN -
COME ON, REF! NO, HE MISSED IT!
AND -
CRACK!
AARRGGHH!!
THERE'S ONLY A MINUTE TO GO, KID - AND I'M MAKING SURE WE WIN!
KITO MAKES A DANGEROUS RUN...
TAKE A BREAK, LOSER!
AIEEE!!!
WHAAM!
GOODNESS! WHAT A BAD TACKLE. AND IT'S BEEN SUCH A CLEAN GAME...
FREE KICK!
WHAT? ARE YOU BLIND?
GET UP, SAP - SO I CAN KNOCK YOU DOWN AGAIN!
THAT DOES IT! IT'S NINJA NO. 9 TIME!

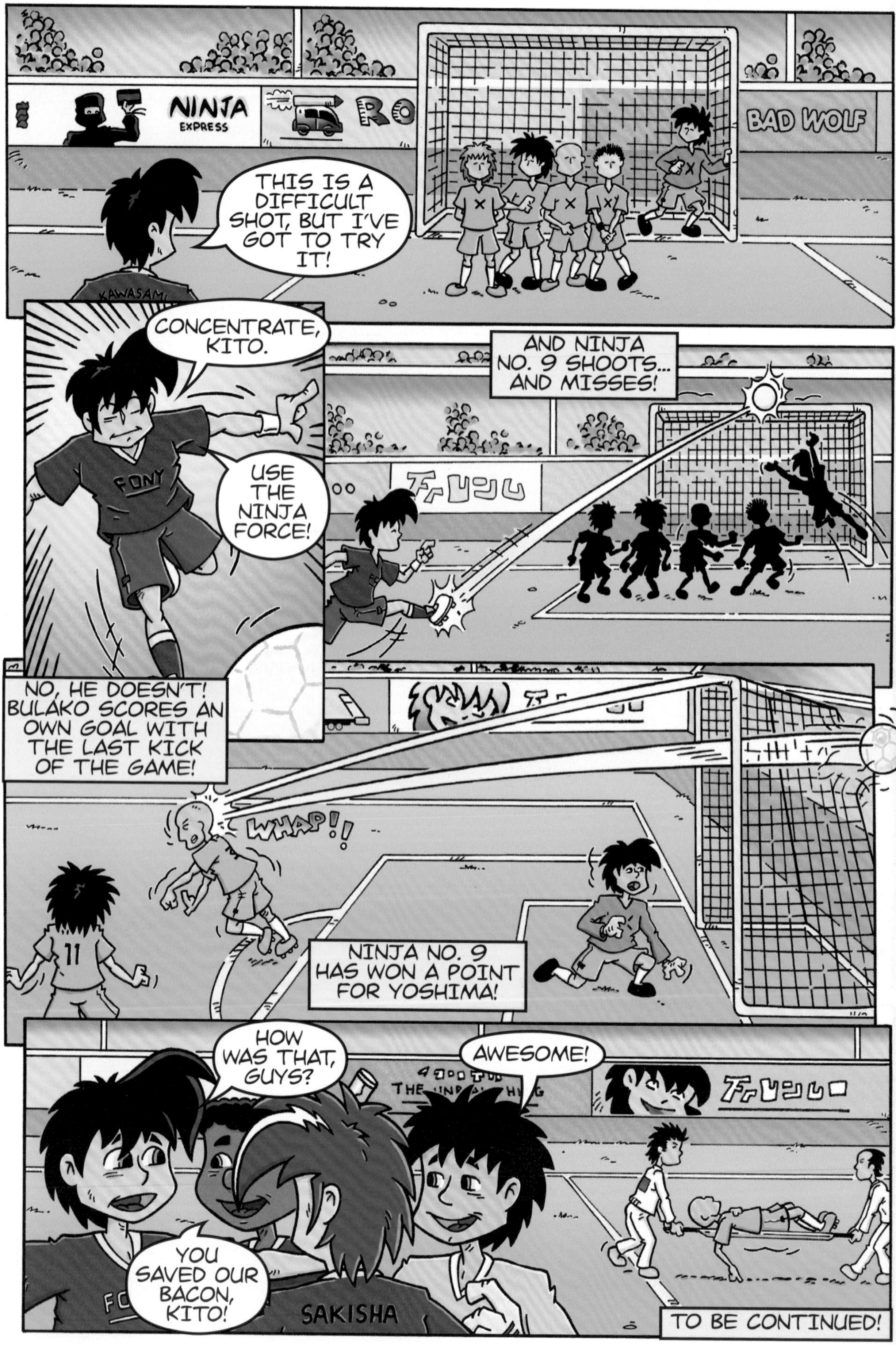
NINJA EXPRESS
BAD WOLF
THIS IS A DIFFICULT SHOT, BUT I'VE GOT TO TRY IT!
KAWASAMI
CONCENTRATE, KITO.
USE THE NINJA FORCE!
FONY
AND NINJA NO. 9 SHOOTS... AND MISSES!
NO, HE DOESN'T! BULAKO SCORES AN OWN GOAL WITH THE LAST KICK OF THE GAME!
WHAP!!
11
NINJA NO. 9 HAS WON A POINT FOR YOSHIMA!
HOW WAS THAT, GUYS?
AWESOME!
YOU SAVED OUR BACON, KITO!
SAKISHA
TO BE CONTINUED!

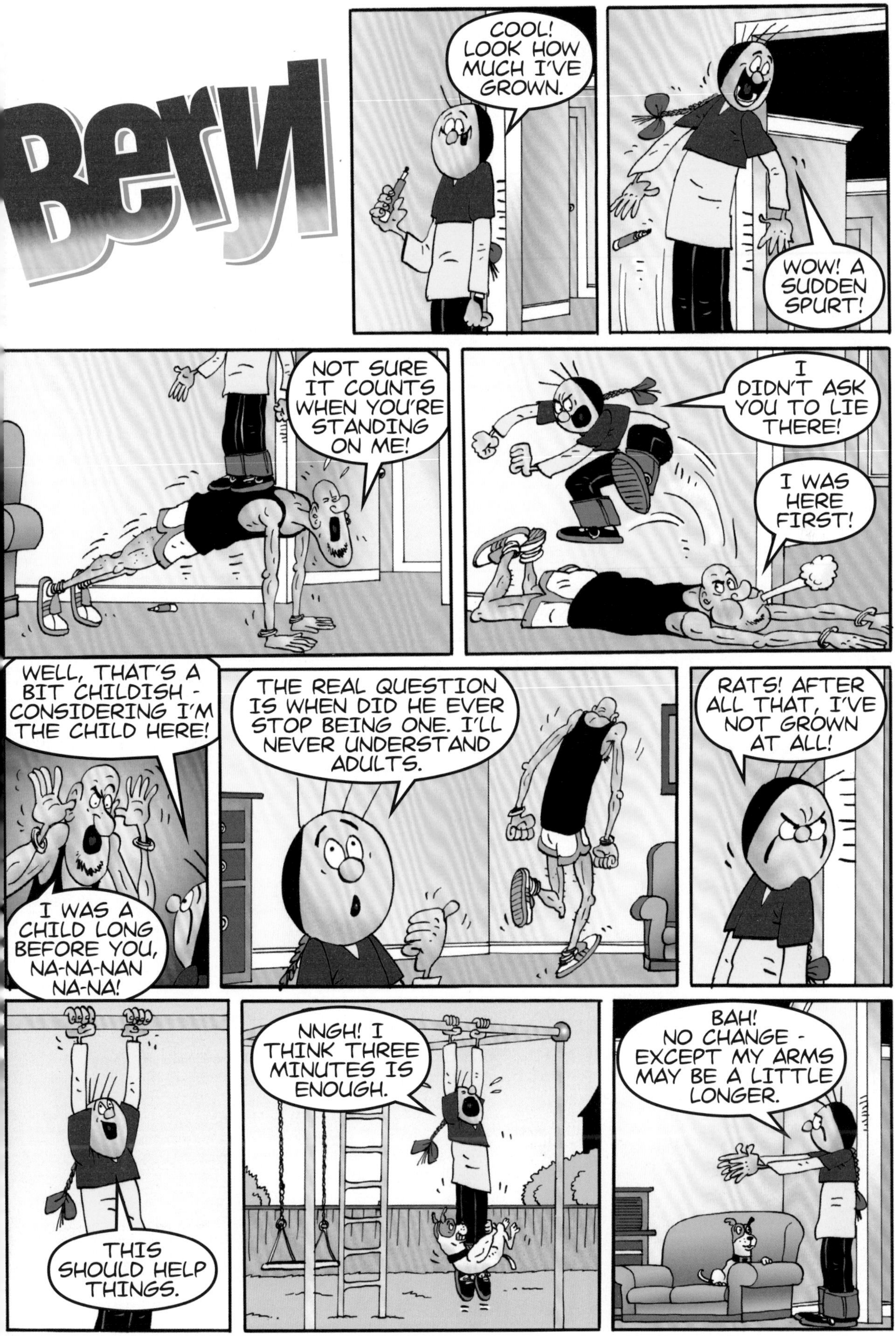
Beryl
COOL! LOOK HOW MUCH I'VE GROWN.
WOW! A SUDDEN SPURT!
NOT SURE IT COUNTS WHEN YOU'RE STANDING ON ME!
I DIDN'T ASK YOU TO LIE THERE!
I WAS HERE FIRST!
WELL, THAT'S A BIT CHILDISH - CONSIDERING I'M THE CHILD HERE!
I WAS A CHILD LONG BEFORE YOU, NA-NA-NAN NA-NA!
THE REAL QUESTION IS WHEN DID HE EVER STOP BEING ONE. I'LL NEVER UNDERSTAND ADULTS.
RATS! AFTER ALL THAT, I'VE NOT GROWN AT ALL!
THIS SHOULD HELP THINGS.
NNGH! I THINK THREE MINUTES IS ENOUGH.
BAH! NO CHANGE - EXCEPT MY ARMS MAY BE A LITTLE LONGER.

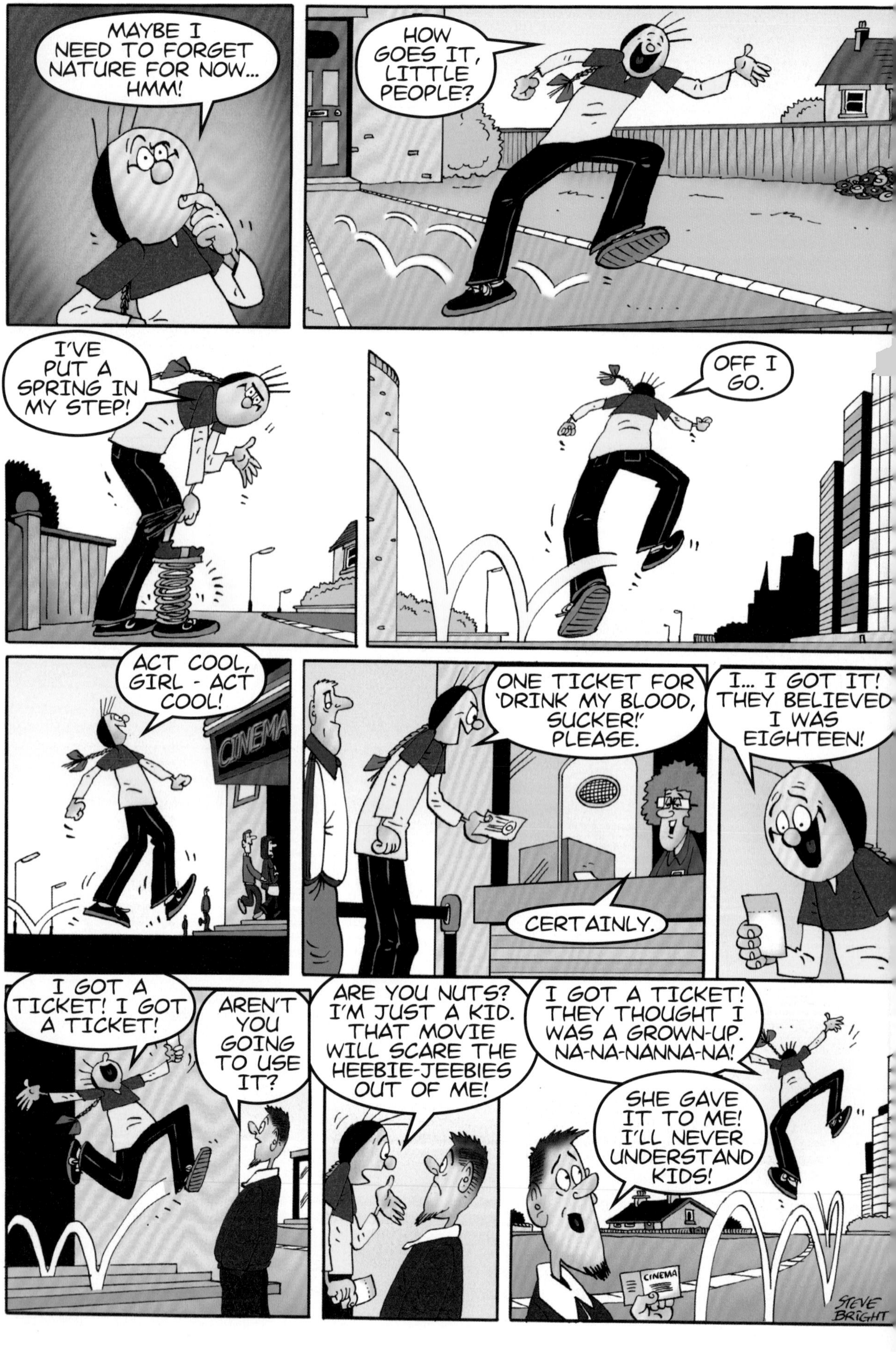
MAYBE I NEED TO FORGET NATURE FOR NOW... HMM!
HOW GOES IT, LITTLE PEOPLE?
I'VE PUT A SPRING IN MY STEP!
OFF I GO.
ACT COOL, GIRL - ACT COOL!
CINEMA
ONE TICKET FOR 'DRINK MY BLOOD, SUCKER!' PLEASE.
CERTAINLY.
I... I GOT IT! THEY BELIEVED I WAS EIGHTEEN!
I GOT A TICKET! I GOT A TICKET!
AREN'T YOU GOING TO USE IT?
ARE YOU NUTS? I'M JUST A KID. THAT MOVIE WILL SCARE THE HEEBIE-JEEBIES OUT OF ME!
I GOT A TICKET! THEY THOUGHT I WAS A GROWN-UP. NA-NA-NANNA-NA!
SHE GAVE IT TO ME! I'LL NEVER UNDERSTAND KIDS!
CINEMA
STEVE BRIGHT

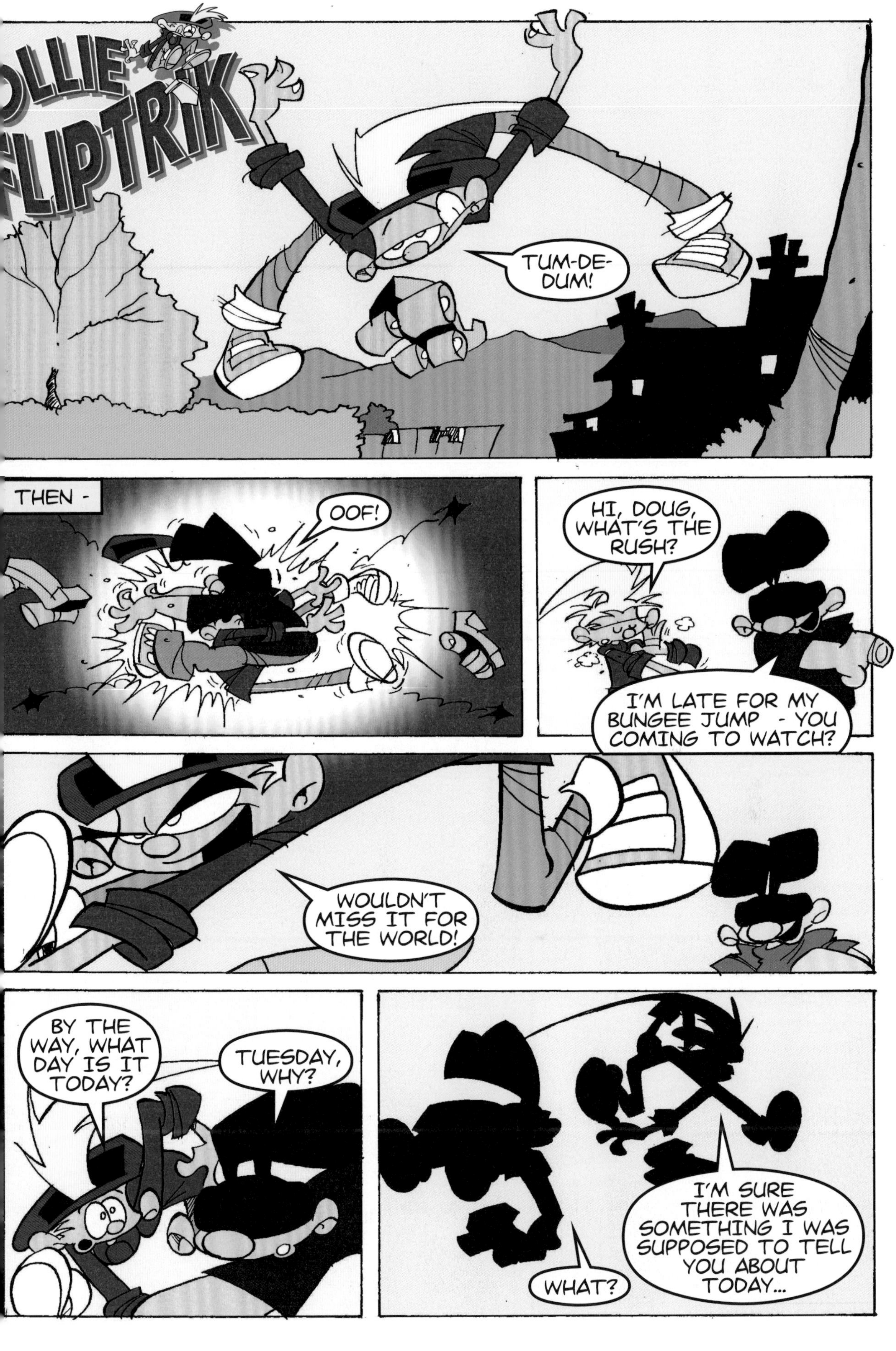
OLLIE FLIPTRIK
TUM-DE-DUM!
THEN -
OOF!
HI, DOUG, WHAT'S THE RUSH?
I'M LATE FOR MY BUNGEE JUMP - YOU COMING TO WATCH?
WOULDN'T MISS IT FOR THE WORLD!
BY THE WAY, WHAT DAY IS IT TODAY?
TUESDAY, WHY?
I'M SURE THERE WAS SOMETHING I WAS SUPPOSED TO TELL YOU ABOUT TODAY...
WHAT?

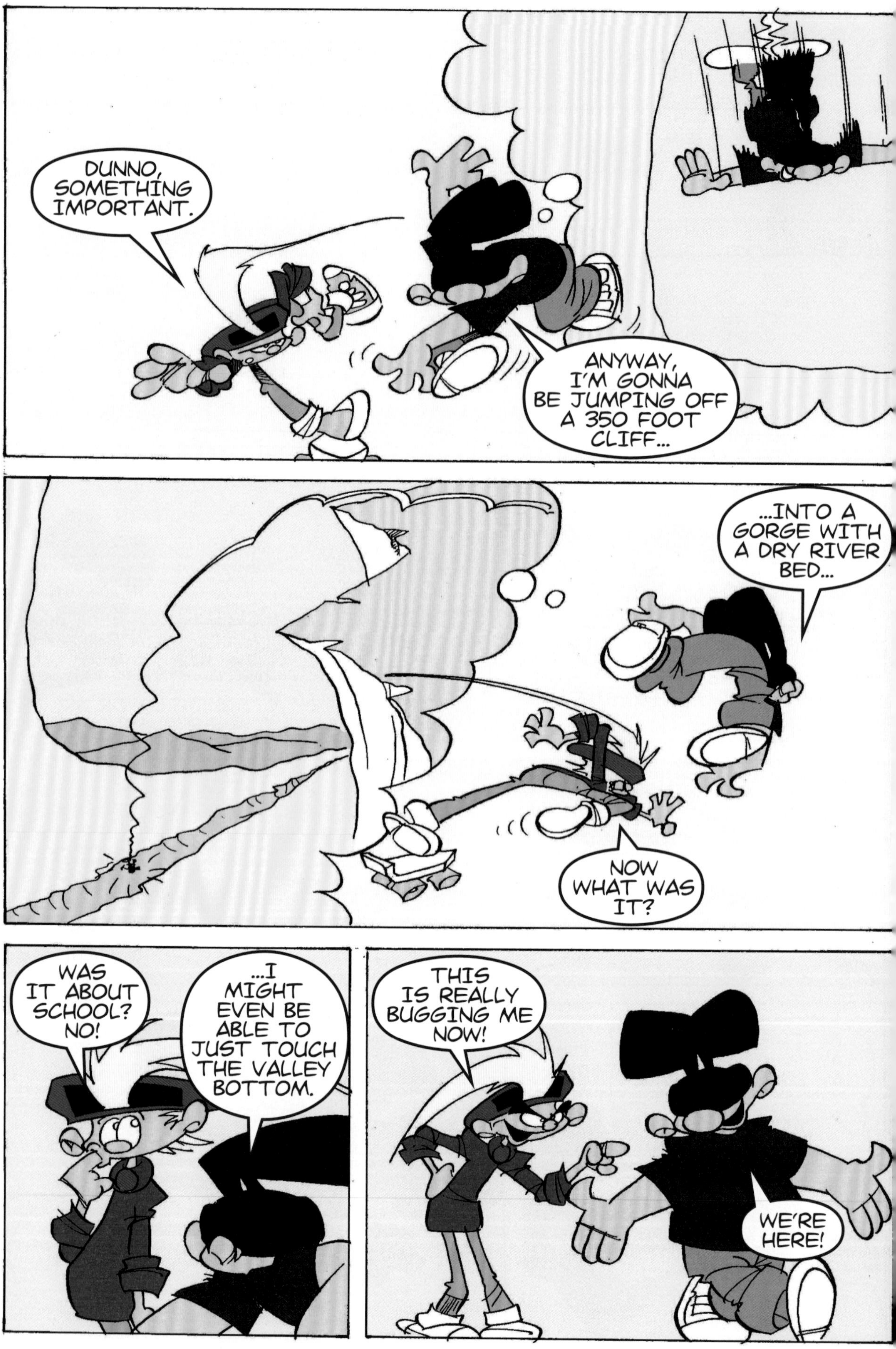

DUNNO, SOMETHING IMPORTANT.
ANYWAY, I'M GONNA BE JUMPING OFF A 350 FOOT CLIFF...
...INTO A GORGE WITH A DRY RIVER BED...
NOW WHAT WAS IT?
WAS IT ABOUT SCHOOL? NO!
...I MIGHT EVEN BE ABLE TO JUST TOUCH THE VALLEY BOTTOM.
THIS IS REALLY BUGGING ME NOW!
WE'RE HERE!

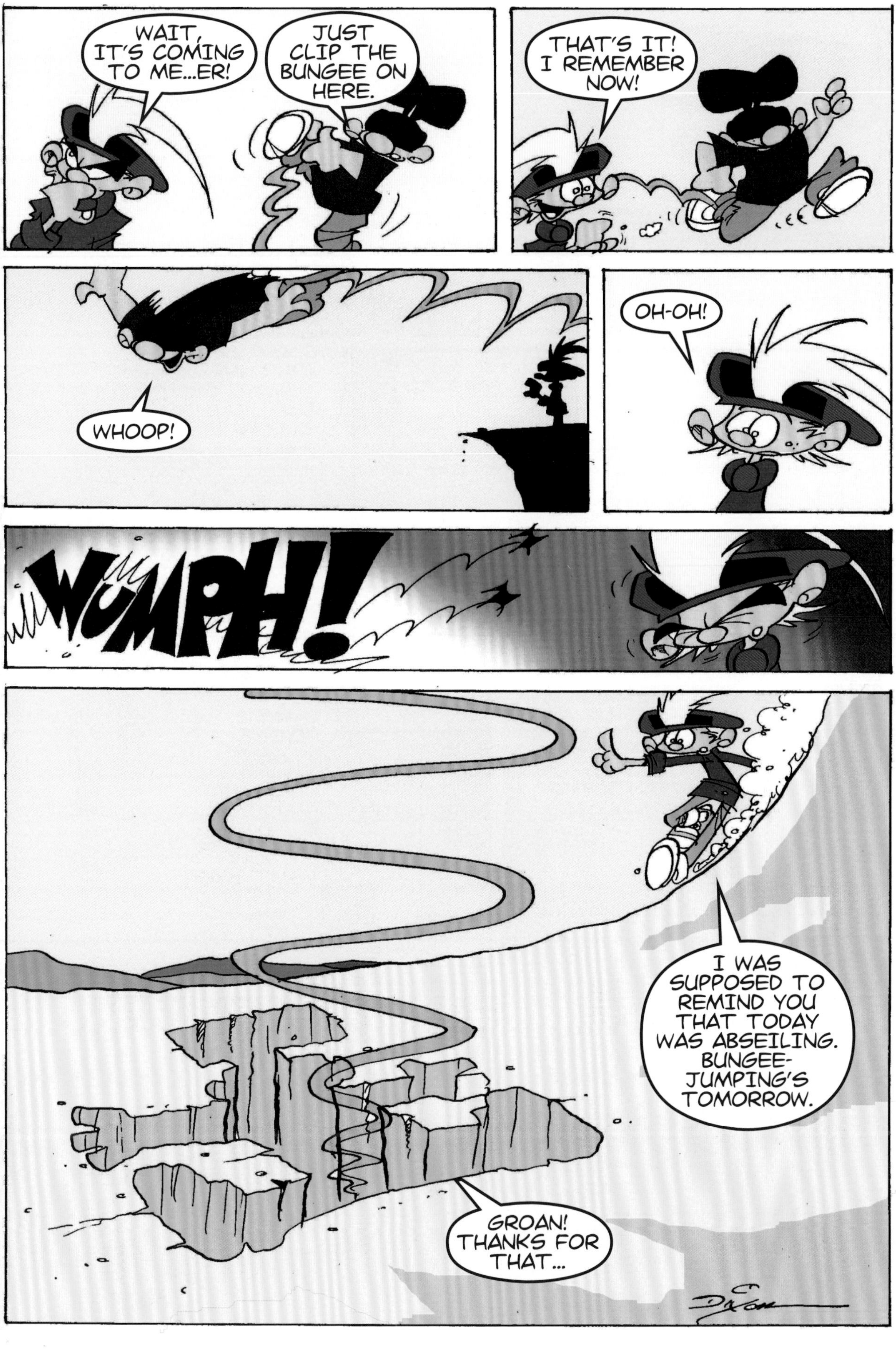
WAIT, IT'S COMING TO ME...ER!
JUST CLIP THE BUNGEE ON HERE.
THAT'S IT! I REMEMBER NOW!
WHOOP!
OH-OH!
WUMPH!
I WAS SUPPOSED TO REMIND YOU THAT TODAY WAS ABSEILING. BUNGEE-JUMPING'S TOMORROW.
GROAN! THANKS FOR THAT...

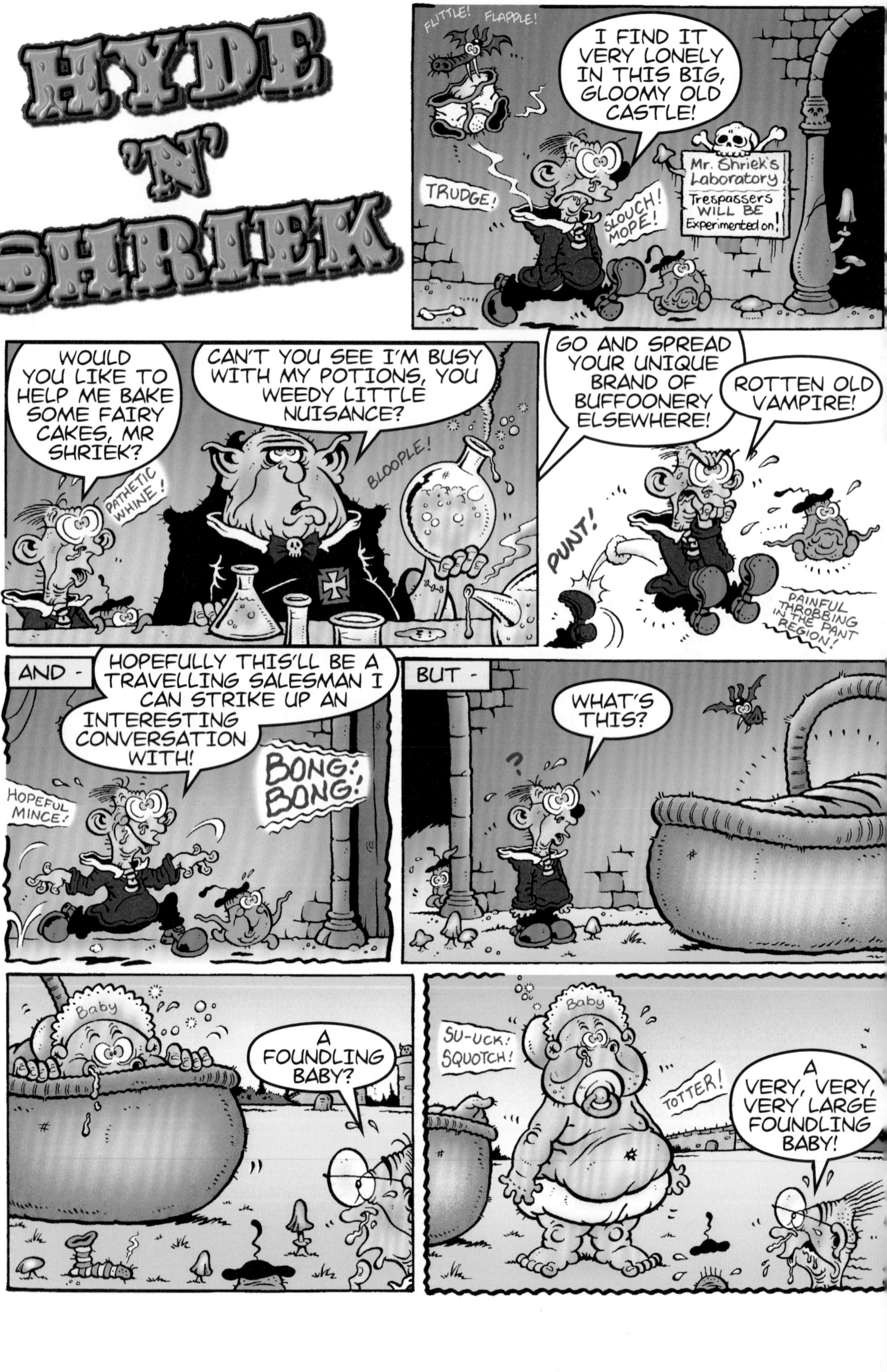
HYDE 'N' SHRIEK
FLITTLE! FLAPPLE!
I FIND IT VERY LONELY IN THIS BIG, GLOOMY OLD CASTLE!
TRUDGE!
SLOUCH! MOPE!
Mr. Shriek's Laboratory
Trespassers WILL BE Experimented on!
WOULD YOU LIKE TO HELP ME BAKE SOME FAIRY CAKES, MR SHRIEK?
PATHETIC WHINE!
CAN'T YOU SEE I'M BUSY WITH MY POTIONS, YOU WEEDY LITTLE NUISANCE?
BLOOPLE!
GO AND SPREAD YOUR UNIQUE BRAND OF BUFFOONERY ELSEWHERE!
ROTTEN OLD VAMPIRE!
PUNT!
PAINFUL THROBBING IN THE PANT REGION!
AND -
HOPEFULLY THIS'LL BE A TRAVELLING SALESMAN I CAN STRIKE UP AN INTERESTING CONVERSATION WITH!
BONG! BONG!
HOPEFUL MINCE!
BUT -
WHAT'S THIS?
Baby
A FOUNDLING BABY?
SU-UCK! SQUOTCH!
TOTTER!
Baby
A VERY, VERY, VERY LARGE FOUNDLING BABY!

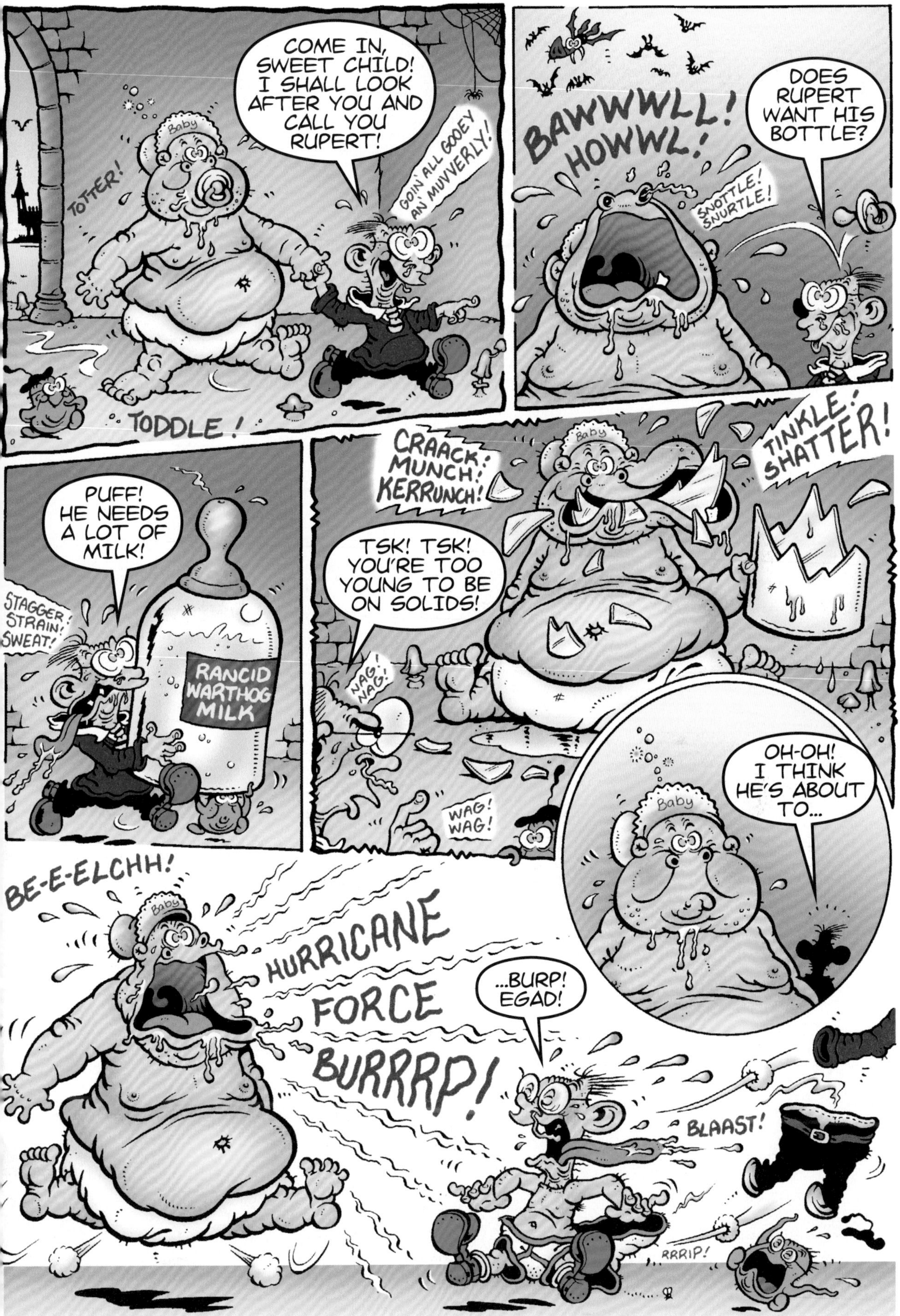
COME IN, SWEET CHILD! I SHALL LOOK AFTER YOU AND CALL YOU RUPERT!
GO'IN ALL GOOEY AN' MUVVERLY!
TOTTER!
TODDLE!
BAWWWLL! HOWWL!
DOES RUPERT WANT HIS BOTTLE?
SNOTTLE! SNURTLE!
PUFF! HE NEEDS A LOT OF MILK!
STAGGER! STRAIN! SWEAT!
RANCID WARTHOG MILK
CRAACK! MUNCH! KERRUNCH!
TINKLE! SHATTER!
TSK! TSK! YOU'RE TOO YOUNG TO BE ON SOLIDS!
NAG! NAG!
WAG! WAG!
OH-OH! I THINK HE'S ABOUT TO...
BE-E-ELCHH!
HURRICANE FORCE BURRRP!
...BURP! EGAD!
BLAAST!
RRRIP!

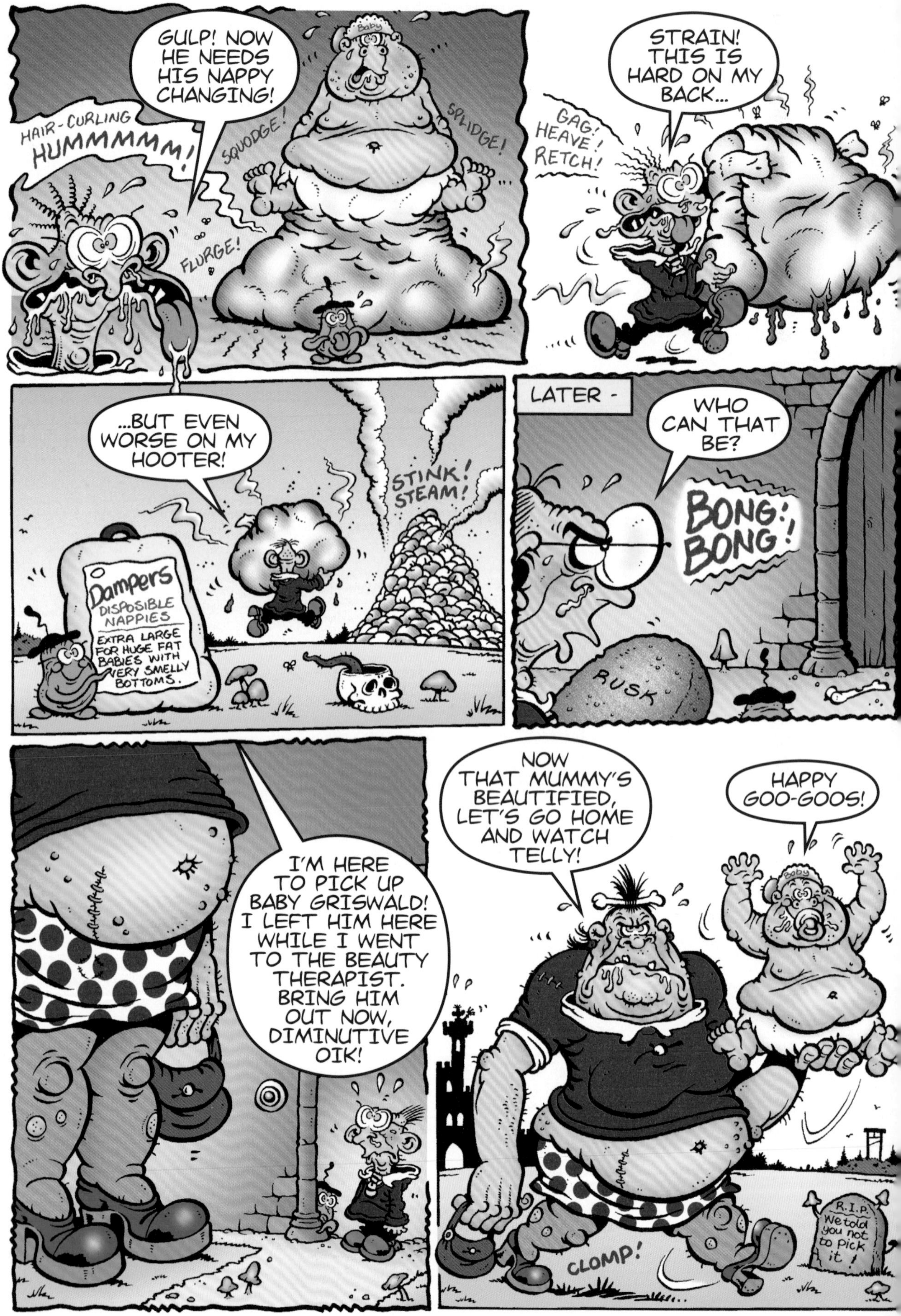
GULP! NOW HE NEEDS HIS NAPPY CHANGING!
Baby
HAIR-CURLING HUMMMMMM!
SQUODGE!
SPLIDGE!
FLURGE!
STRAIN! THIS IS HARD ON MY BACK...
GAG! HEAVE! RETCH!
...BUT EVEN WORSE ON MY HOOTER!
STINK! STEAM!
Dampers
DISPOSIBLE NAPPIES
EXTRA LARGE FOR HUGE FAT BABIES WITH VERY SMELLY BOTTOMS.
LATER -
WHO CAN THAT BE?
BONG! BONG!
RUSK
I'M HERE TO PICK UP BABY GRISWALD! I LEFT HIM HERE WHILE I WENT TO THE BEAUTY THERAPIST. BRING HIM OUT NOW, DIMINUTIVE OIK!
NOW THAT MUMMY'S BEAUTIFIED, LET'S GO HOME AND WATCH TELLY!
HAPPY GOO-GOOS!
Baby
CLOMP!
R.I.P. We told you not to pick it!

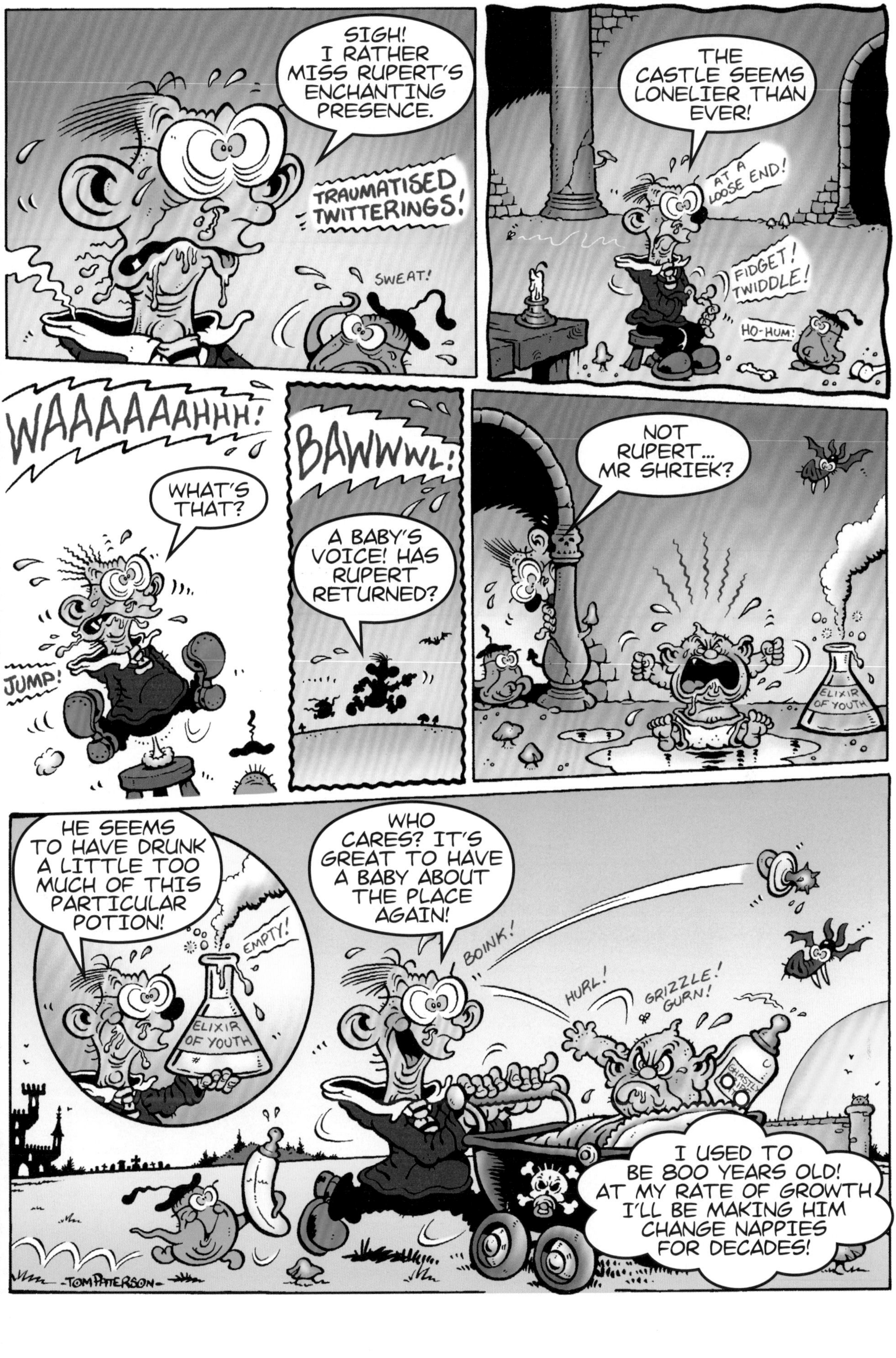
SIGH! I RATHER MISS RUPERT'S ENCHANTING PRESENCE.
TRAUMATISED TWITTERINGS!
SWEAT!
THE CASTLE SEEMS LONELIER THAN EVER!
AT A LOOSE END!
FIDGET! TWIDDLE!
HO-HUM!
WAAAAAAHHH!
WHAT'S THAT?
JUMP!
BAWWWL!
A BABY'S VOICE! HAS RUPERT RETURNED?
NOT RUPERT... MR SHRIEK?
ELIXIR OF YOUTH
HE SEEMS TO HAVE DRUNK A LITTLE TOO MUCH OF THIS PARTICULAR POTION!
EMPTY!
ELIXIR OF YOUTH
WHO CARES? IT'S GREAT TO HAVE A BABY ABOUT THE PLACE AGAIN!
BOINK!
HURL!
GRIZZLE! GURN!
I USED TO BE 800 YEARS OLD! AT MY RATE OF GROWTH I'LL BE MAKING HIM CHANGE NAPPIES FOR DECADES!
TOM PATERSON

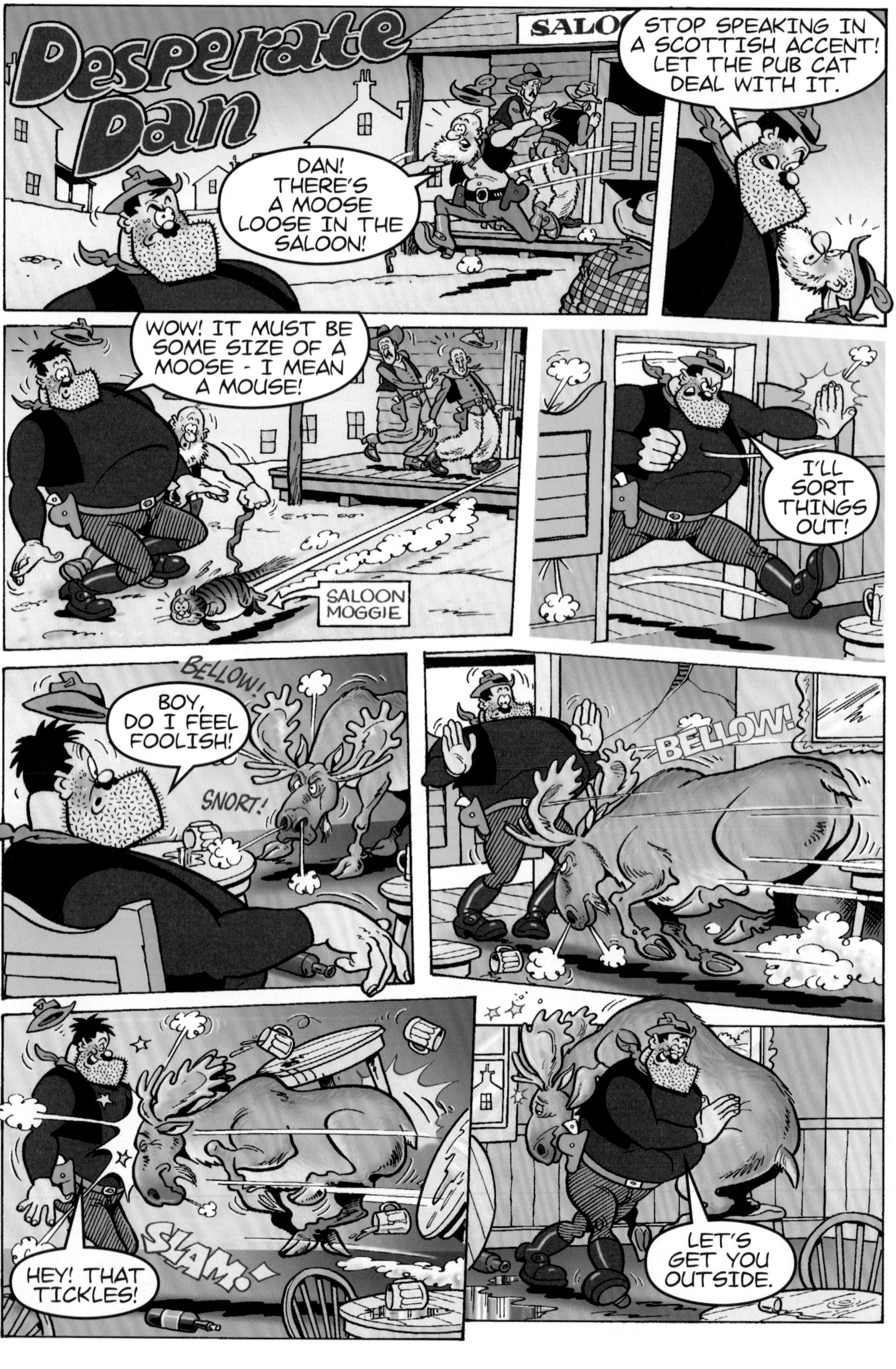
Desperate Dan
SALOO
DAN! THERE'S A MOOSE LOOSE IN THE SALOON!
STOP SPEAKING IN A SCOTTISH ACCENT! LET THE PUB CAT DEAL WITH IT.
WOW! IT MUST BE SOME SIZE OF A MOOSE - I MEAN A MOUSE!
SALOON MOGGIE
I'LL SORT THINGS OUT!
BELLOW!
BOY, DO I FEEL FOOLISH!
SNORT!
BELLOW!
SLAM!
HEY! THAT TICKLES!
LET'S GET YOU OUTSIDE.

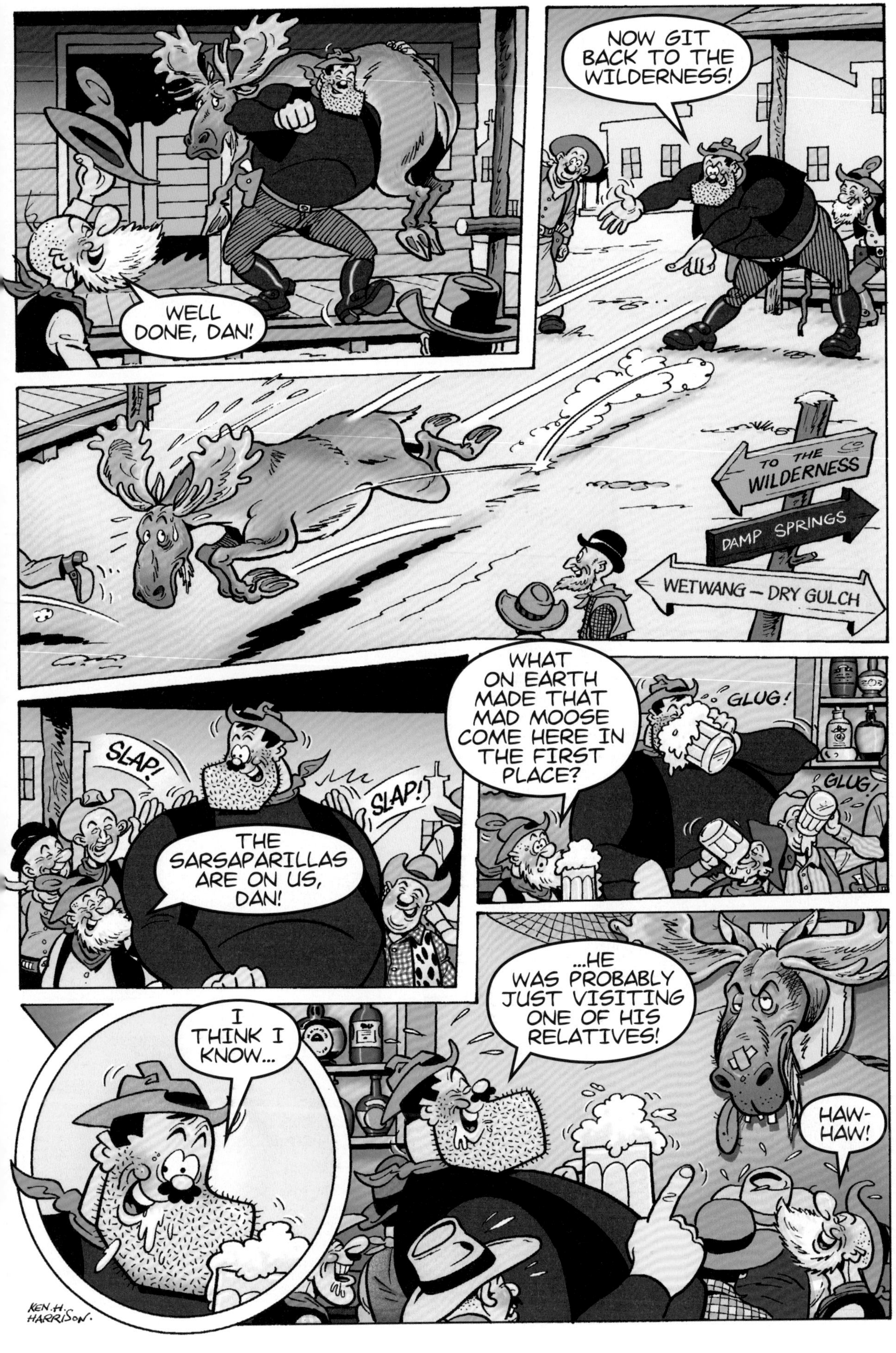
WELL DONE, DAN!
NOW GIT BACK TO THE WILDERNESS!
TO THE WILDERNESS
DAMP SPRINGS
WETWANG – DRY GULCH
SLAP!
SLAP!
THE SARSAPARILLAS ARE ON US, DAN!
WHAT ON EARTH MADE THAT MAD MOOSE COME HERE IN THE FIRST PLACE?
GLUG!
GLUG!
I THINK I KNOW...
...HE WAS PROBABLY JUST VISITING ONE OF HIS RELATIVES!
HAW-HAW!
KEN. H. HARRISON.

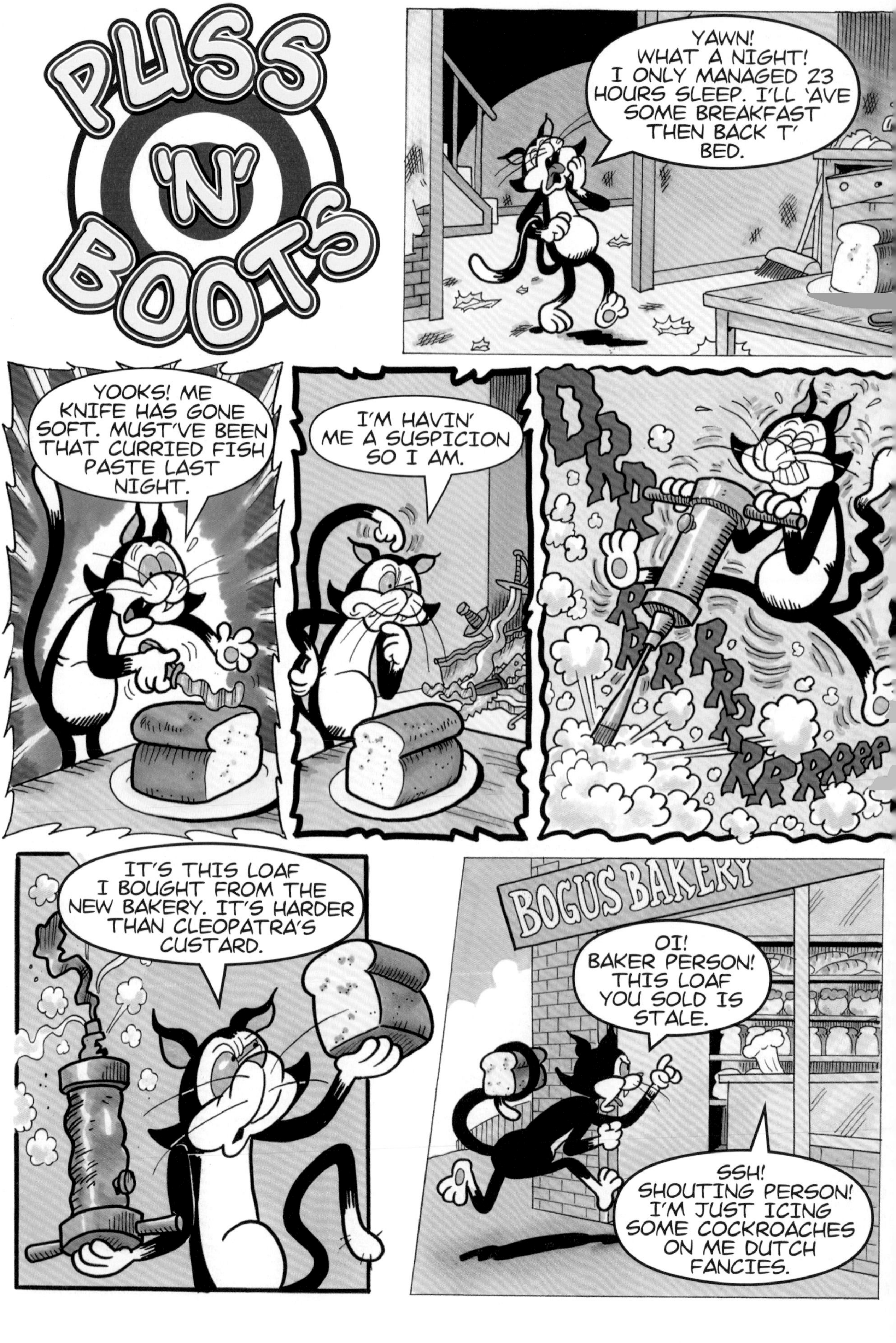
PUSS 'N' BOOTS
YAWN! WHAT A NIGHT! I ONLY MANAGED 23 HOURS SLEEP. I'LL 'AVE SOME BREAKFAST THEN BACK T' BED.
YOOKS! ME KNIFE HAS GONE SOFT. MUST'VE BEEN THAT CURRIED FISH PASTE LAST NIGHT.
I'M HAVIN' ME A SUSPICION SO I AM.
DRRRRRRRRRRRRRRRRRRPP
IT'S THIS LOAF I BOUGHT FROM THE NEW BAKERY. IT'S HARDER THAN CLEOPATRA'S CUSTARD.
BOGUS BAKERY
OI! BAKER PERSON! THIS LOAF YOU SOLD IS STALE.
SSH! SHOUTING PERSON! I'M JUST ICING SOME COCKROACHES ON ME DUTCH FANCIES.

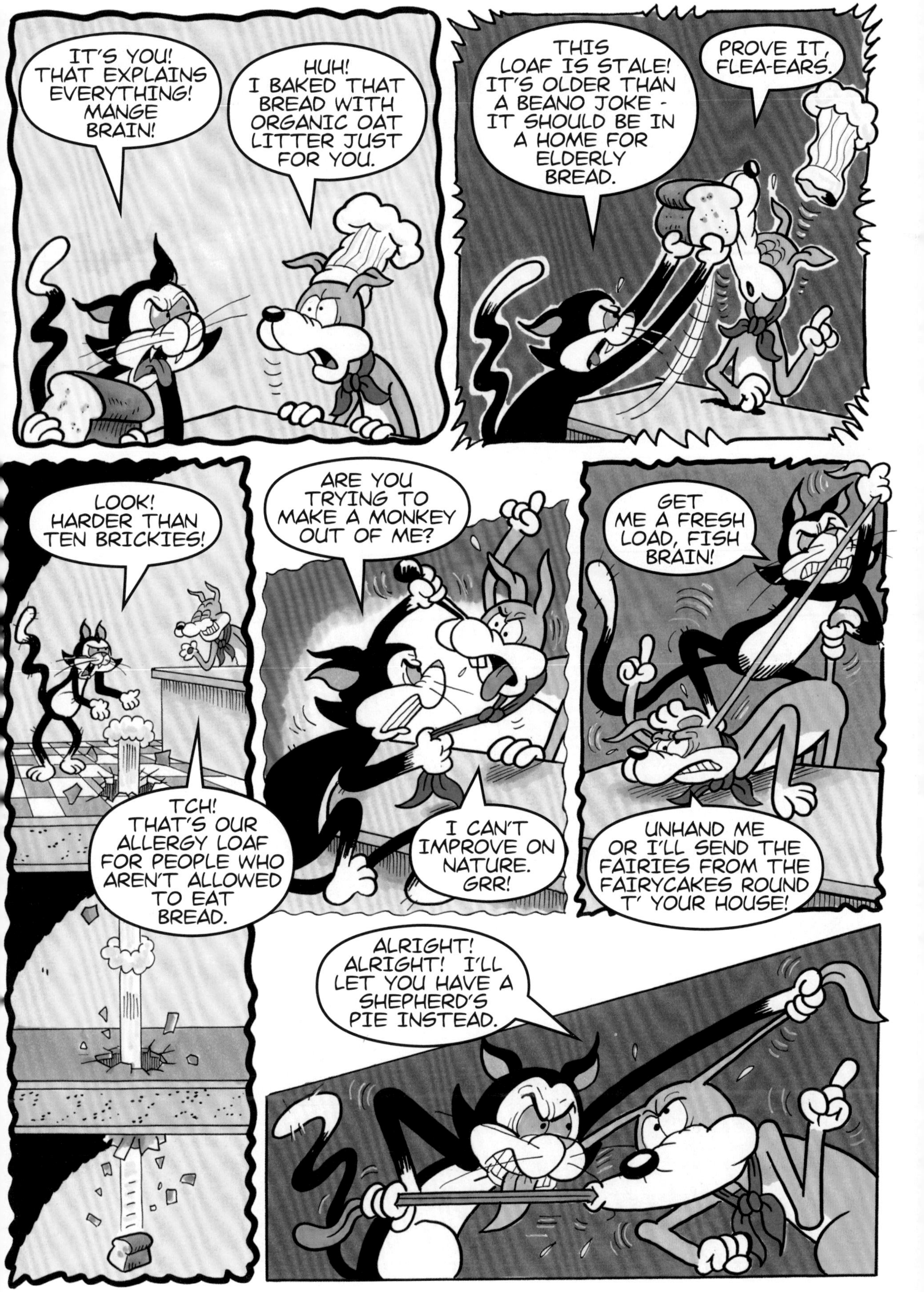
IT'S YOU! THAT EXPLAINS EVERYTHING! MANGE BRAIN!
HUH! I BAKED THAT BREAD WITH ORGANIC OAT LITTER JUST FOR YOU.
THIS LOAF IS STALE! IT'S OLDER THAN A BEANO JOKE - IT SHOULD BE IN A HOME FOR ELDERLY BREAD.
PROVE IT, FLEA-EARS.
LOOK! HARDER THAN TEN BRICKIES!
TCH! THAT'S OUR ALLERGY LOAF FOR PEOPLE WHO AREN'T ALLOWED TO EAT BREAD.
ARE YOU TRYING TO MAKE A MONKEY OUT OF ME?
I CAN'T IMPROVE ON NATURE. GRR!
GET ME A FRESH LOAD, FISH BRAIN!
UNHAND ME OR I'LL SEND THE FAIRIES FROM THE FAIRYCAKES ROUND T' YOUR HOUSE!
ALRIGHT! ALRIGHT! I'LL LET YOU HAVE A SHEPHERD'S PIE INSTEAD.

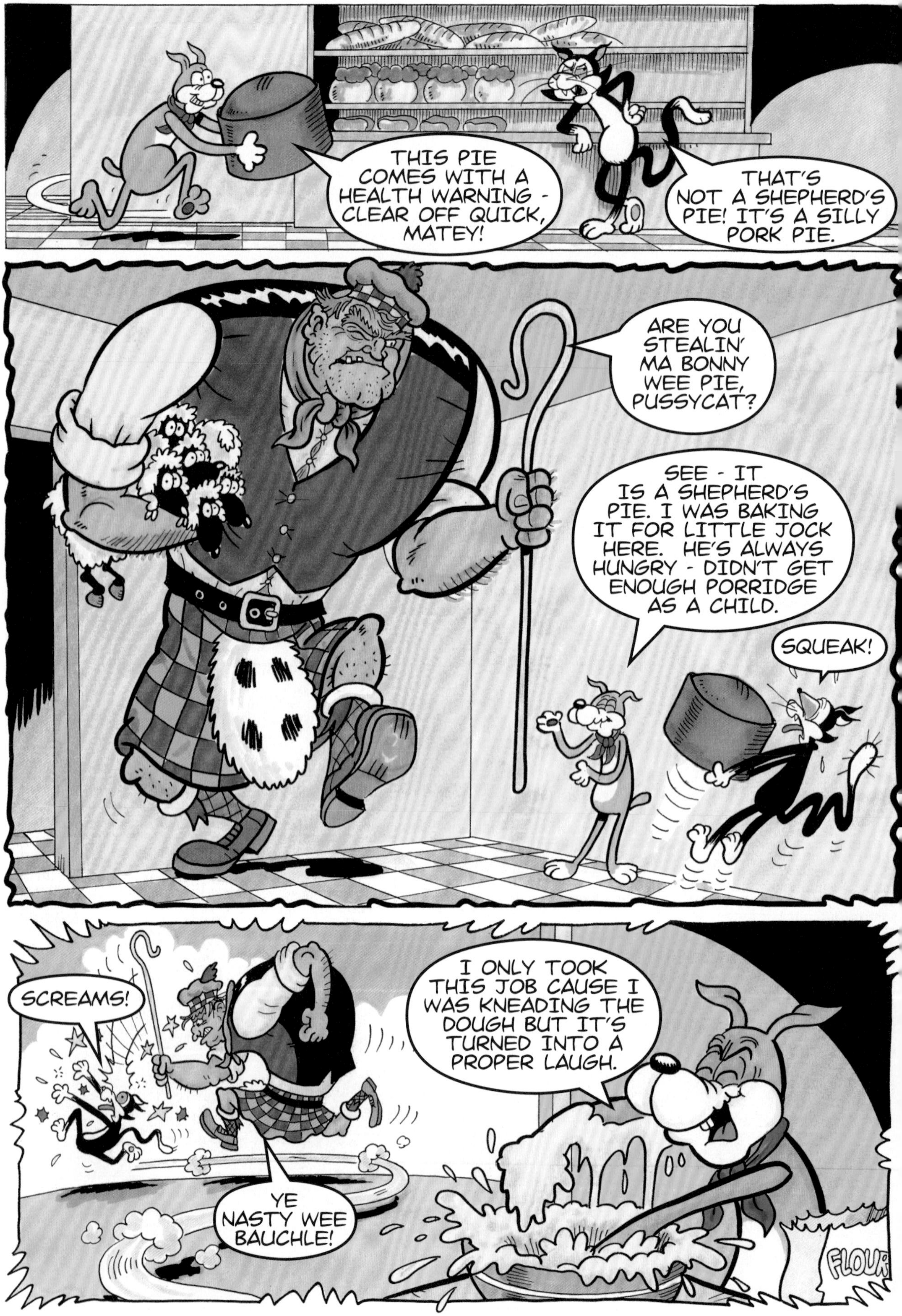
THIS PIE COMES WITH A HEALTH WARNING - CLEAR OFF QUICK, MATEY!
THAT'S NOT A SHEPHERD'S PIE! IT'S A SILLY PORK PIE.
ARE YOU STEALIN' MA BONNY WEE PIE, PUSSYCAT?
SEE - IT IS A SHEPHERD'S PIE. I WAS BAKING IT FOR LITTLE JOCK HERE. HE'S ALWAYS HUNGRY - DIDN'T GET ENOUGH PORRIDGE AS A CHILD.
SQUEAK!
SCREAMS!
YE NASTY WEE BAUCHLE!
I ONLY TOOK THIS JOB CAUSE I WAS KNEADING THE DOUGH BUT IT'S TURNED INTO A PROPER LAUGH.
FLOUR

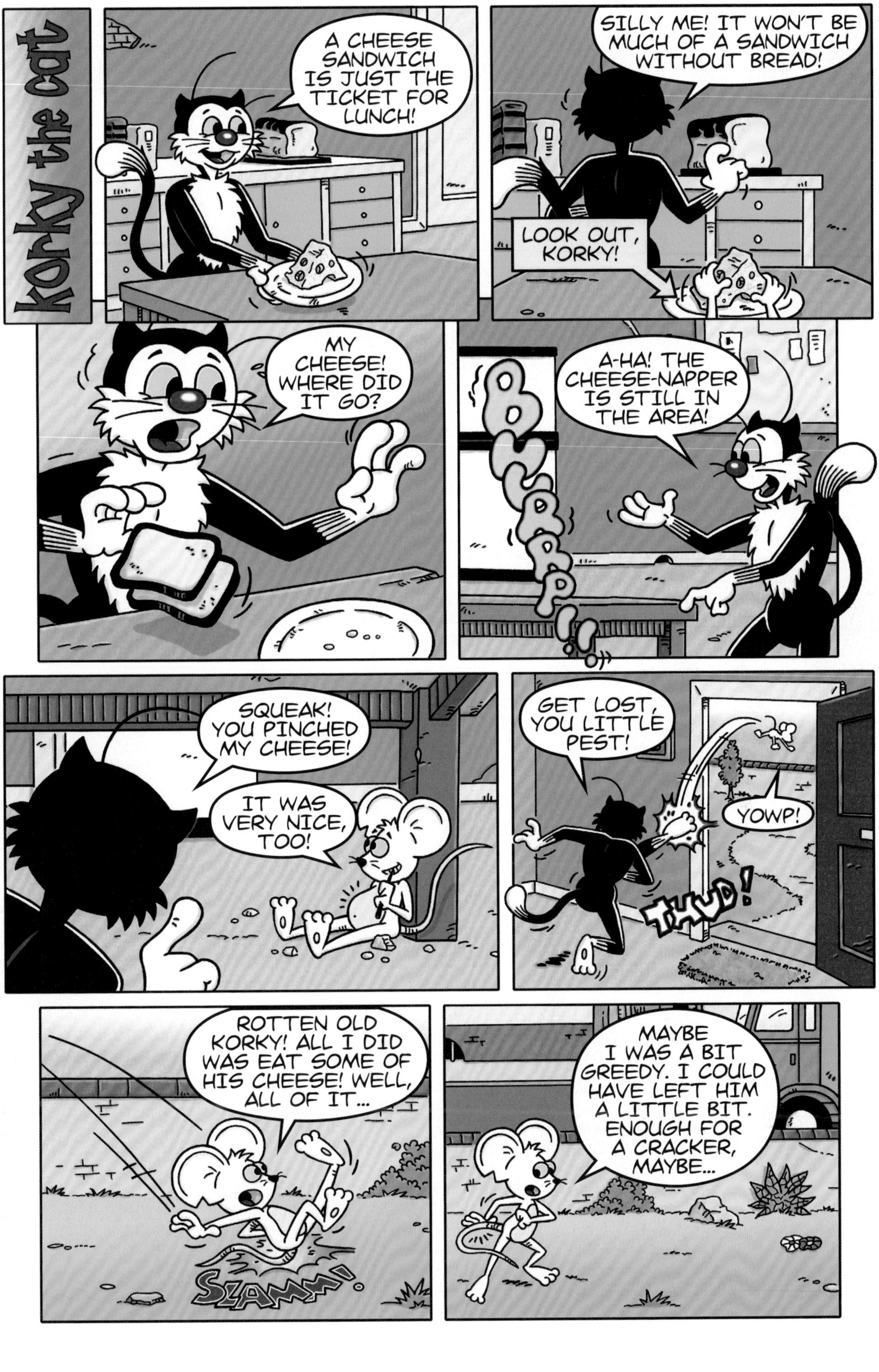
Korky the cat
A CHEESE SANDWICH IS JUST THE TICKET FOR LUNCH!
SILLY ME! IT WON'T BE MUCH OF A SANDWICH WITHOUT BREAD!
LOOK OUT, KORKY!
MY CHEESE! WHERE DID IT GO?
BURRP!!
A-HA! THE CHEESE-NAPPER IS STILL IN THE AREA!
SQUEAK! YOU PINCHED MY CHEESE!
IT WAS VERY NICE, TOO!
GET LOST, YOU LITTLE PEST!
YOWP!
THUD!
ROTTEN OLD KORKY! ALL I DID WAS EAT SOME OF HIS CHEESE! WELL, ALL OF IT...
SLAMM!
MAYBE I WAS A BIT GREEDY. I COULD HAVE LEFT HIM A LITTLE BIT. ENOUGH FOR A CRACKER, MAYBE...

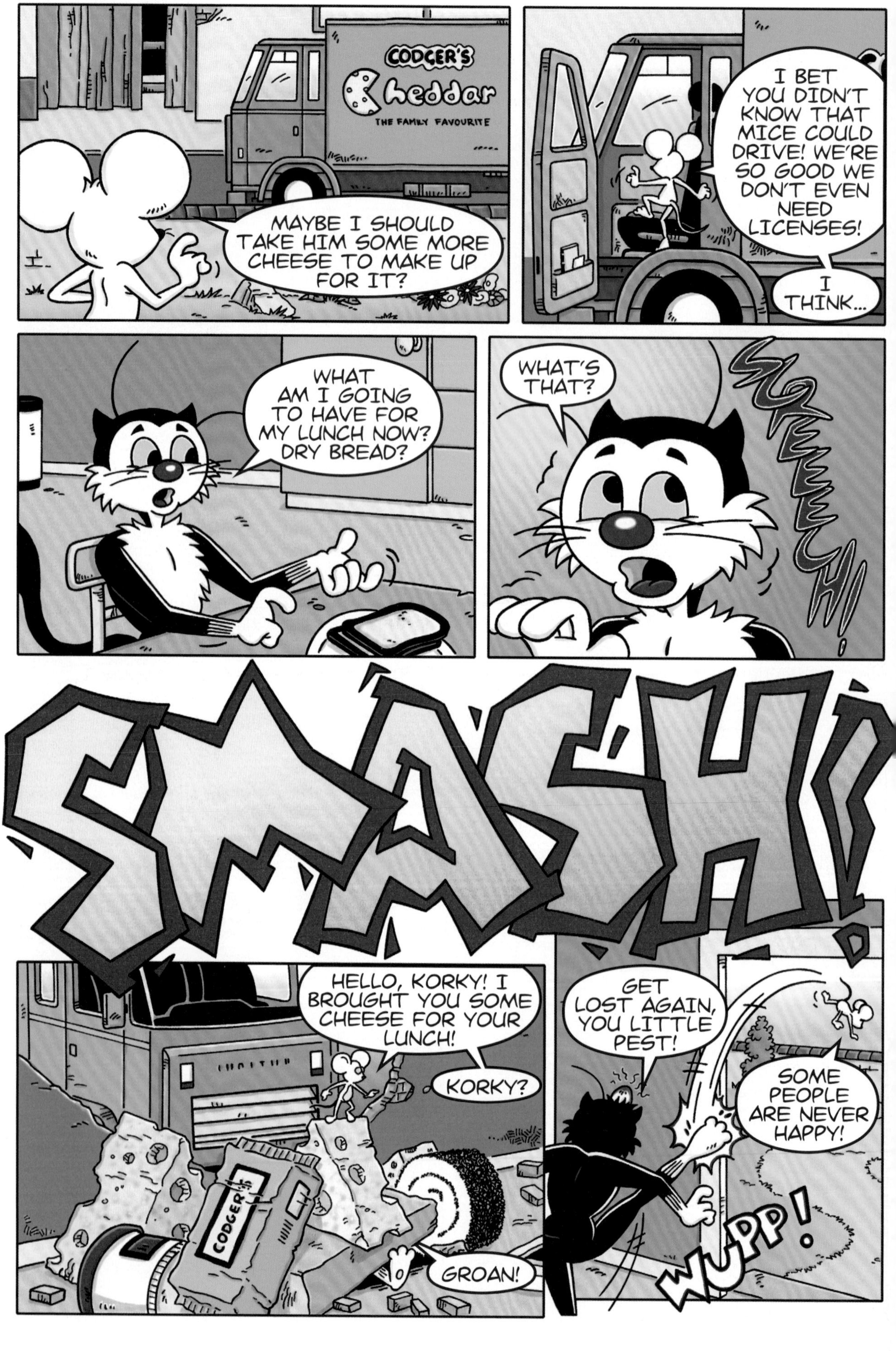
CODGER'S
Cheddar
THE FAMILY FAVOURITE
MAYBE I SHOULD TAKE HIM SOME MORE CHEESE TO MAKE UP FOR IT?
I BET YOU DIDN'T KNOW THAT MICE COULD DRIVE! WE'RE SO GOOD WE DON'T EVEN NEED LICENSES!
I THINK...
WHAT AM I GOING TO HAVE FOR MY LUNCH NOW? DRY BREAD?
WHAT'S THAT?
SKREEEEEEECH!
SMASH!
HELLO, KORKY! I BROUGHT YOU SOME CHEESE FOR YOUR LUNCH!
KORKY?
CODGER'S
GROAN!
GET LOST AGAIN, YOU LITTLE PEST!
SOME PEOPLE ARE NEVER HAPPY!
WUPP!

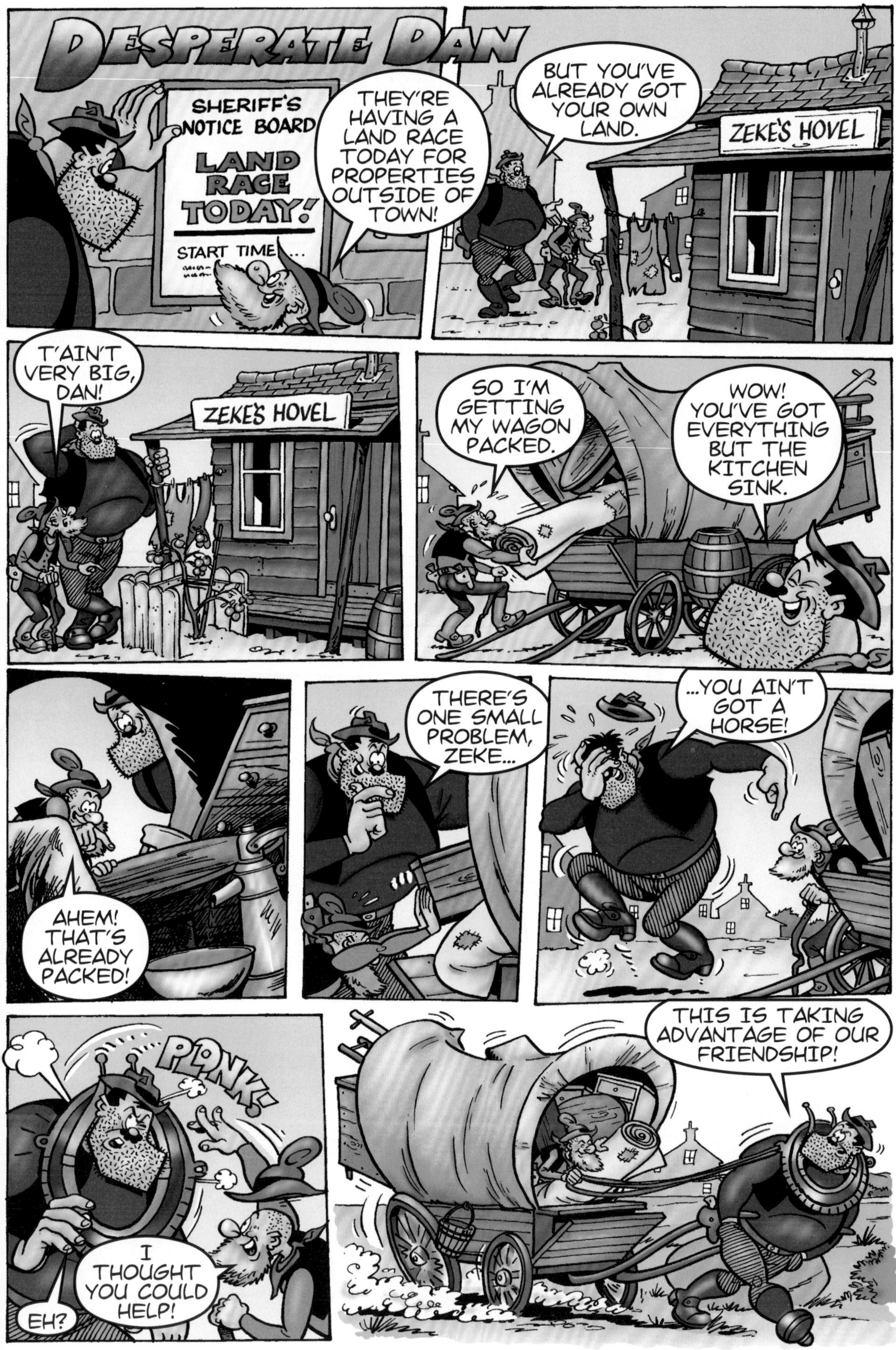
DESPERATE DAN
SHERIFF'S NOTICE BOARD
LAND RACE TODAY!
START TIME....
THEY'RE HAVING A LAND RACE TODAY FOR PROPERTIES OUTSIDE OF TOWN!
BUT YOU'VE ALREADY GOT YOUR OWN LAND.
ZEKE'S HOVEL
T'AIN'T VERY BIG, DAN!
ZEKE'S HOVEL
SO I'M GETTING MY WAGON PACKED.
WOW! YOU'VE GOT EVERYTHING BUT THE KITCHEN SINK.
AHEM! THAT'S ALREADY PACKED!
THERE'S ONE SMALL PROBLEM, ZEKE...
...YOU AIN'T GOT A HORSE!
PLONK!
EH?
I THOUGHT YOU COULD HELP!
THIS IS TAKING ADVANTAGE OF OUR FRIENDSHIP!

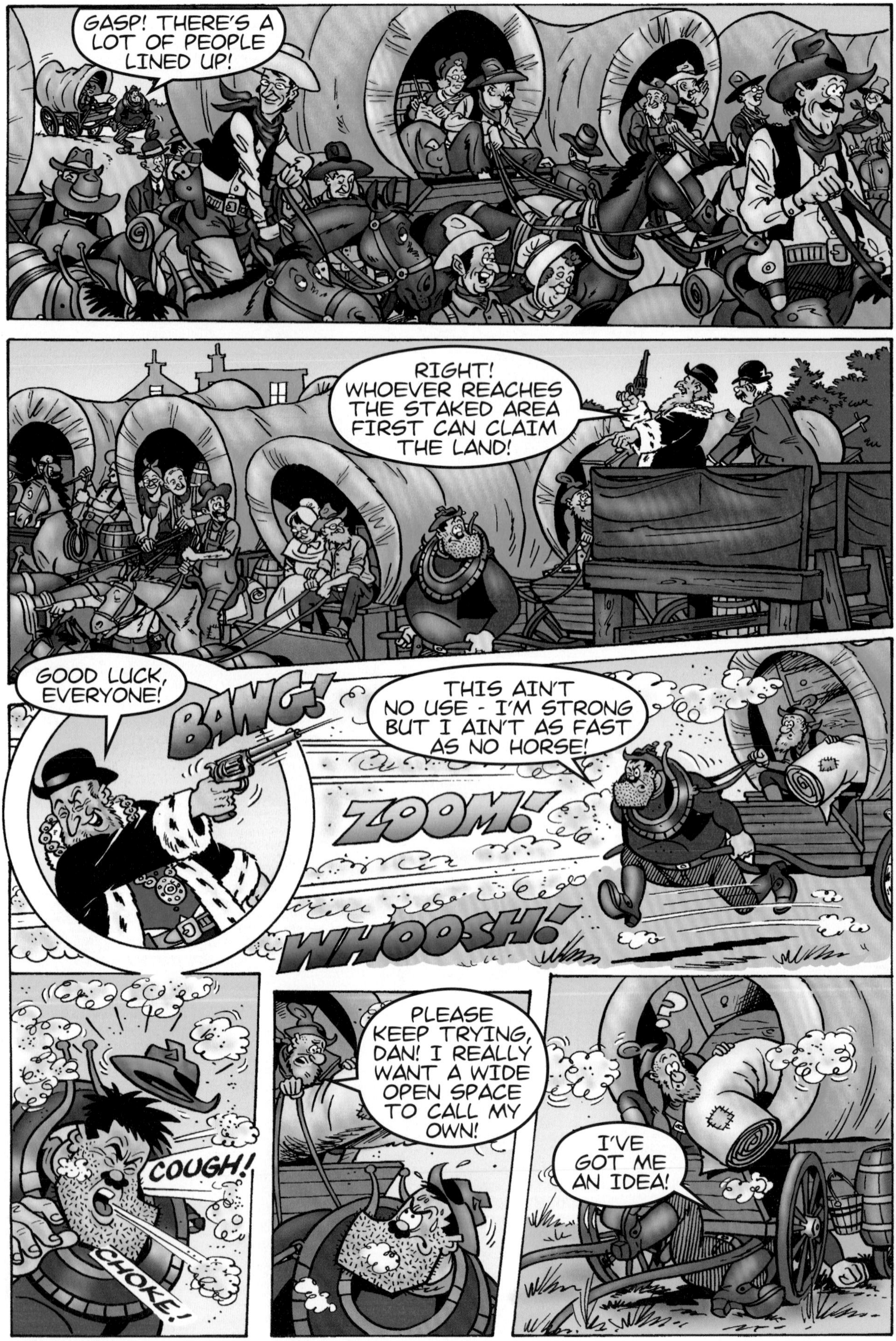
GASP! THERE'S A LOT OF PEOPLE LINED UP!
RIGHT! WHOEVER REACHES THE STAKED AREA FIRST CAN CLAIM THE LAND!
GOOD LUCK, EVERYONE!
BANG!
THIS AIN'T NO USE - I'M STRONG BUT I AIN'T AS FAST AS NO HORSE!
ZOOM!
WHOOSH!
COUGH!
CHOKE!
PLEASE KEEP TRYING, DAN! I REALLY WANT A WIDE OPEN SPACE TO CALL MY OWN!
I'VE GOT ME AN IDEA!

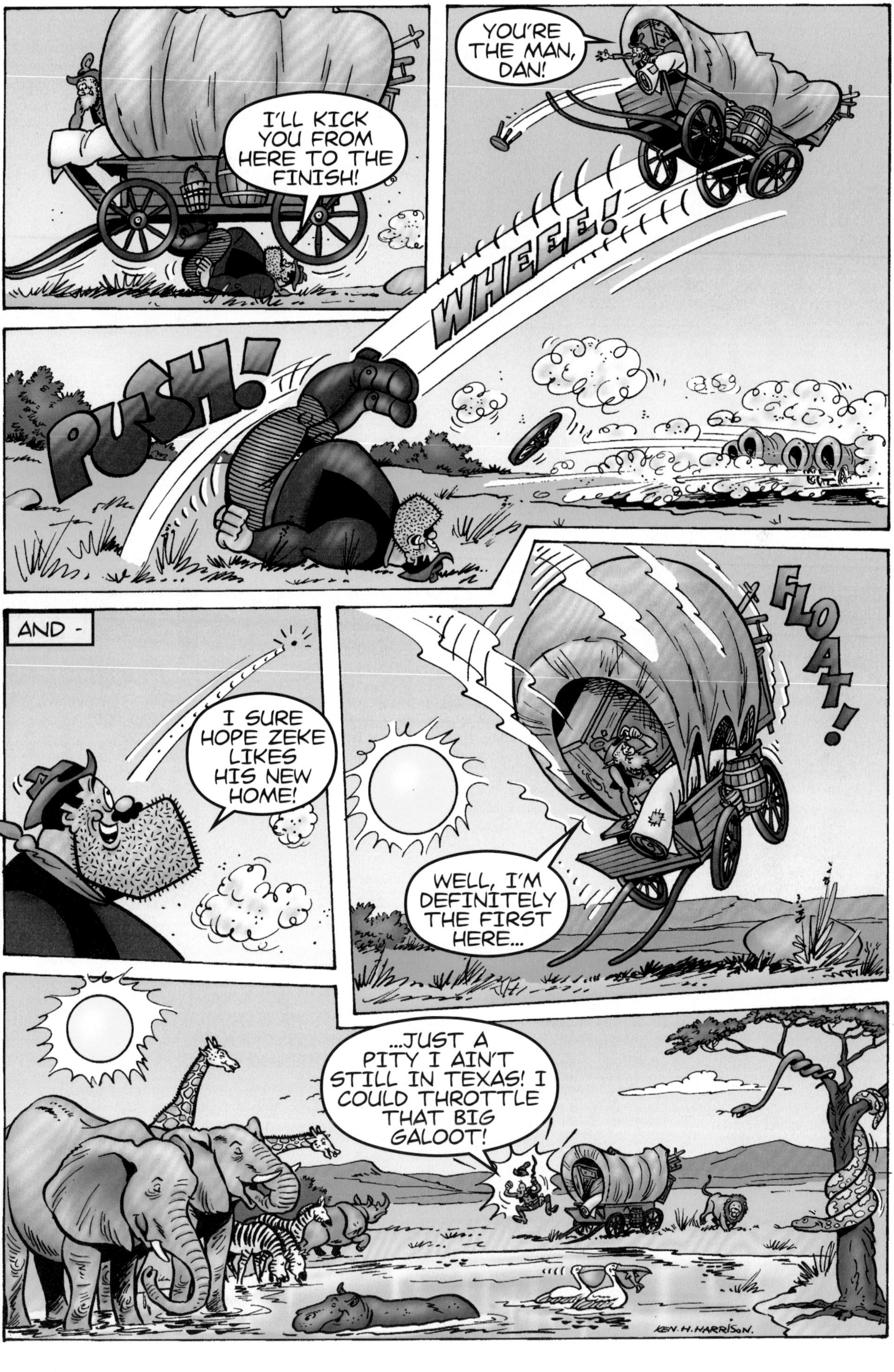
I'LL KICK YOU FROM HERE TO THE FINISH!
YOU'RE THE MAN, DAN!
WHEEE!
PUSH!
AND -
I SURE HOPE ZEKE LIKES HIS NEW HOME!
FLOAT!
WELL, I'M DEFINITELY THE FIRST HERE...
...JUST A PITY I AIN'T STILL IN TEXAS! I COULD THROTTLE THAT BIG GALOOT!
KEN H. HARRISON.

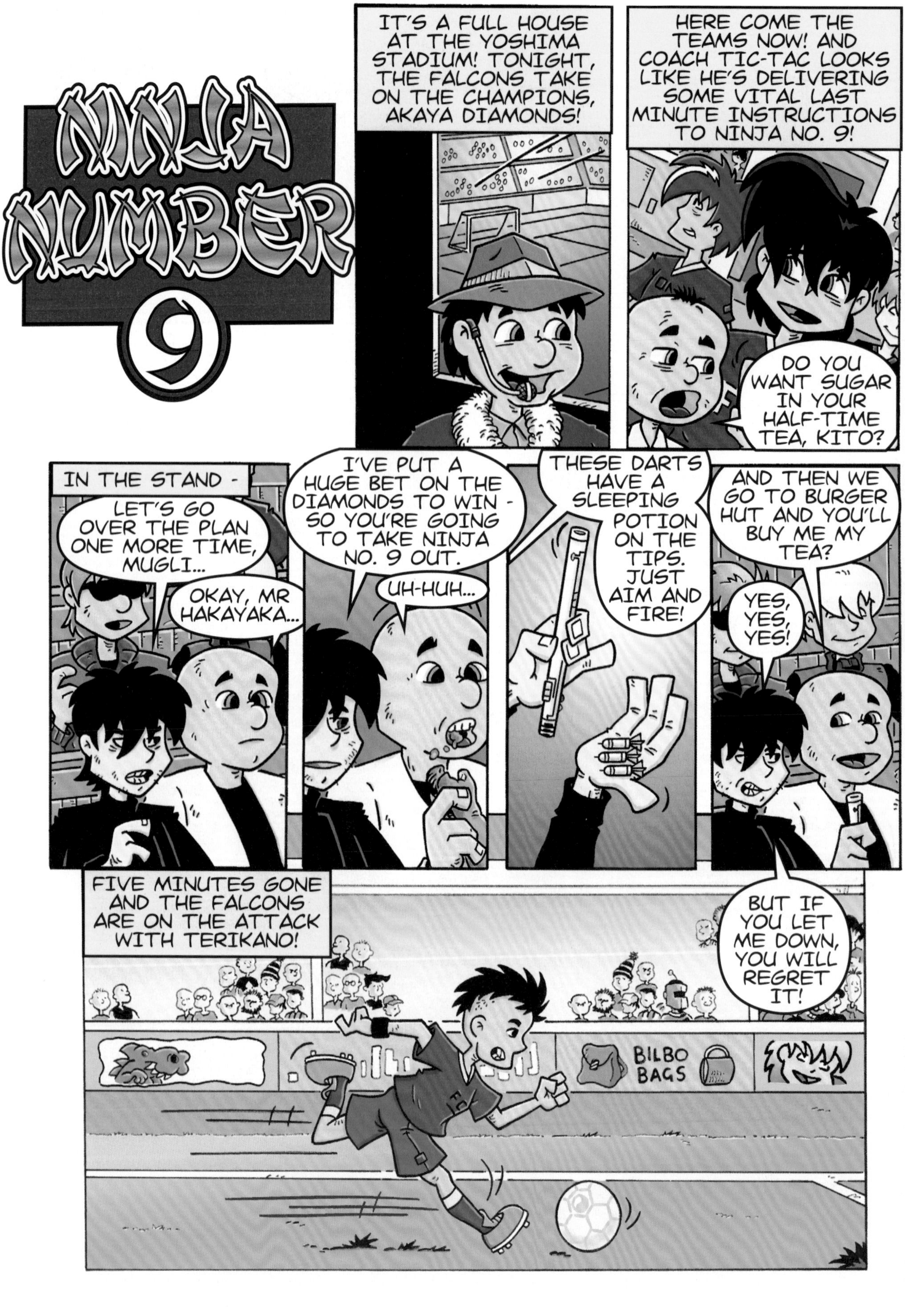
NINJA NUMBER 9
IT'S A FULL HOUSE AT THE YOSHIMA STADIUM! TONIGHT, THE FALCONS TAKE ON THE CHAMPIONS, AKAYA DIAMONDS!
HERE COME THE TEAMS NOW! AND COACH TIC-TAC LOOKS LIKE HE'S DELIVERING SOME VITAL LAST MINUTE INSTRUCTIONS TO NINJA NO. 9!
DO YOU WANT SUGAR IN YOUR HALF-TIME TEA, KITO?
IN THE STAND -
LET'S GO OVER THE PLAN ONE MORE TIME, MUGLI...
OKAY, MR HAKAYAKA...
I'VE PUT A HUGE BET ON THE DIAMONDS TO WIN - SO YOU'RE GOING TO TAKE NINJA NO. 9 OUT.
UH-HUH...
THESE DARTS HAVE A SLEEPING POTION ON THE TIPS. JUST AIM AND FIRE!
AND THEN WE GO TO BURGER HUT AND YOU'LL BUY ME MY TEA?
YES, YES, YES!
BUT IF YOU LET ME DOWN, YOU WILL REGRET IT!
FIVE MINUTES GONE AND THE FALCONS ARE ON THE ATTACK WITH TERIKANO!
BILBO BAGS

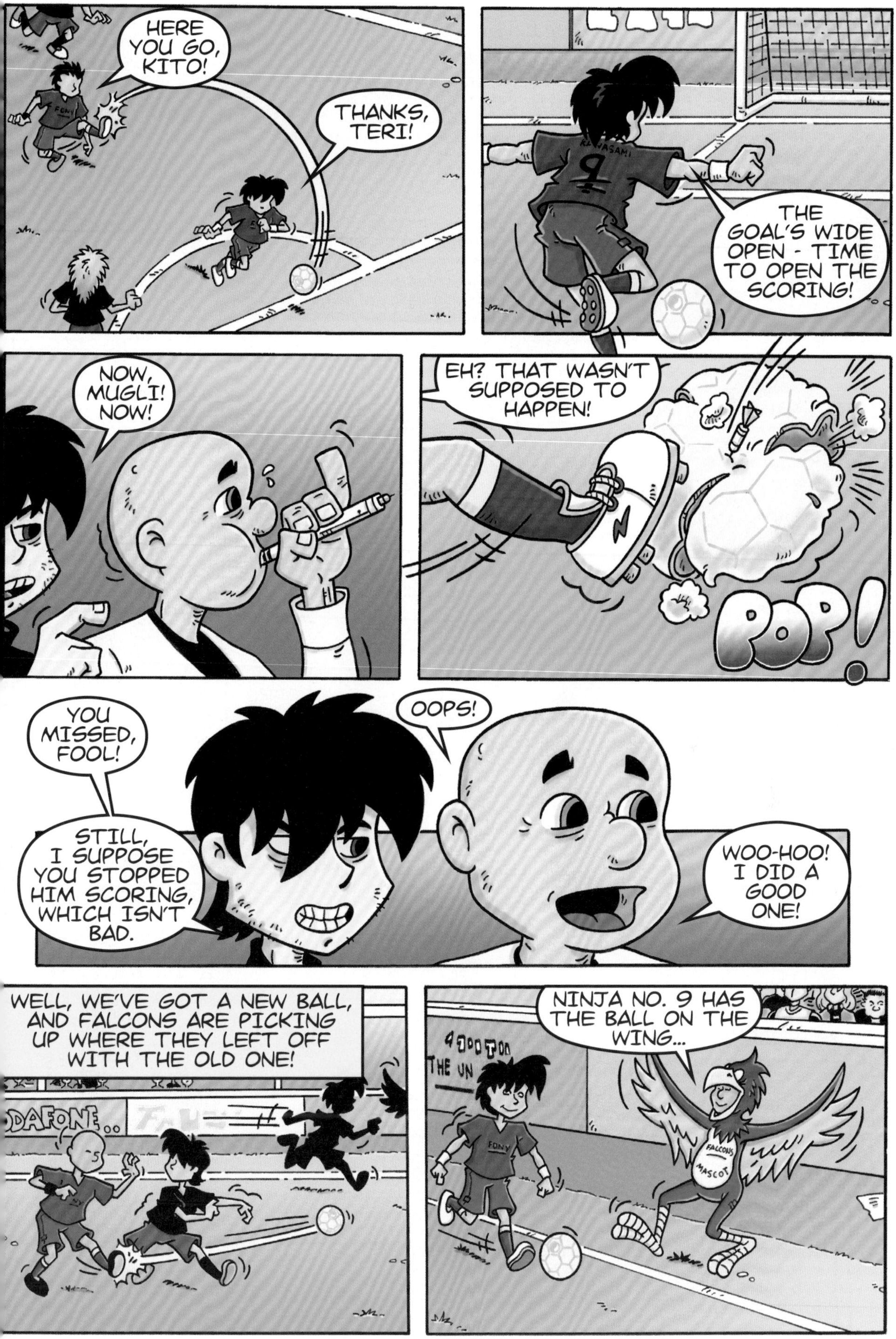
HERE YOU GO, KITO!
THANKS, TERI!
THE GOAL'S WIDE OPEN - TIME TO OPEN THE SCORING!
NOW, MUGLI! NOW!
EH? THAT WASN'T SUPPOSED TO HAPPEN!
POP!
YOU MISSED, FOOL!
OOPS!
STILL, I SUPPOSE YOU STOPPED HIM SCORING, WHICH ISN'T BAD.
WOO-HOO! I DID A GOOD ONE!
WELL, WE'VE GOT A NEW BALL, AND FALCONS ARE PICKING UP WHERE THEY LEFT OFF WITH THE OLD ONE!
NINJA NO. 9 HAS THE BALL ON THE WING...

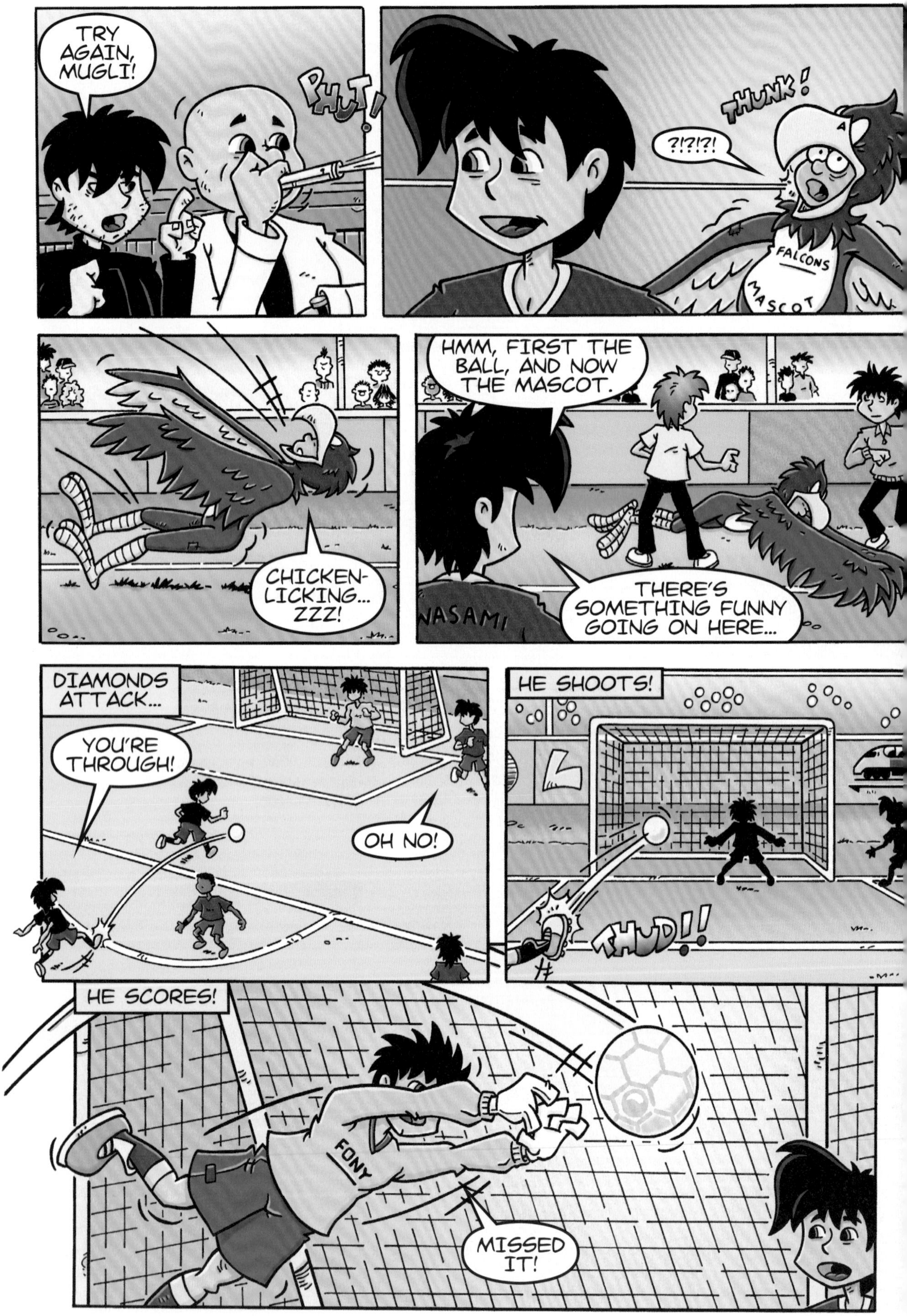
TRY AGAIN, MUGLI!
PHUT!
THUNK!
?!?!?!
FALCONS MASCOT
CHICKEN-LICKING... ZZZ!
HMM, FIRST THE BALL, AND NOW THE MASCOT.
THERE'S SOMETHING FUNNY GOING ON HERE...
WASAMI
DIAMONDS ATTACK...
YOU'RE THROUGH!
OH NO!
HE SHOOTS!
THUD!!
HE SCORES!
FONY
MISSED IT!

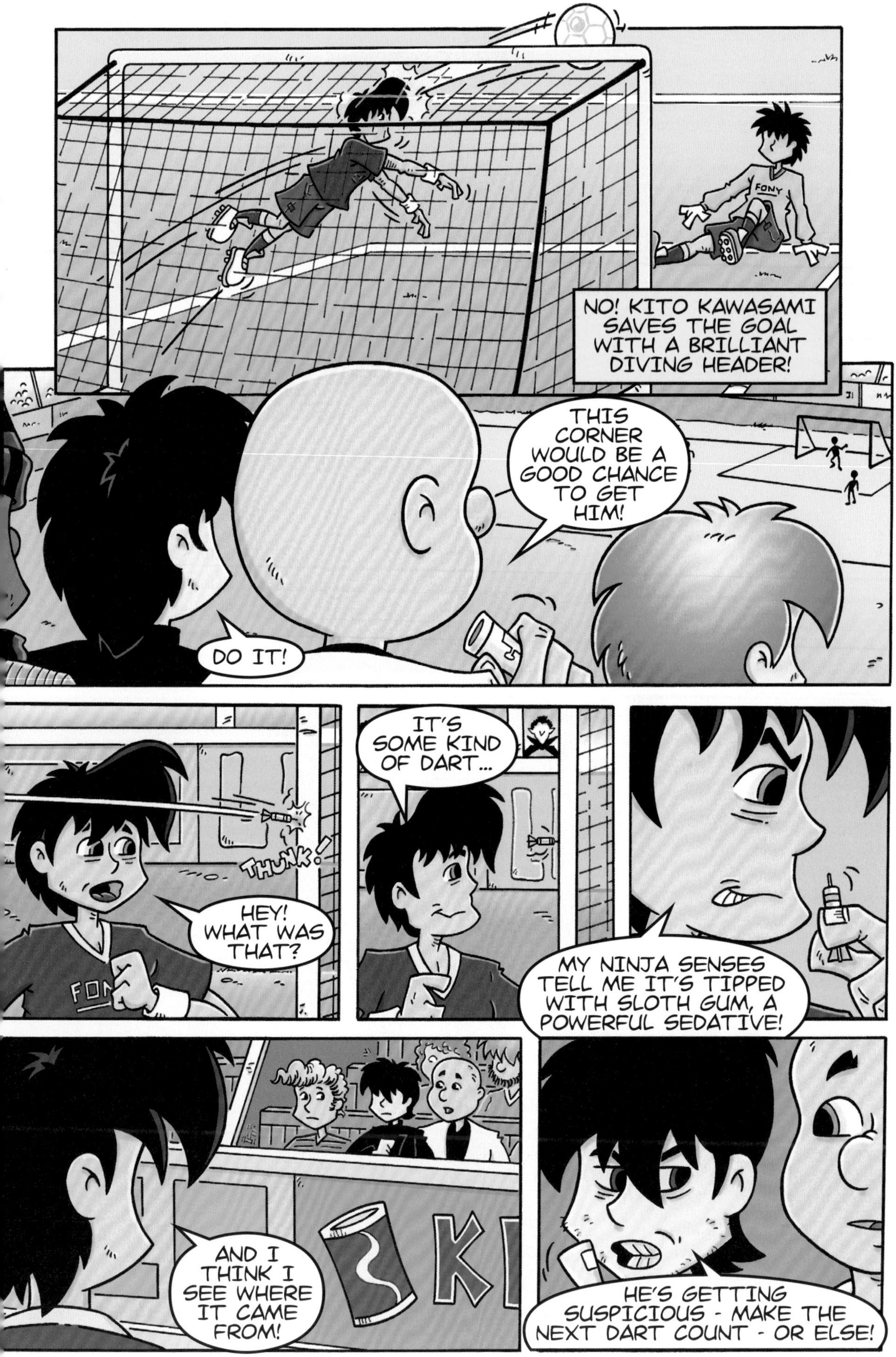
NO! KITO KAWASAMI SAVES THE GOAL WITH A BRILLIANT DIVING HEADER!
FONY
THIS CORNER WOULD BE A GOOD CHANCE TO GET HIM!
DO IT!
HEY! WHAT WAS THAT?
THUNK!
IT'S SOME KIND OF DART...
MY NINJA SENSES TELL ME IT'S TIPPED WITH SLOTH GUM, A POWERFUL SEDATIVE!
AND I THINK I SEE WHERE IT CAME FROM!
HE'S GETTING SUSPICIOUS - MAKE THE NEXT DART COUNT - OR ELSE!

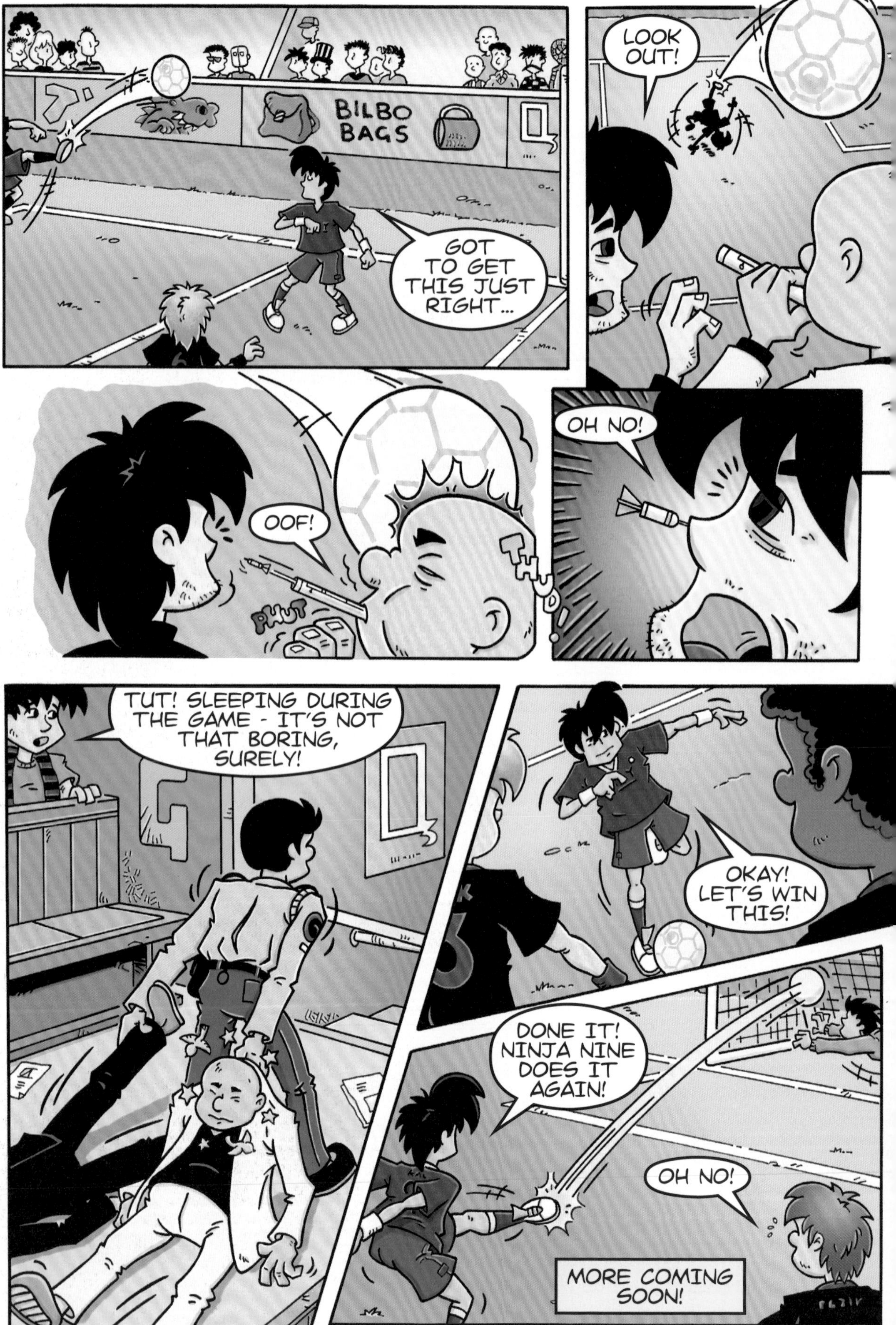
BILBO BAGS
GOT TO GET THIS JUST RIGHT...
LOOK OUT!
OOF!
PHUT
THUD!
OH NO!
TUT! SLEEPING DURING THE GAME - IT'S NOT THAT BORING, SURELY!
OKAY! LET'S WIN THIS!
DONE IT! NINJA NINE DOES IT AGAIN!
OH NO!
MORE COMING SOON!

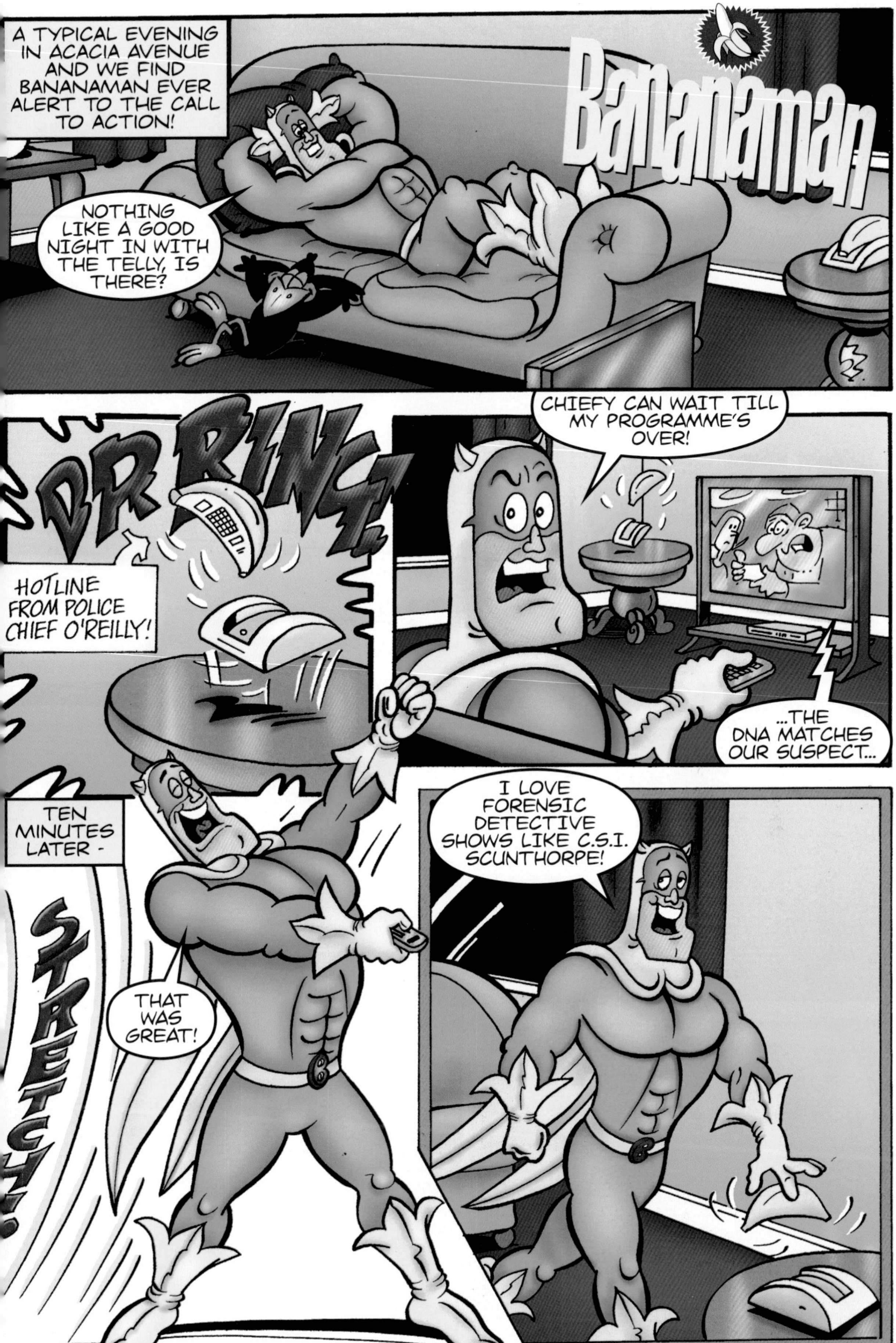
Bananaman
A TYPICAL EVENING IN ACACIA AVENUE AND WE FIND BANANAMAN EVER ALERT TO THE CALL TO ACTION!
NOTHING LIKE A GOOD NIGHT IN WITH THE TELLY, IS THERE?
DRRING!
HOTLINE FROM POLICE CHIEF O'REILLY!
CHIEFY CAN WAIT TILL MY PROGRAMME'S OVER!
...THE DNA MATCHES OUR SUSPECT...
TEN MINUTES LATER -
STRETCH!
THAT WAS GREAT!
I LOVE FORENSIC DETECTIVE SHOWS LIKE C.S.I. SCUNTHORPE!

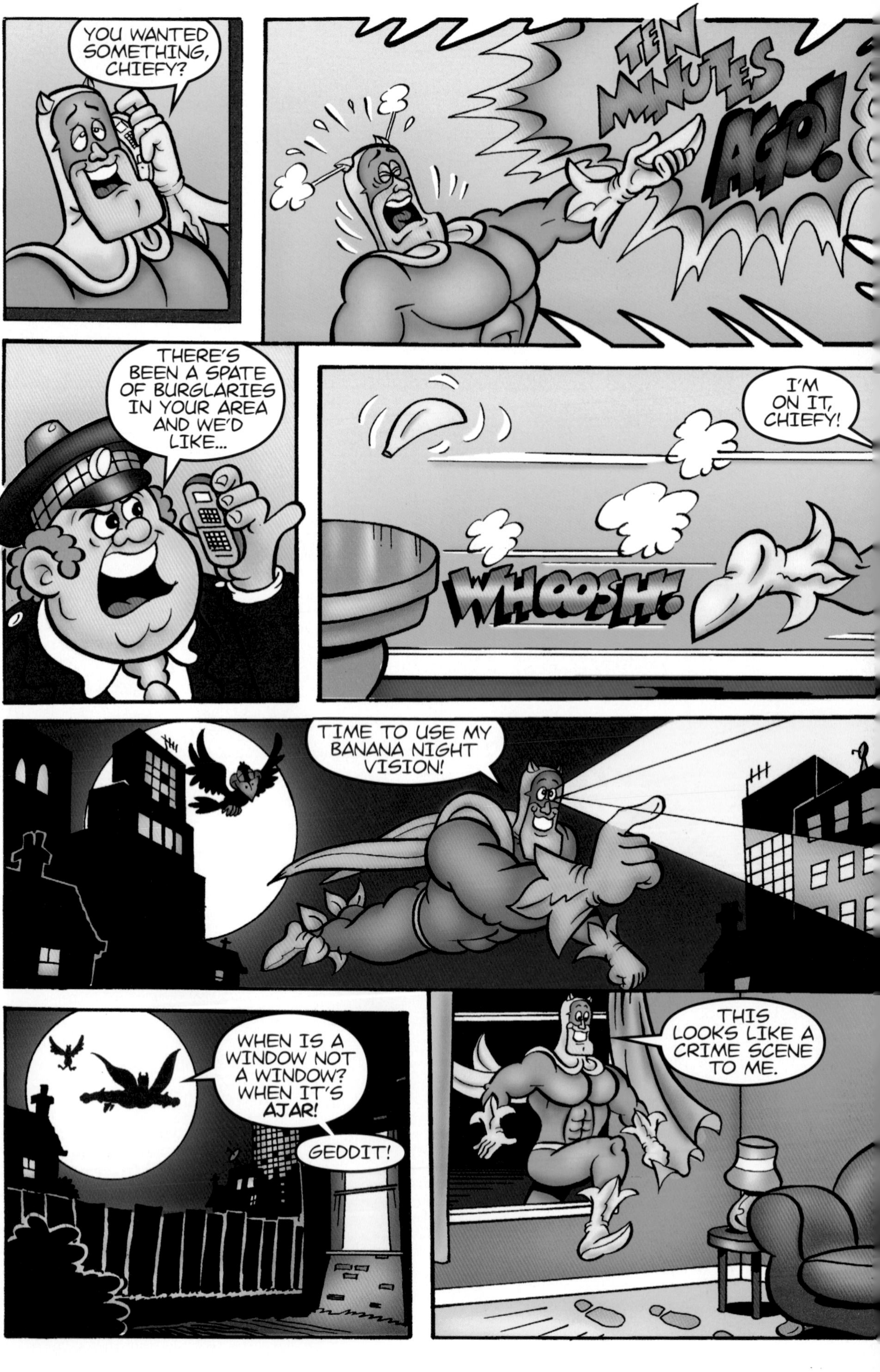

YOU WANTED SOMETHING, CHIEFY?
TEN MINUTES AGO!
THERE'S BEEN A SPATE OF BURGLARIES IN YOUR AREA AND WE'D LIKE...
I'M ON IT, CHIEFY!
WHOOSH!
TIME TO USE MY BANANA NIGHT VISION!
WHEN IS A WINDOW NOT A WINDOW? WHEN IT'S **AJAR**!
GEDDIT!
THIS LOOKS LIKE A CRIME SCENE TO ME.

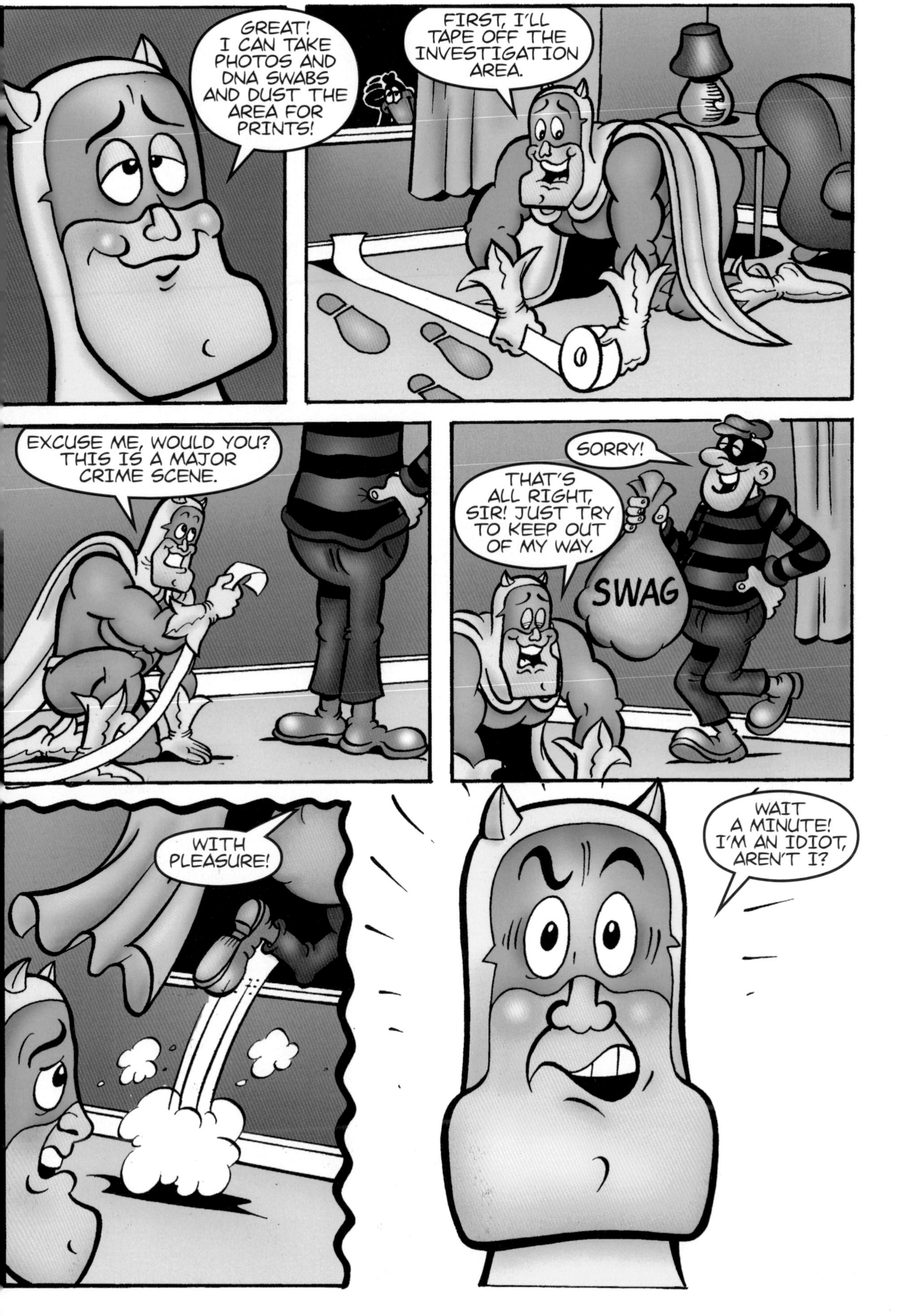
GREAT! I CAN TAKE PHOTOS AND DNA SWABS AND DUST THE AREA FOR PRINTS!
FIRST, I'LL TAPE OFF THE INVESTIGATION AREA.
EXCUSE ME, WOULD YOU? THIS IS A MAJOR CRIME SCENE.
SORRY!
THAT'S ALL RIGHT, SIR! JUST TRY TO KEEP OUT OF MY WAY.
SWAG
WITH PLEASURE!
WAIT A MINUTE! I'M AN IDIOT, AREN'T I?

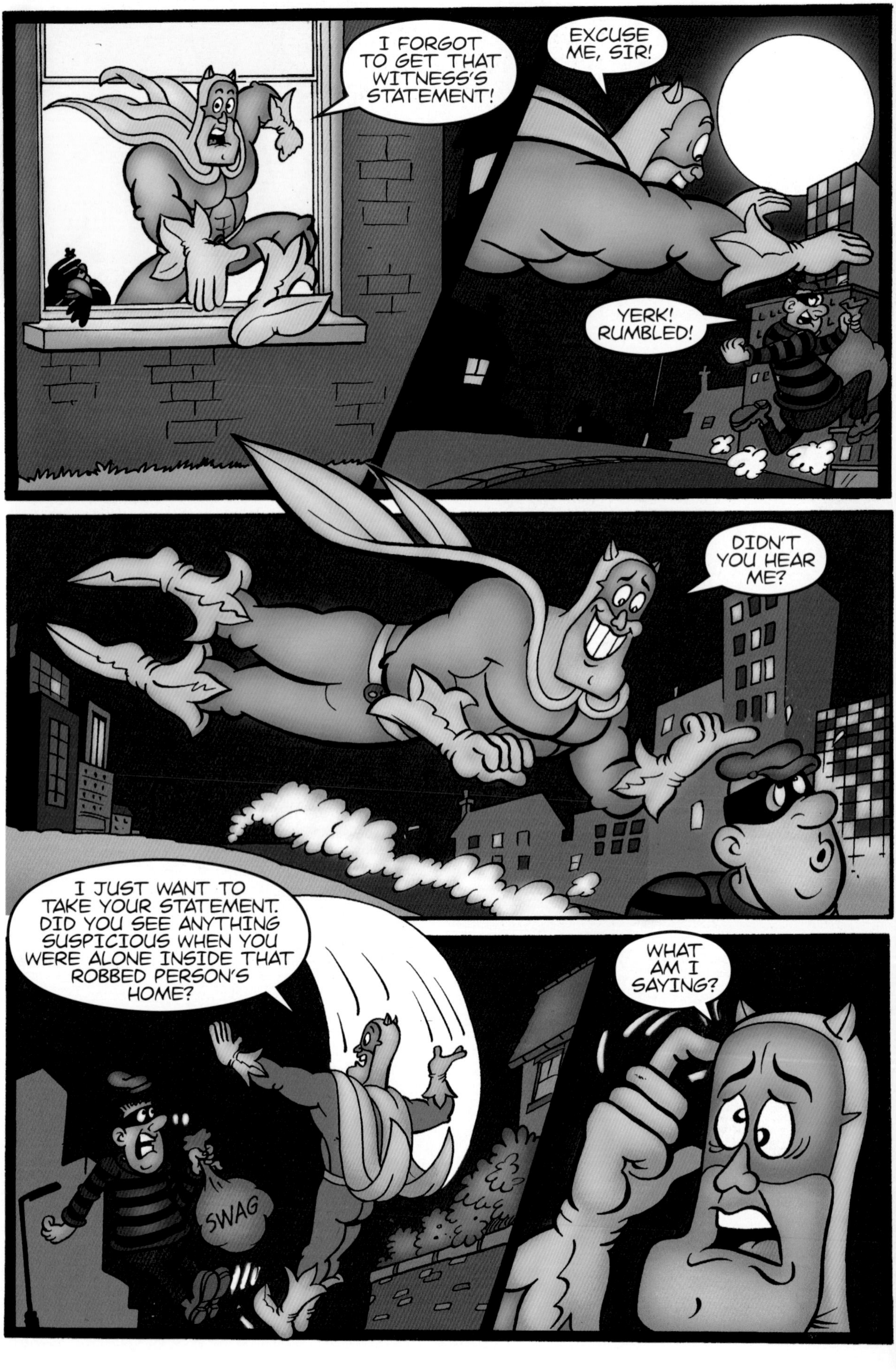
I FORGOT TO GET THAT WITNESS'S STATEMENT!
EXCUSE ME, SIR!
YERK! RUMBLED!
DIDN'T YOU HEAR ME?
I JUST WANT TO TAKE YOUR STATEMENT. DID YOU SEE ANYTHING SUSPICIOUS WHEN YOU WERE ALONE INSIDE THAT ROBBED PERSON'S HOME?
SWAG
WHAT AM I SAYING?

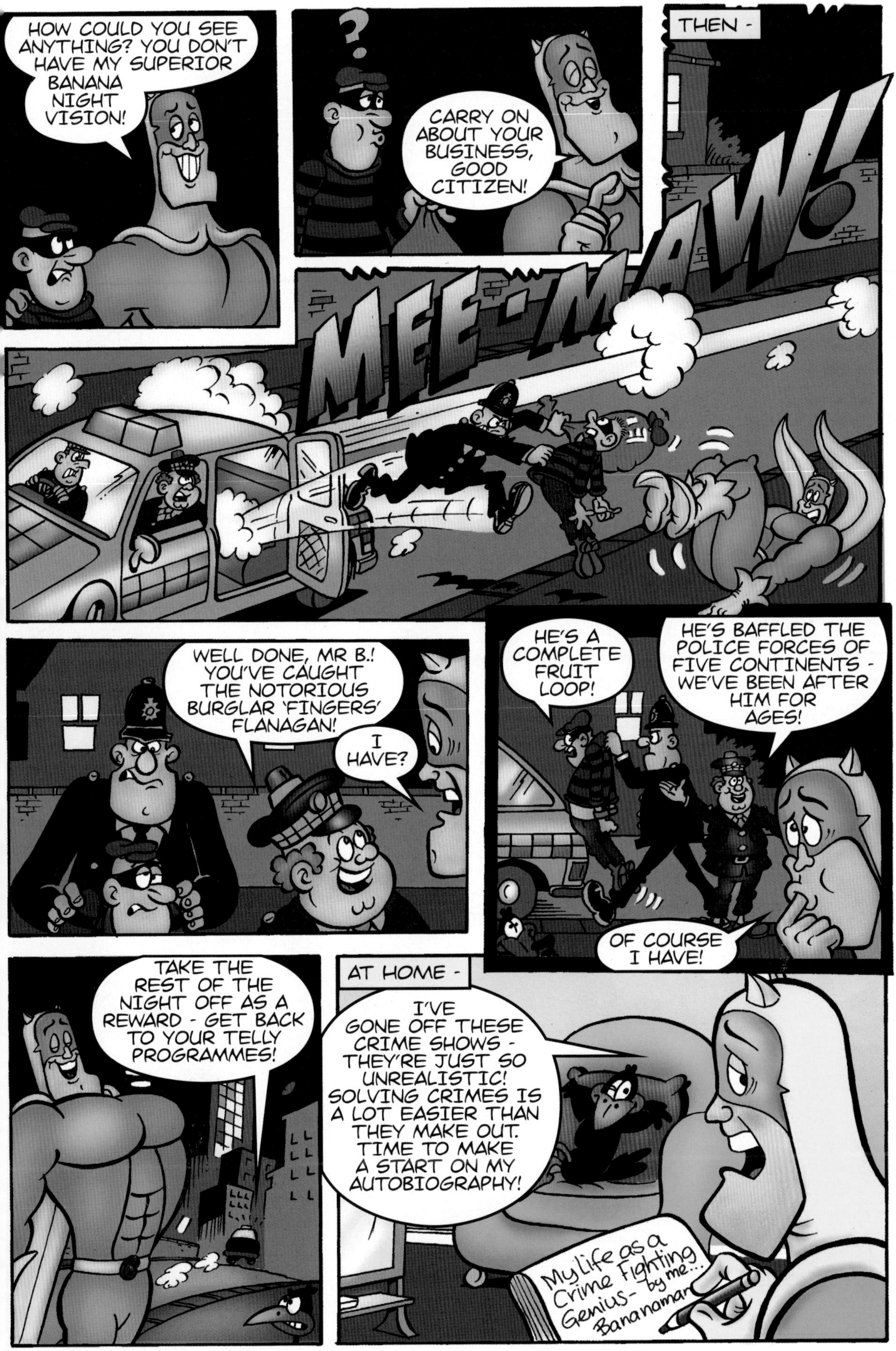
HOW COULD YOU SEE ANYTHING? YOU DON'T HAVE MY SUPERIOR BANANA NIGHT VISION!
?
CARRY ON ABOUT YOUR BUSINESS, GOOD CITIZEN!
THEN -
MEE-MAW!
WELL DONE, MR B.! YOU'VE CAUGHT THE NOTORIOUS BURGLAR 'FINGERS' FLANAGAN!
I HAVE?
HE'S A COMPLETE FRUIT LOOP!
HE'S BAFFLED THE POLICE FORCES OF FIVE CONTINENTS - WE'VE BEEN AFTER HIM FOR AGES!
OF COURSE I HAVE!
TAKE THE REST OF THE NIGHT OFF AS A REWARD - GET BACK TO YOUR TELLY PROGRAMMES!
AT HOME -
I'VE GONE OFF THESE CRIME SHOWS - THEY'RE JUST SO UNREALISTIC! SOLVING CRIMES IS A LOT EASIER THAN THEY MAKE OUT. TIME TO MAKE A START ON MY AUTOBIOGRAPHY!
My Life as a Crime Fighting Genius - by me... Bananaman

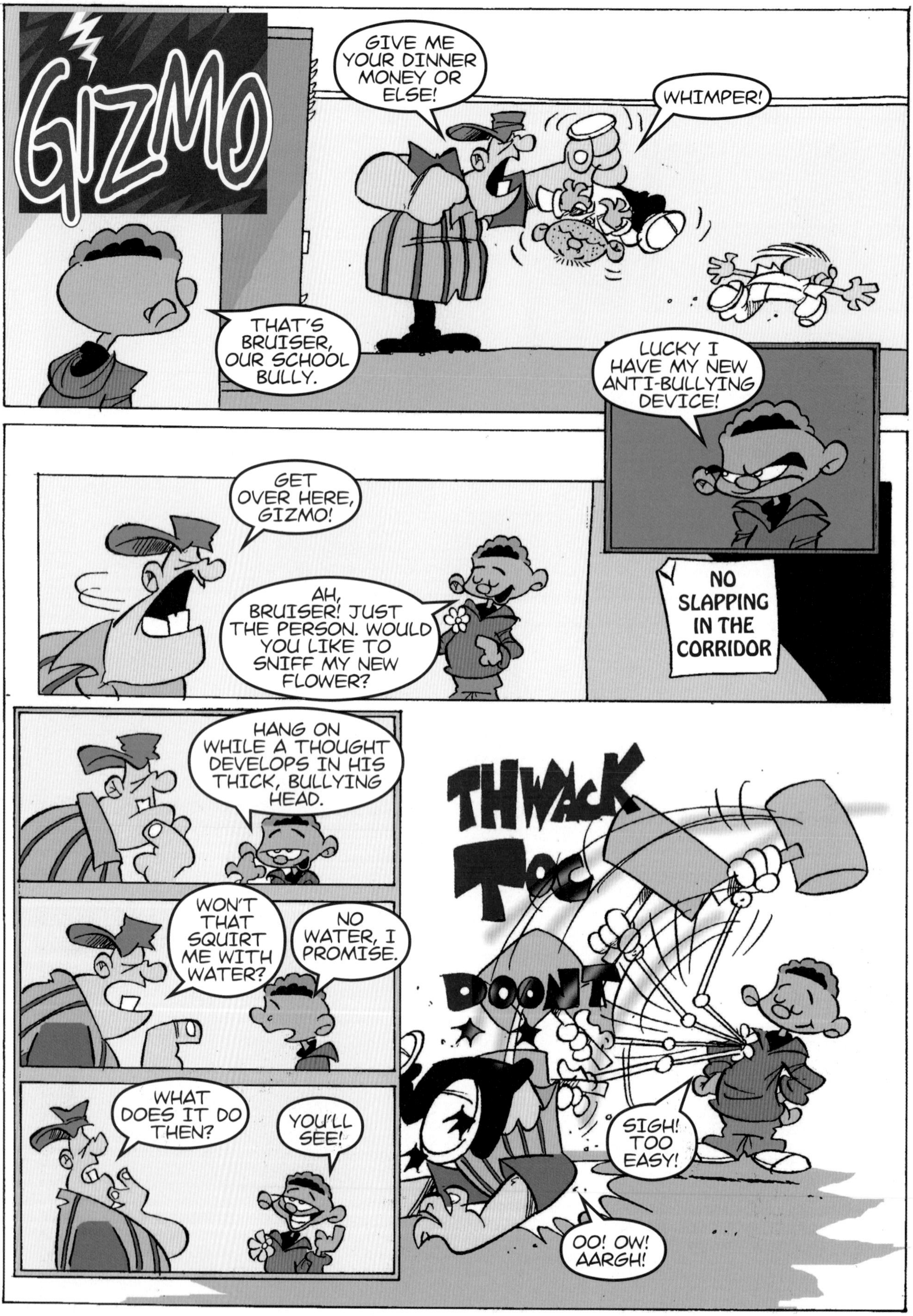
GIZMO
GIVE ME YOUR DINNER MONEY OR ELSE!
WHIMPER!
THAT'S BRUISER, OUR SCHOOL BULLY.
LUCKY I HAVE MY NEW ANTI-BULLYING DEVICE!
GET OVER HERE, GIZMO!
AH, BRUISER! JUST THE PERSON. WOULD YOU LIKE TO SNIFF MY NEW FLOWER?
NO SLAPPING IN THE CORRIDOR
HANG ON WHILE A THOUGHT DEVELOPS IN HIS THICK, BULLYING HEAD.
WON'T THAT SQUIRT ME WITH WATER?
NO WATER, I PROMISE.
WHAT DOES IT DO THEN?
YOU'LL SEE!
THWACK
DOONT
SIGH! TOO EASY!
OO! OW! AARGH!

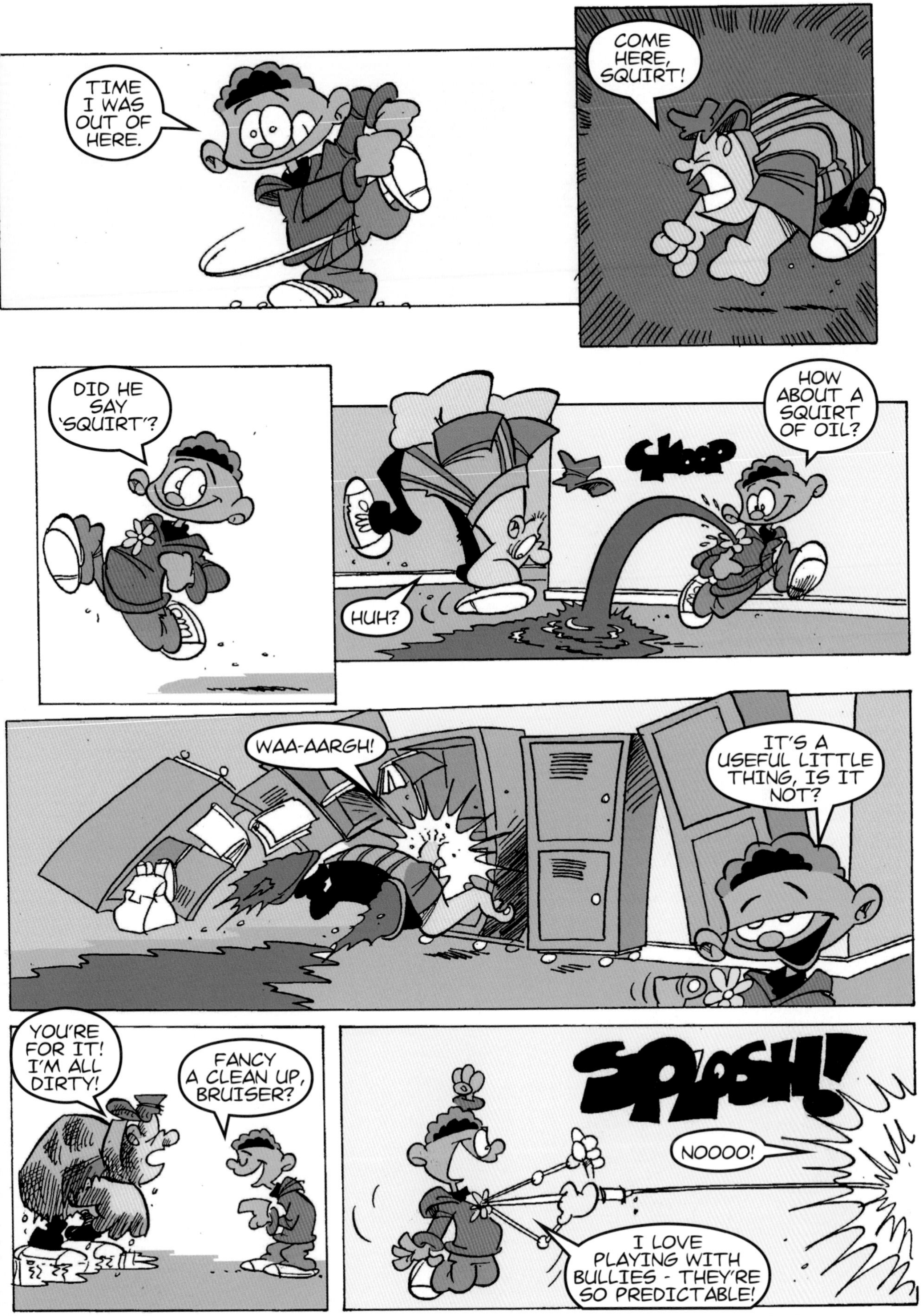
TIME I WAS OUT OF HERE.
COME HERE, SQUIRT!
DID HE SAY 'SQUIRT'?
SKOOP
HOW ABOUT A SQUIRT OF OIL?
HUH?
WAA-AARGH!
IT'S A USEFUL LITTLE THING, IS IT NOT?
YOU'RE FOR IT! I'M ALL DIRTY!
FANCY A CLEAN UP, BRUISER?
SPLOSH!
NOOOO!
I LOVE PLAYING WITH BULLIES - THEY'RE SO PREDICTABLE!

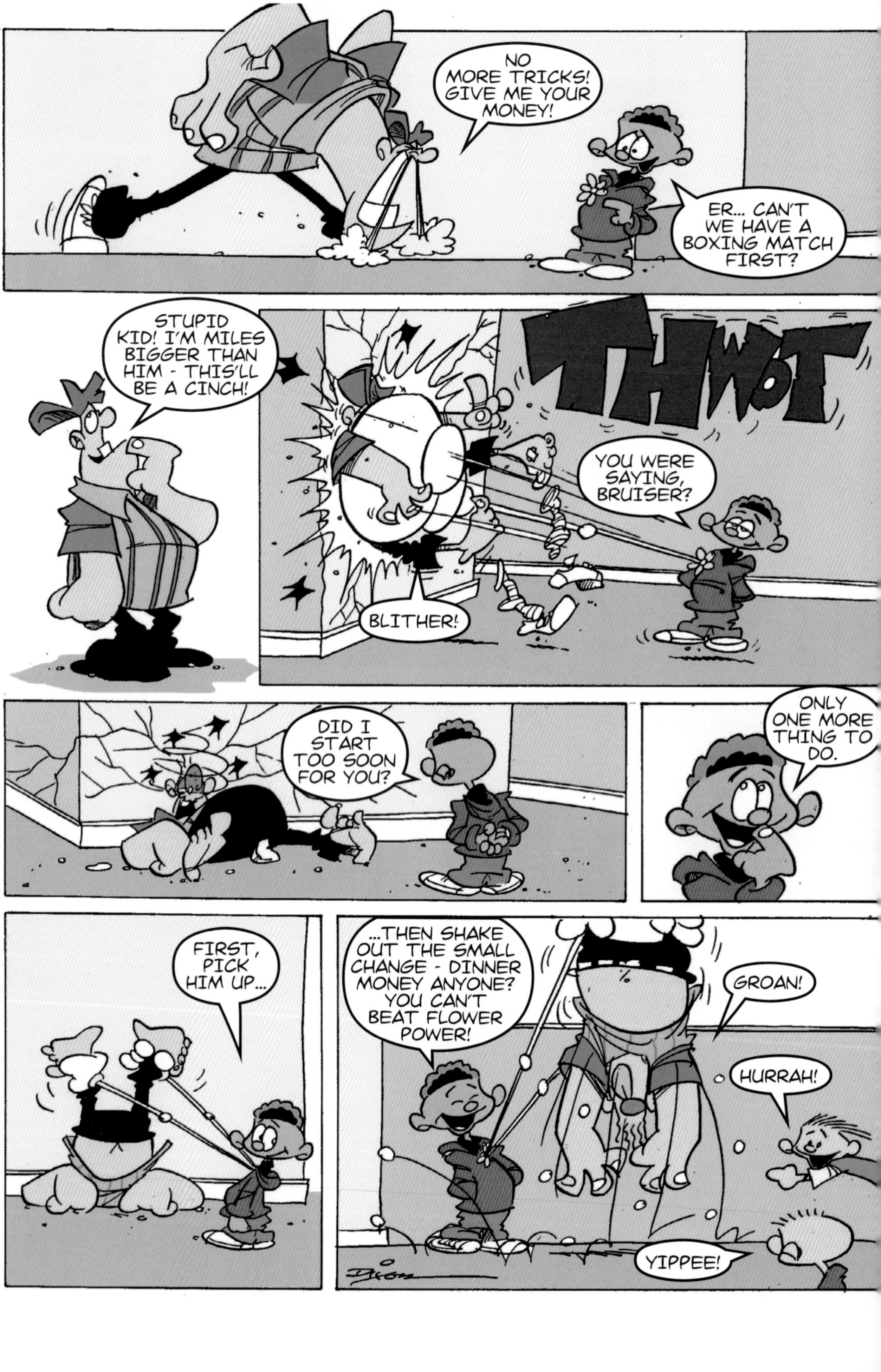

NO MORE TRICKS! GIVE ME YOUR MONEY!
ER... CAN'T WE HAVE A BOXING MATCH FIRST?
STUPID KID! I'M MILES BIGGER THAN HIM - THIS'LL BE A CINCH!
THWOT
YOU WERE SAYING, BRUISER?
BLITHER!
DID I START TOO SOON FOR YOU?
ONLY ONE MORE THING TO DO.
FIRST, PICK HIM UP...
...THEN SHAKE OUT THE SMALL CHANGE - DINNER MONEY ANYONE? YOU CAN'T BEAT FLOWER POWER!
GROAN!
HURRAH!
YIPPEE!

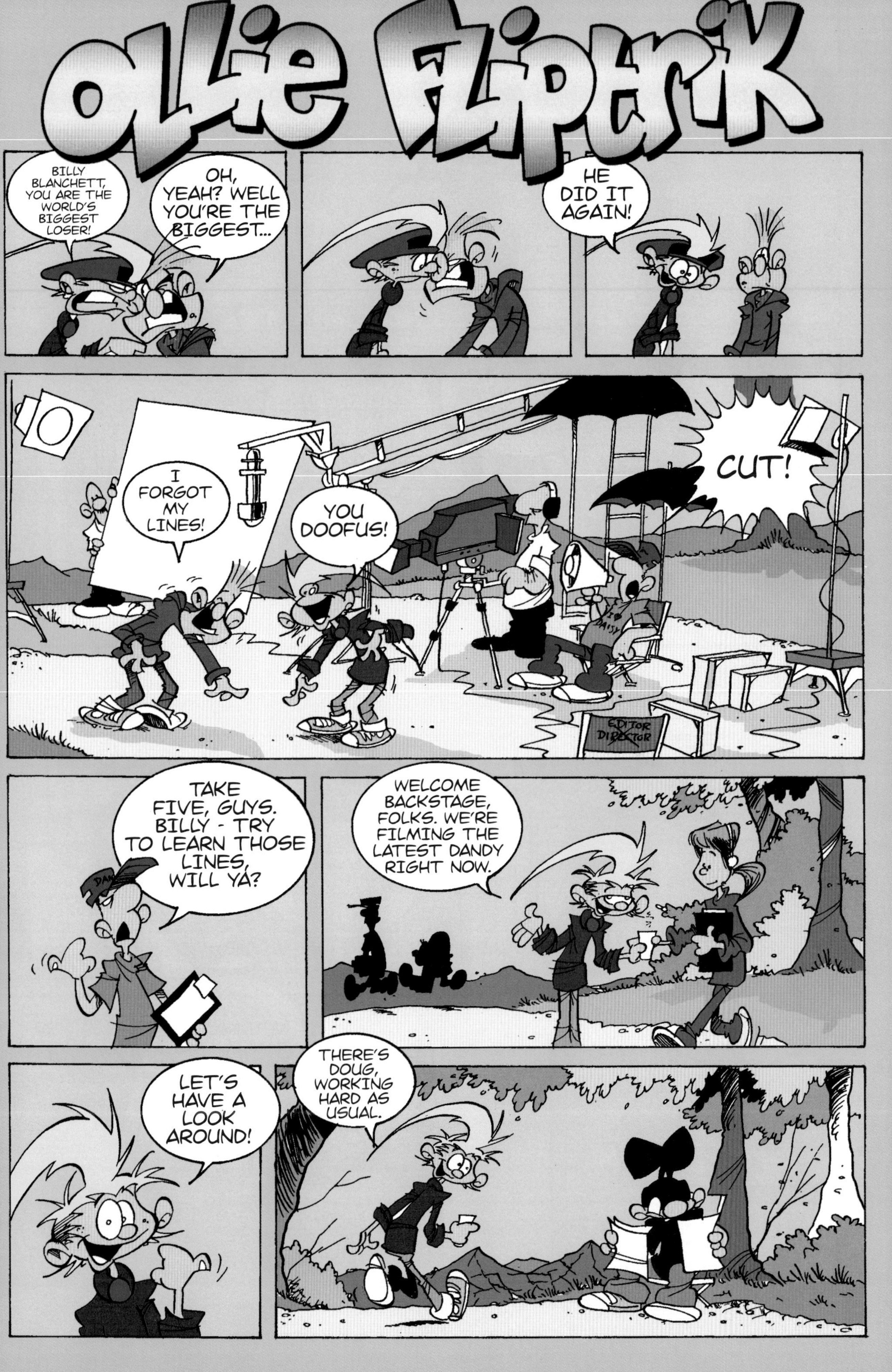
OLLIE FLIPTRIK
BILLY BLANCHETT, YOU ARE THE WORLD'S BIGGEST LOSER!
OH, YEAH? WELL YOU'RE THE BIGGEST...
HE DID IT AGAIN!
CUT!
I FORGOT MY LINES!
YOU DOOFUS!
DAISY
EDITOR DIRECTOR
TAKE FIVE, GUYS. BILLY - TRY TO LEARN THOSE LINES, WILL YA?
WELCOME BACKSTAGE, FOLKS. WE'RE FILMING THE LATEST DANDY RIGHT NOW.
LET'S HAVE A LOOK AROUND!
THERE'S DOUG, WORKING HARD AS USUAL.

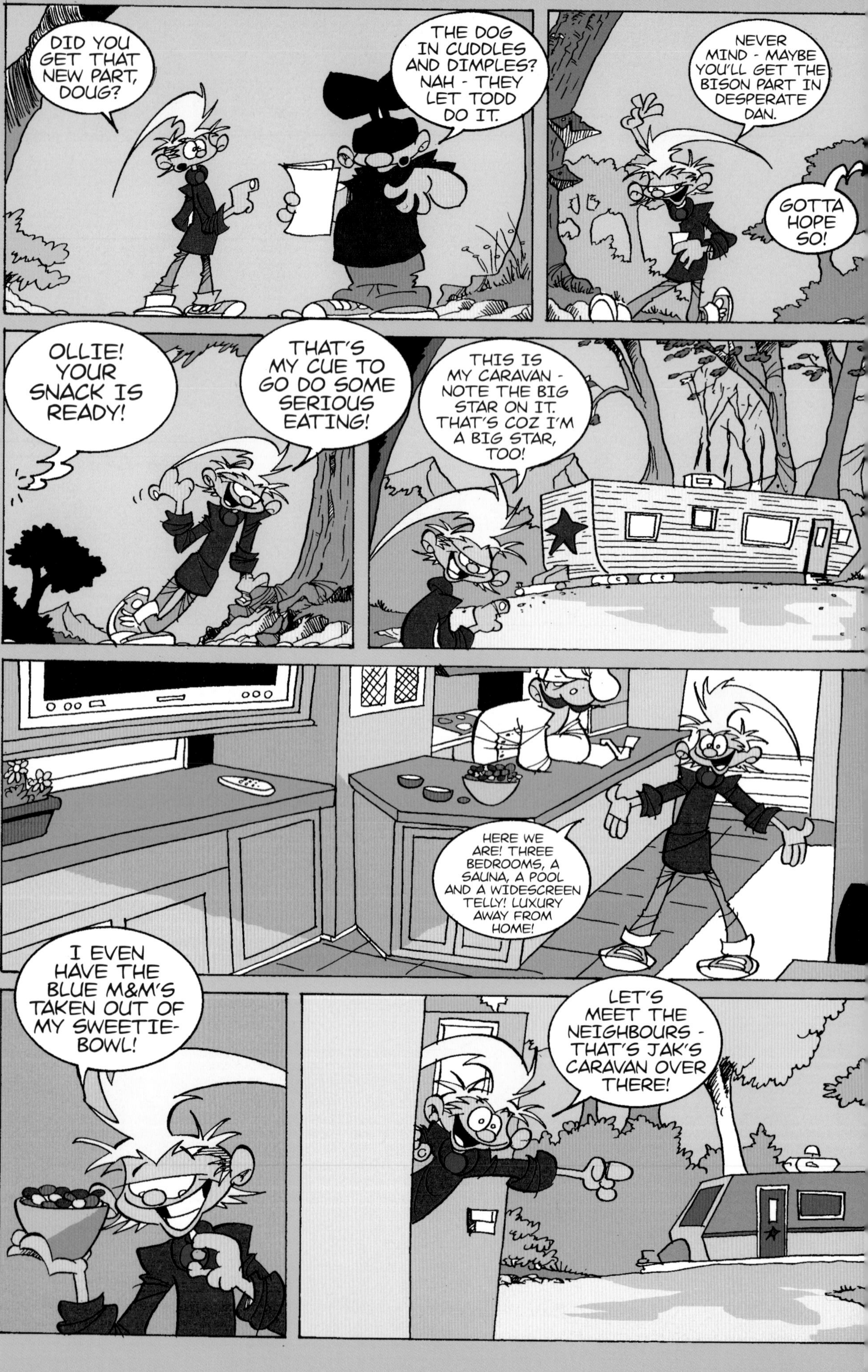
DID YOU GET THAT NEW PART, DOUG?
THE DOG IN CUDDLES AND DIMPLES? NAH - THEY LET TODD DO IT.
NEVER MIND - MAYBE YOU'LL GET THE BISON PART IN DESPERATE DAN.
GOTTA HOPE SO!
OLLIE! YOUR SNACK IS READY!
THAT'S MY CUE TO GO DO SOME SERIOUS EATING!
THIS IS MY CARAVAN - NOTE THE BIG STAR ON IT. THAT'S COZ I'M A BIG STAR, TOO!
HERE WE ARE! THREE BEDROOMS, A SAUNA, A POOL AND A WIDESCREEN TELLY! LUXURY AWAY FROM HOME!
I EVEN HAVE THE BLUE M&M'S TAKEN OUT OF MY SWEETIE-BOWL!
LET'S MEET THE NEIGHBOURS - THAT'S JAK'S CARAVAN OVER THERE!

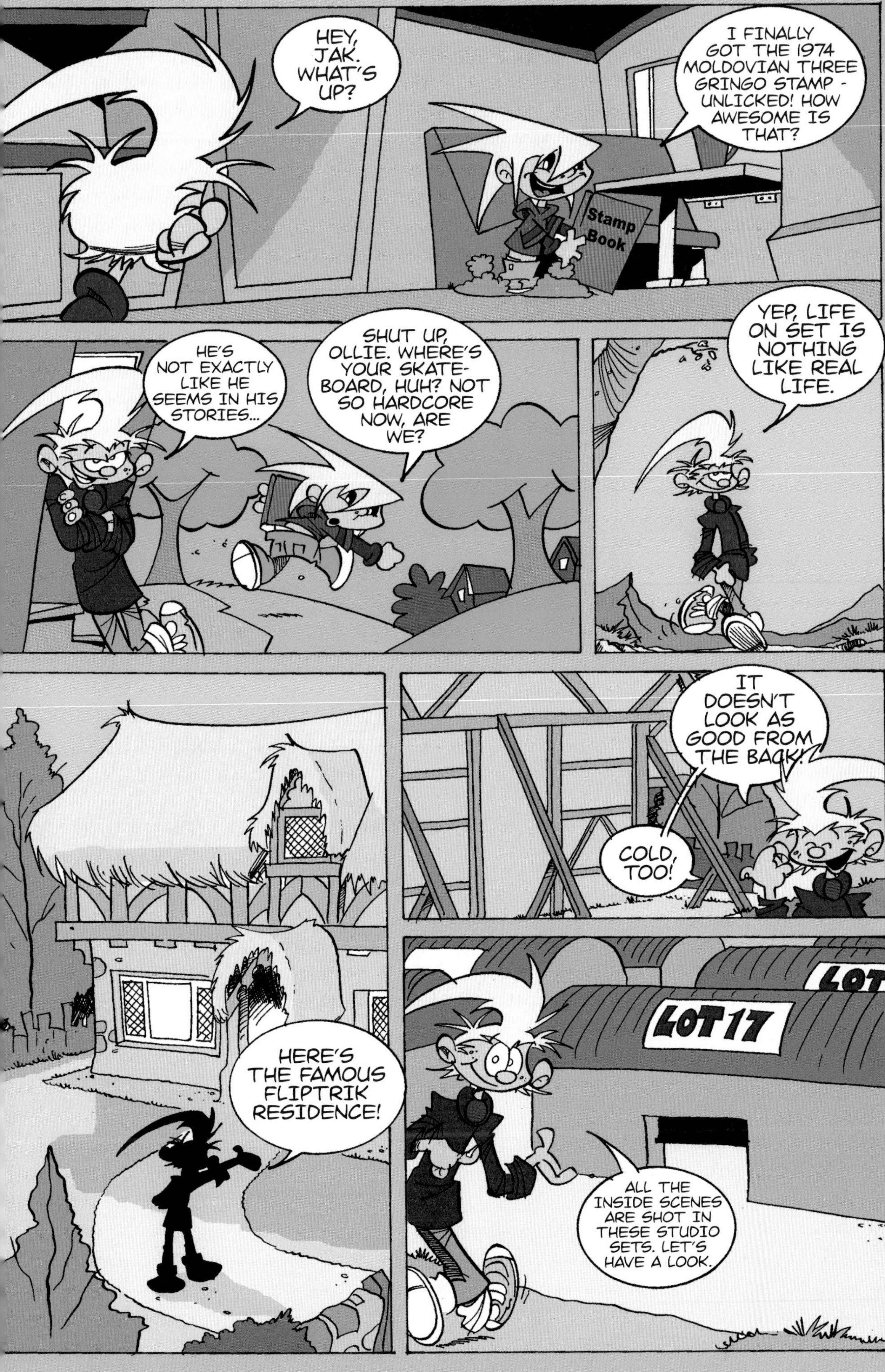
HEY, JAK. WHAT'S UP?
I FINALLY GOT THE 1974 MOLDOVIAN THREE GRINGO STAMP - UNLICKED! HOW AWESOME IS THAT?
Stamp Book
HE'S NOT EXACTLY LIKE HE SEEMS IN HIS STORIES...
SHUT UP, OLLIE. WHERE'S YOUR SKATE-BOARD, HUH? NOT SO HARDCORE NOW, ARE WE?
YEP, LIFE ON SET IS NOTHING LIKE REAL LIFE.
HERE'S THE FAMOUS FLIPTRIK RESIDENCE!
IT DOESN'T LOOK AS GOOD FROM THE BACK!
COLD, TOO!
LOT 17
ALL THE INSIDE SCENES ARE SHOT IN THESE STUDIO SETS. LET'S HAVE A LOOK.

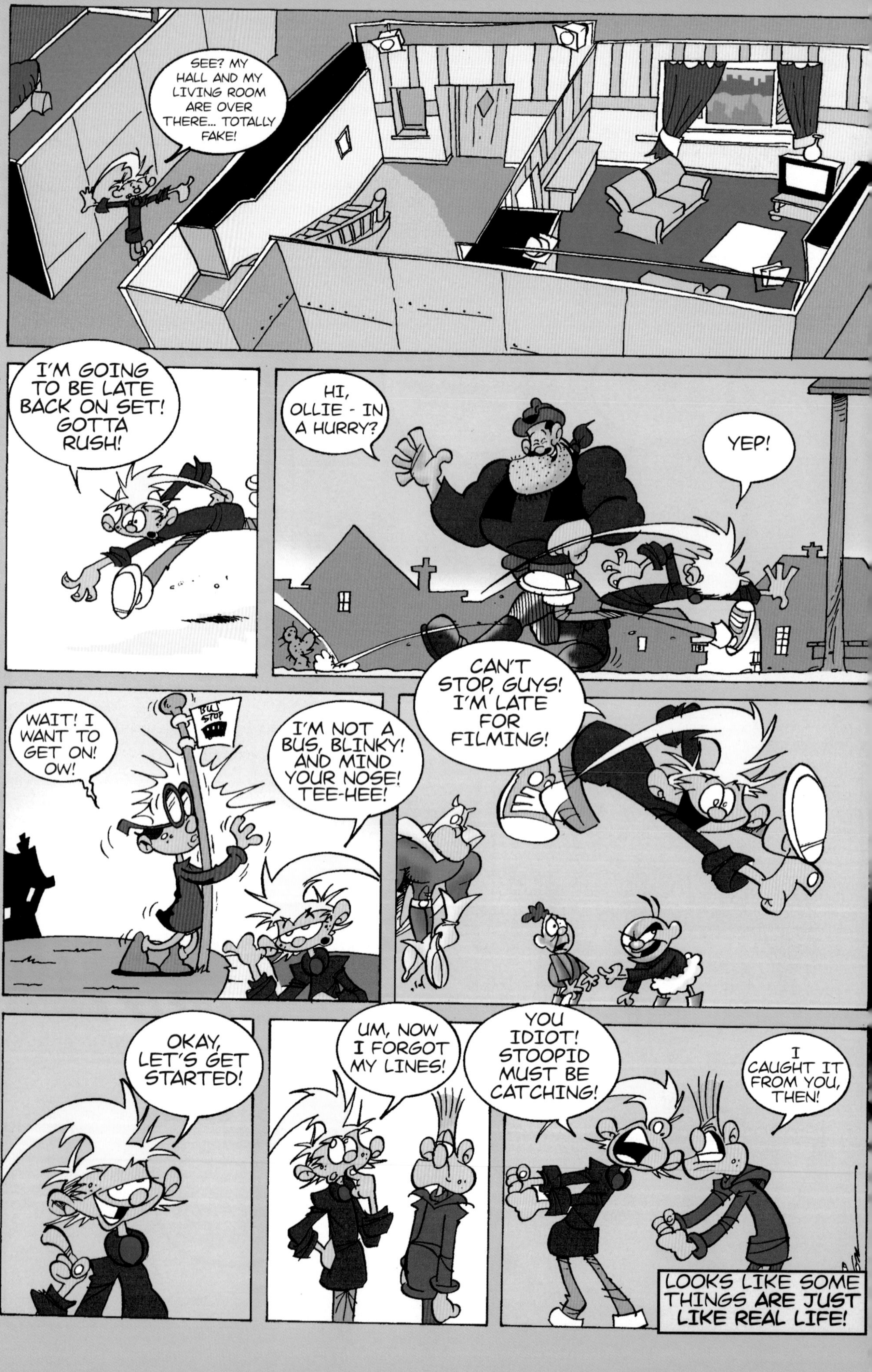
SEE? MY HALL AND MY LIVING ROOM ARE OVER THERE... TOTALLY FAKE!
I'M GOING TO BE LATE BACK ON SET! GOTTA RUSH!
HI, OLLIE - IN A HURRY?
YEP!
WAIT! I WANT TO GET ON! OW!
BUS STOP
I'M NOT A BUS, BLINKY! AND MIND YOUR NOSE! TEE-HEE!
CAN'T STOP, GUYS! I'M LATE FOR FILMING!
OKAY, LET'S GET STARTED!
UM, NOW I FORGOT MY LINES!
YOU IDIOT! STOOPID MUST BE CATCHING!
I CAUGHT IT FROM YOU, THEN!
LOOKS LIKE SOME THINGS ARE JUST LIKE REAL LIFE!

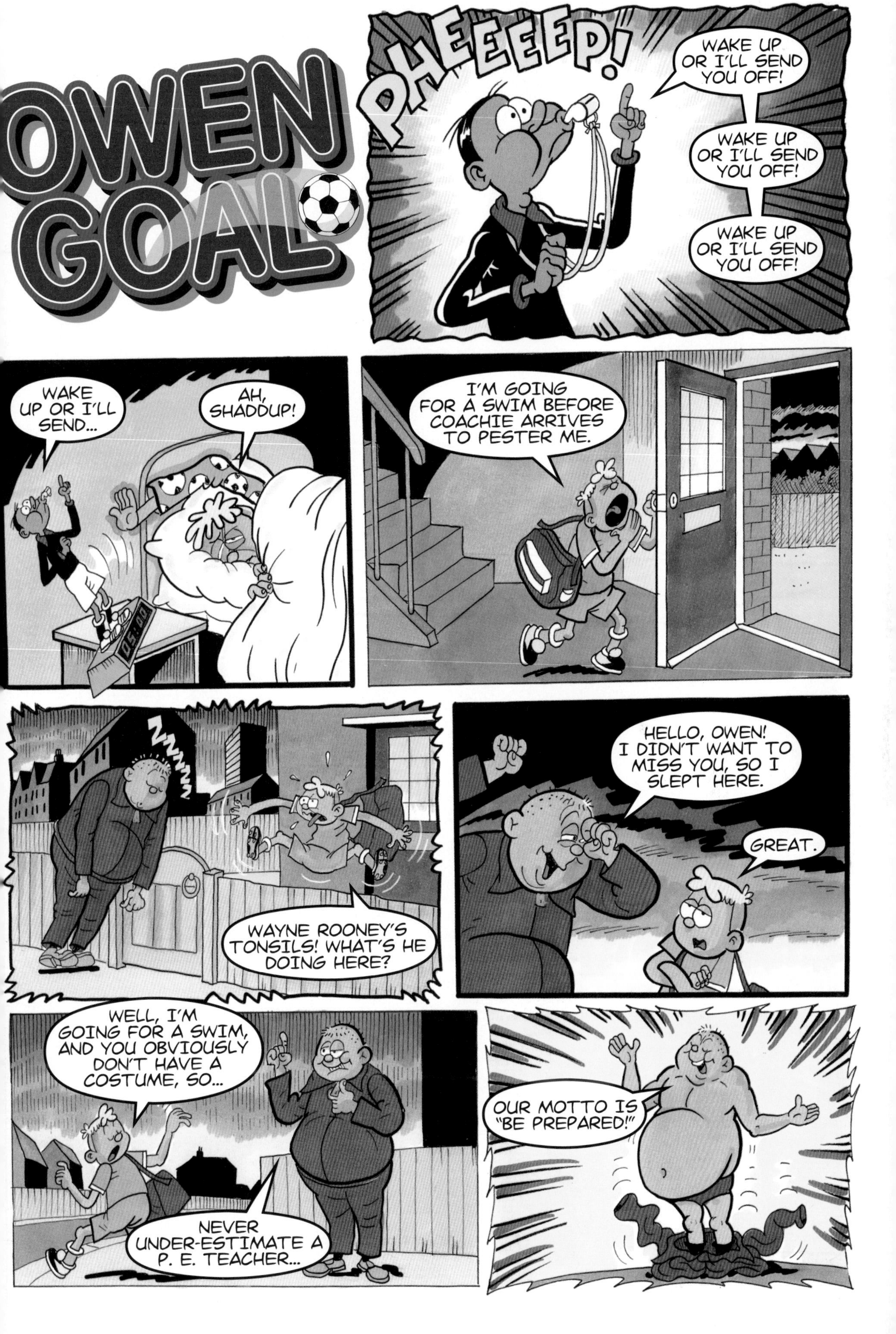
OWEN GOAL
PHEEEEP!
WAKE UP OR I'LL SEND YOU OFF!
WAKE UP OR I'LL SEND YOU OFF!
WAKE UP OR I'LL SEND YOU OFF!
WAKE UP OR I'LL SEND...
AH, SHADDUP!
I'M GOING FOR A SWIM BEFORE COACHIE ARRIVES TO PESTER ME.
ZZZZZ
WAYNE ROONEY'S TONSILS! WHAT'S HE DOING HERE?
HELLO, OWEN! I DIDN'T WANT TO MISS YOU, SO I SLEPT HERE.
GREAT.
WELL, I'M GOING FOR A SWIM, AND YOU OBVIOUSLY DON'T HAVE A COSTUME, SO...
NEVER UNDER-ESTIMATE A P. E. TEACHER...
OUR MOTTO IS "BE PREPARED!"

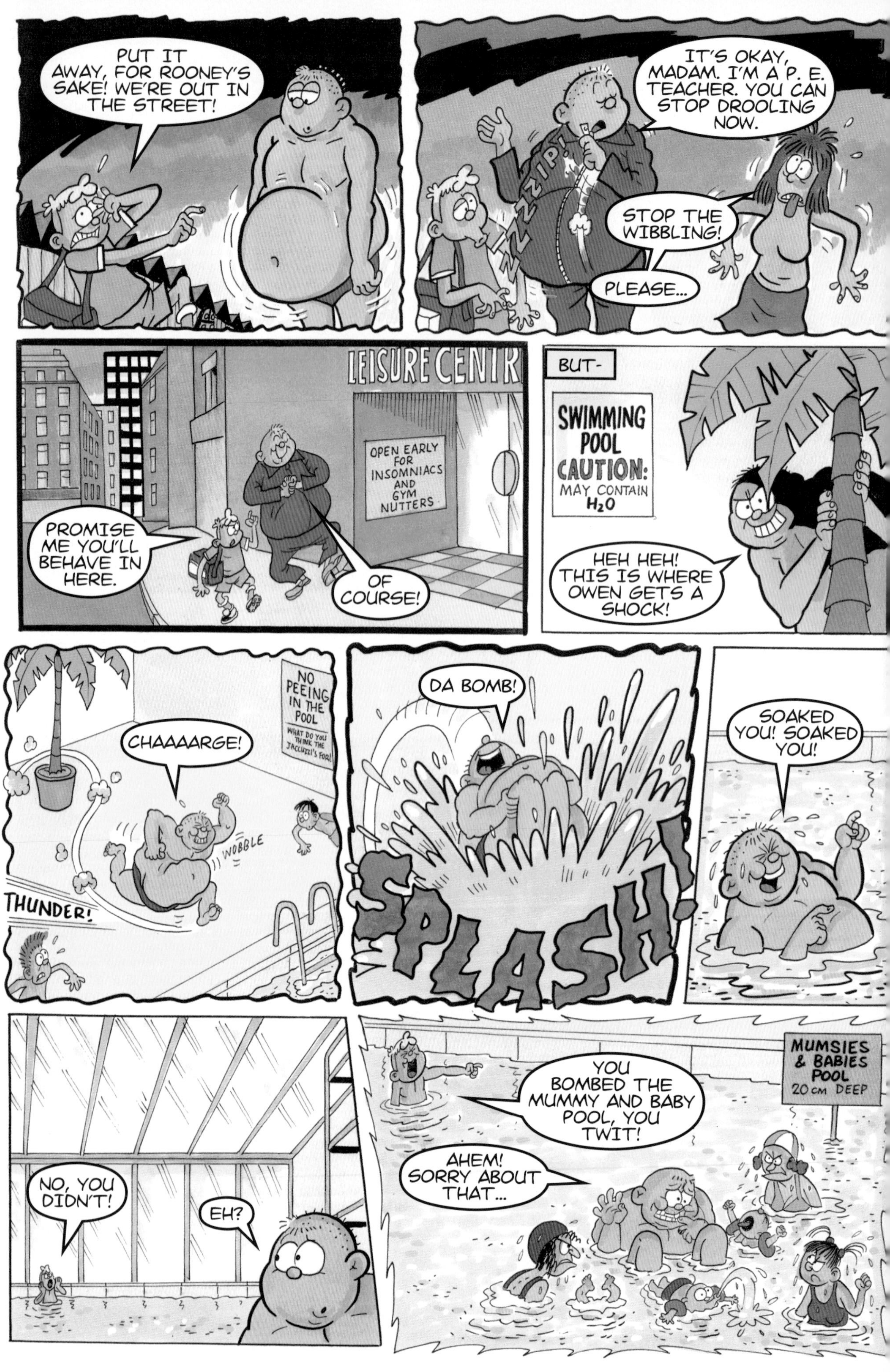

PUT IT AWAY, FOR ROONEY'S SAKE! WE'RE OUT IN THE STREET!
IT'S OKAY, MADAM. I'M A P. E. TEACHER. YOU CAN STOP DROOLING NOW.
ZZZIP!
STOP THE WIBBLING!
PLEASE...
LEISURE CENTR
OPEN EARLY FOR INSOMNIACS AND GYM NUTTERS
PROMISE ME YOU'LL BEHAVE IN HERE.
OF COURSE!
BUT-
SWIMMING POOL CAUTION: MAY CONTAIN H2O
HEH HEH! THIS IS WHERE OWEN GETS A SHOCK!
NO PEEING IN THE POOL
WHAT DO YOU THINK THE JACCUZZI'S FOR!
CHAAAARGE!
WOBBLE
THUNDER!
DA BOMB!
SPLASH!
SOAKED YOU! SOAKED YOU!
NO, YOU DIDN'T!
EH?
YOU BOMBED THE MUMMY AND BABY POOL, YOU TWIT!
MUMSIES & BABIES POOL 20 CM DEEP
AHEM! SORRY ABOUT THAT...

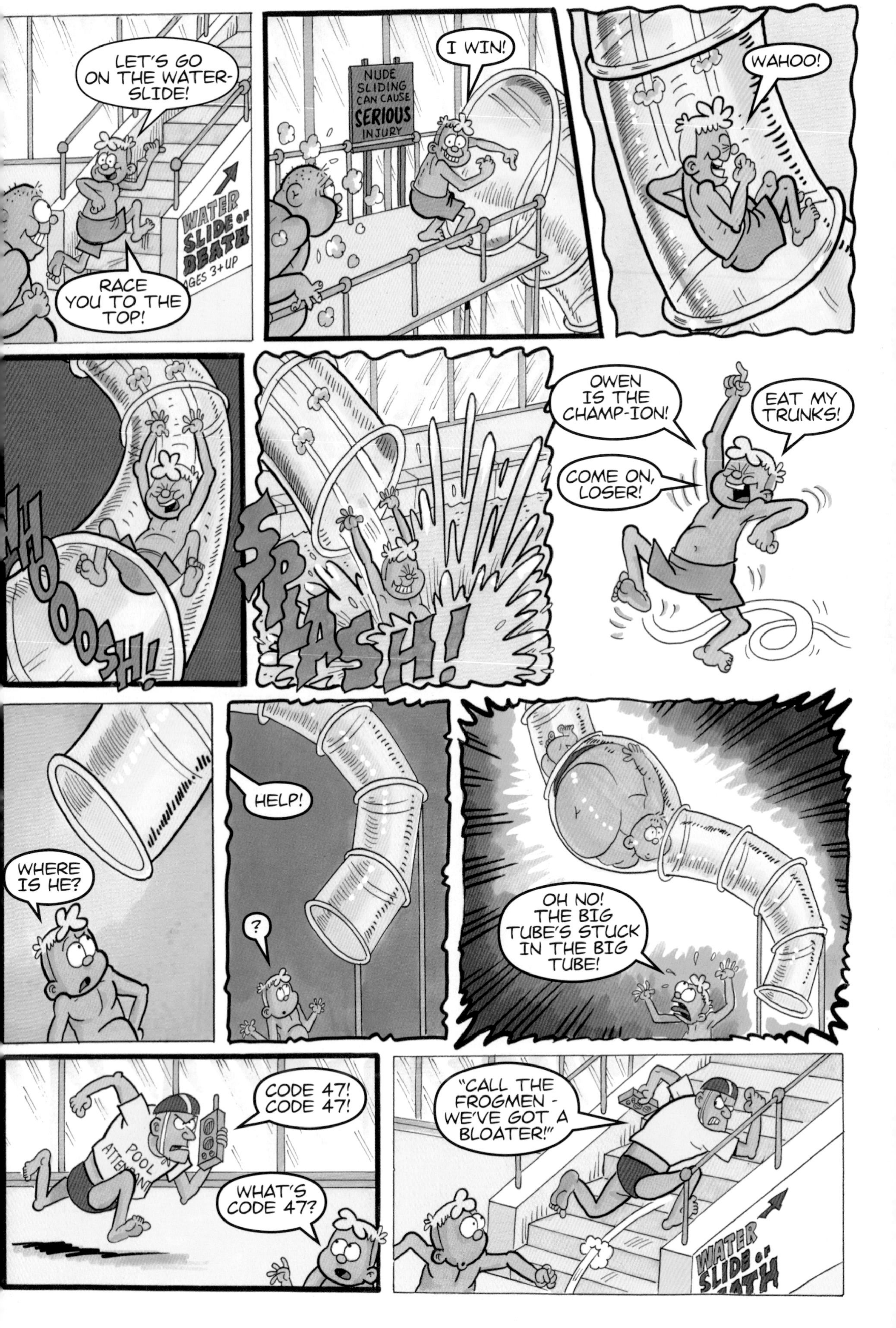
LET'S GO ON THE WATER-SLIDE!
RACE YOU TO THE TOP!
WATER SLIDE OF DEATH
AGES 3+UP
NUDE SLIDING CAN CAUSE SERIOUS INJURY
I WIN!
WAHOO!
WHOOOOSH!
SPLASH!
OWEN IS THE CHAMP-ION!
EAT MY TRUNKS!
COME ON, LOSER!
WHERE IS HE?
HELP!
?
OH NO! THE BIG TUBE'S STUCK IN THE BIG TUBE!
CODE 47! CODE 47!
POOL ATTENDANT
WHAT'S CODE 47?
"CALL THE FROGMEN - WE'VE GOT A BLOATER!"
WATER SLIDE OF DEATH

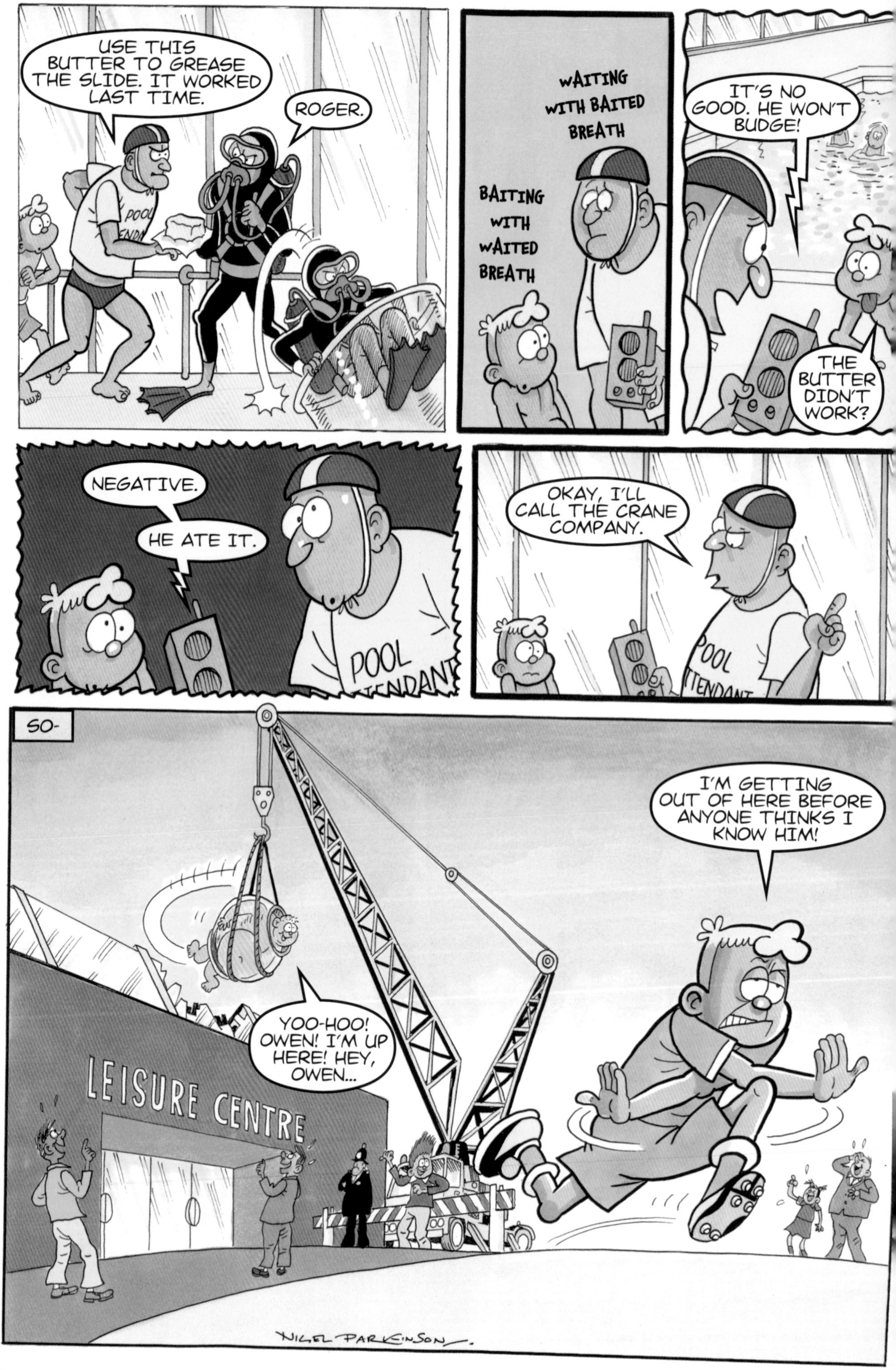
USE THIS BUTTER TO GREASE THE SLIDE. IT WORKED LAST TIME.
ROGER.
POOL TENDA
WAITING WITH BAITED BREATH
BAITING WITH WAITED BREATH
IT'S NO GOOD. HE WON'T BUDGE!
THE BUTTER DIDN'T WORK?
NEGATIVE.
HE ATE IT.
POOL TENDANT
OKAY, I'LL CALL THE CRANE COMPANY.
POOL TENDANT
SO-
I'M GETTING OUT OF HERE BEFORE ANYONE THINKS I KNOW HIM!
YOO-HOO! OWEN! I'M UP HERE! HEY, OWEN...
LEISURE CENTRE
NIGEL PARKINSON

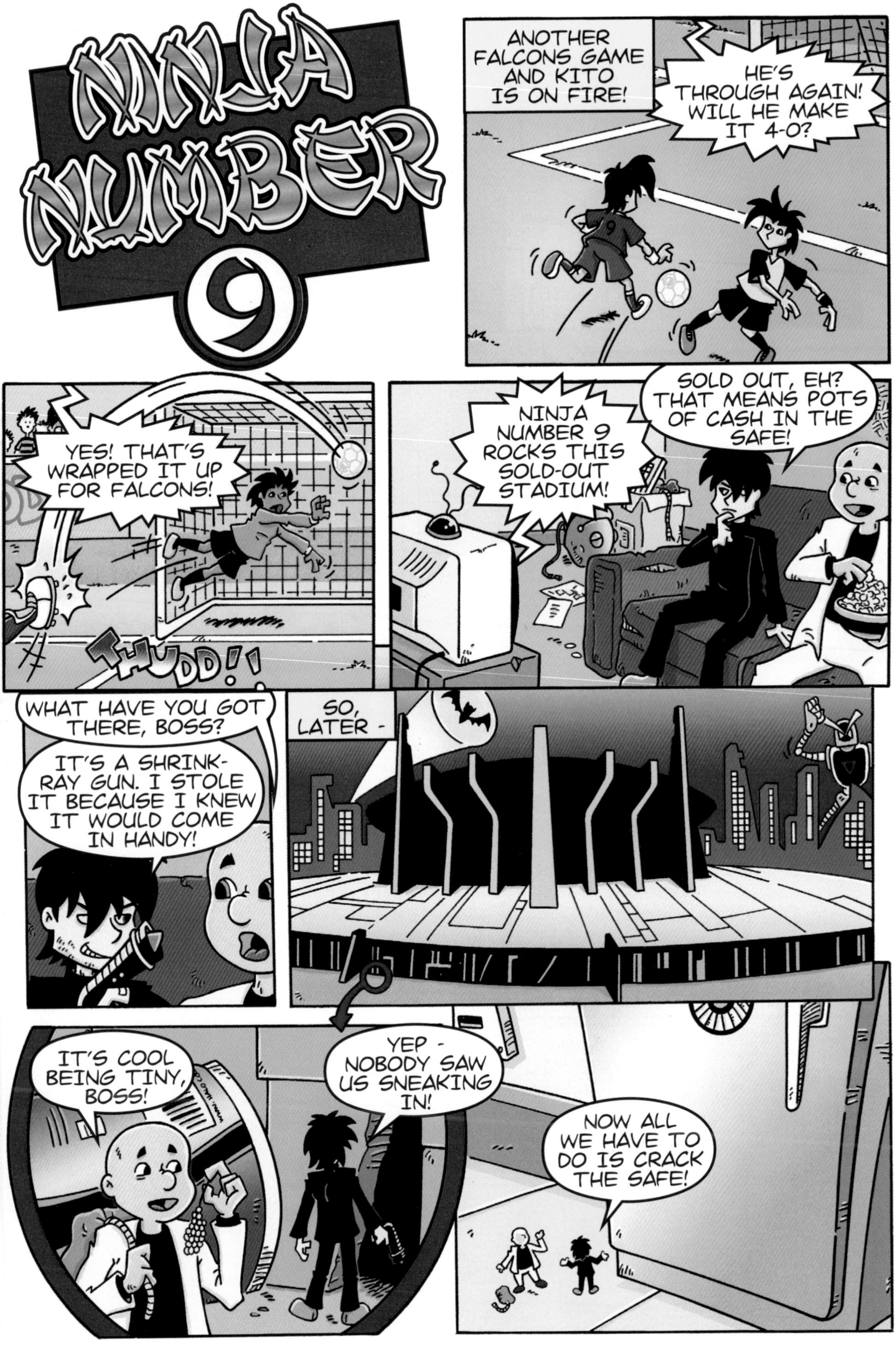
NINJA NUMBER 9
ANOTHER FALCONS GAME AND KITO IS ON FIRE!
HE'S THROUGH AGAIN! WILL HE MAKE IT 4-0?
YES! THAT'S WRAPPED IT UP FOR FALCONS!
THUDD!!
NINJA NUMBER 9 ROCKS THIS SOLD-OUT STADIUM!
SOLD OUT, EH? THAT MEANS POTS OF CASH IN THE SAFE!
WHAT HAVE YOU GOT THERE, BOSS?
IT'S A SHRINK-RAY GUN. I STOLE IT BECAUSE I KNEW IT WOULD COME IN HANDY!
SO, LATER -
IT'S COOL BEING TINY, BOSS!
YEP - NOBODY SAW US SNEAKING IN!
NOW ALL WE HAVE TO DO IS CRACK THE SAFE!

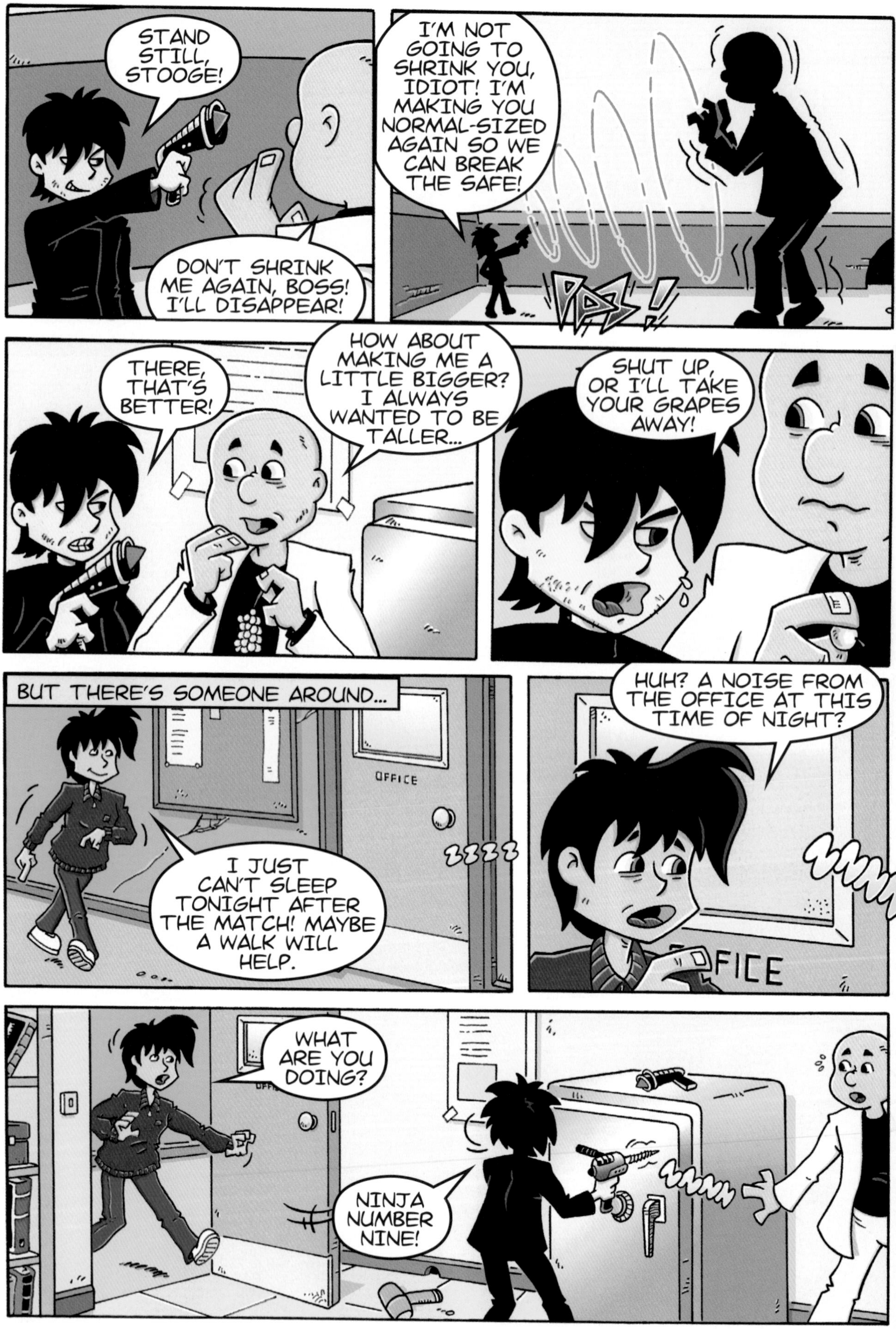
STAND STILL, STOOGE!
DON'T SHRINK ME AGAIN, BOSS! I'LL DISAPPEAR!
I'M NOT GOING TO SHRINK YOU, IDIOT! I'M MAKING YOU NORMAL-SIZED AGAIN SO WE CAN BREAK THE SAFE!
PAZZ!
THERE, THAT'S BETTER!
HOW ABOUT MAKING ME A LITTLE BIGGER? I ALWAYS WANTED TO BE TALLER...
SHUT UP, OR I'LL TAKE YOUR GRAPES AWAY!
BUT THERE'S SOMEONE AROUND...
OFFICE
I JUST CAN'T SLEEP TONIGHT AFTER THE MATCH! MAYBE A WALK WILL HELP.
HUH? A NOISE FROM THE OFFICE AT THIS TIME OF NIGHT?
WHAT ARE YOU DOING?
NINJA NUMBER NINE!

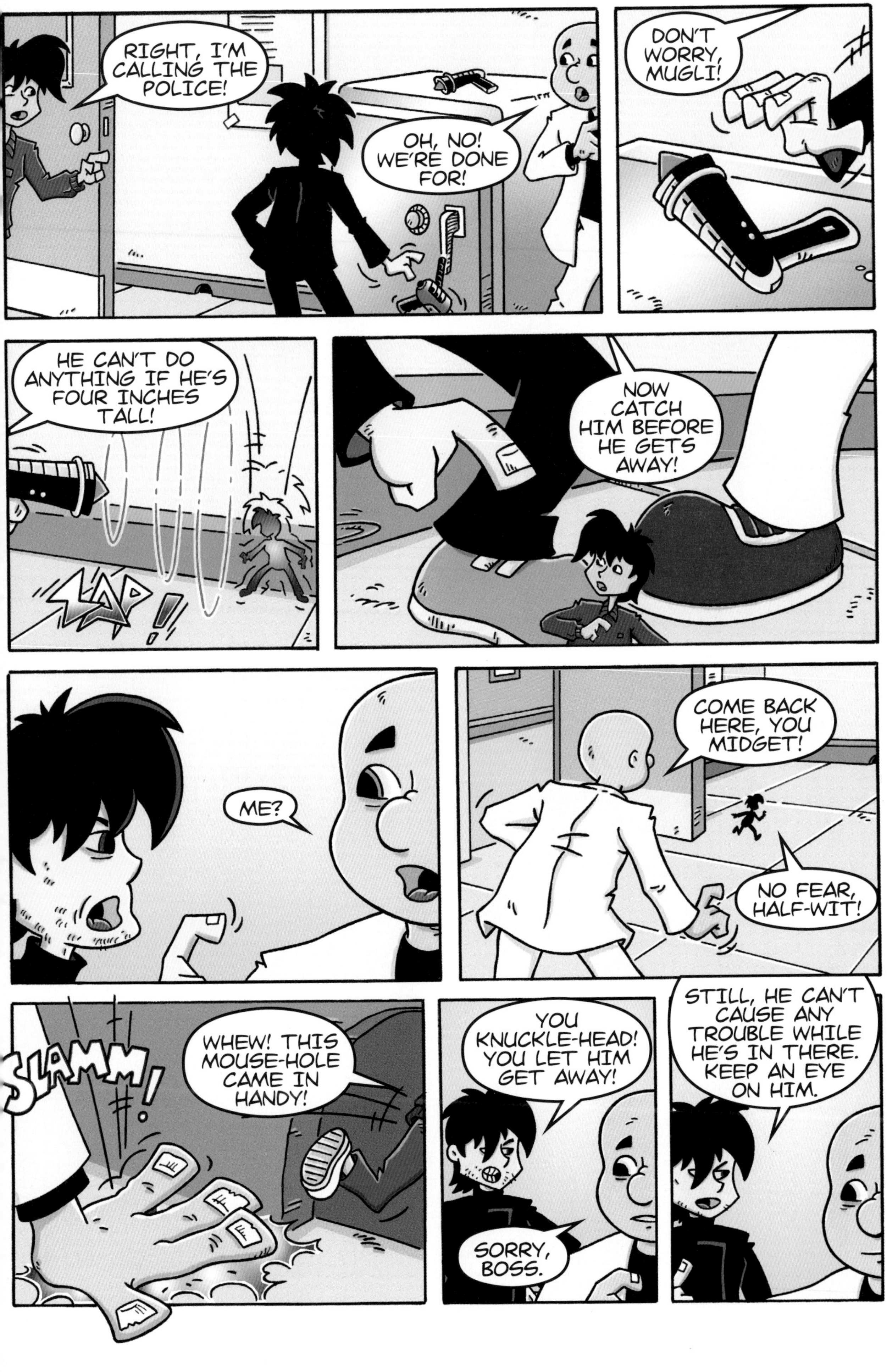
RIGHT, I'M CALLING THE POLICE!
OH, NO! WE'RE DONE FOR!
DON'T WORRY, MUGLI!
HE CAN'T DO ANYTHING IF HE'S FOUR INCHES TALL!
ZAP!
NOW CATCH HIM BEFORE HE GETS AWAY!
ME?
COME BACK HERE, YOU MIDGET!
NO FEAR, HALF-WIT!
SLAMM!
WHEW! THIS MOUSE-HOLE CAME IN HANDY!
YOU KNUCKLE-HEAD! YOU LET HIM GET AWAY!
SORRY, BOSS.
STILL, HE CAN'T CAUSE ANY TROUBLE WHILE HE'S IN THERE. KEEP AN EYE ON HIM.

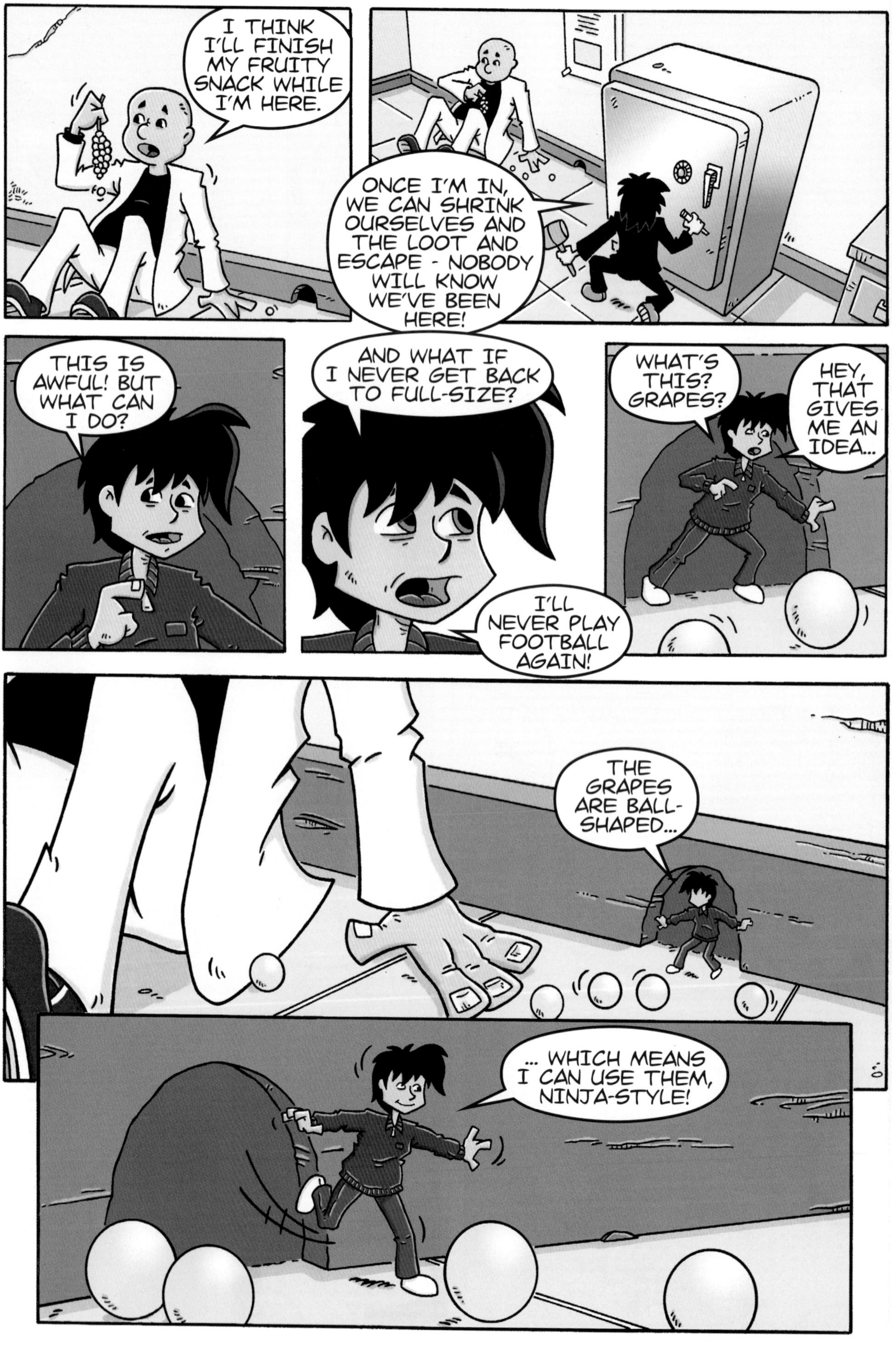
I THINK I'LL FINISH MY FRUITY SNACK WHILE I'M HERE.
ONCE I'M IN, WE CAN SHRINK OURSELVES AND THE LOOT AND ESCAPE - NOBODY WILL KNOW WE'VE BEEN HERE!
THIS IS AWFUL! BUT WHAT CAN I DO?
AND WHAT IF I NEVER GET BACK TO FULL-SIZE?
I'LL NEVER PLAY FOOTBALL AGAIN!
WHAT'S THIS? GRAPES?
HEY, THAT GIVES ME AN IDEA...
THE GRAPES ARE BALL-SHAPED...
... WHICH MEANS I CAN USE THEM, NINJA-STYLE!

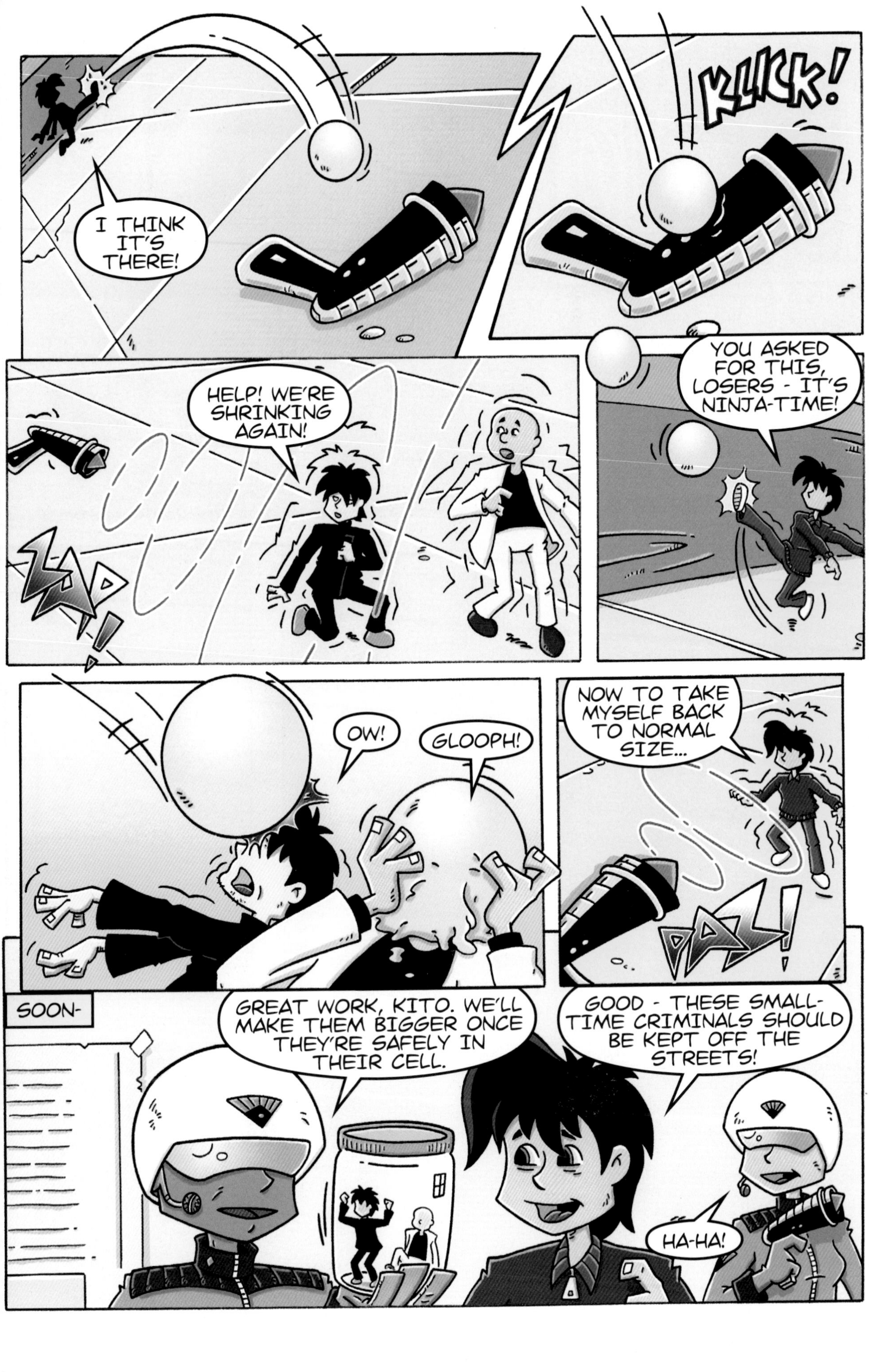
I THINK IT'S THERE!
KLICK!
HELP! WE'RE SHRINKING AGAIN!
ZAP!
YOU ASKED FOR THIS, LOSERS - IT'S NINJA-TIME!
OW!
GLOOPH!
NOW TO TAKE MYSELF BACK TO NORMAL SIZE...
ZAP!
SOON-
GREAT WORK, KITO. WE'LL MAKE THEM BIGGER ONCE THEY'RE SAFELY IN THEIR CELL.
GOOD - THESE SMALL-TIME CRIMINALS SHOULD BE KEPT OFF THE STREETS!
HA-HA!

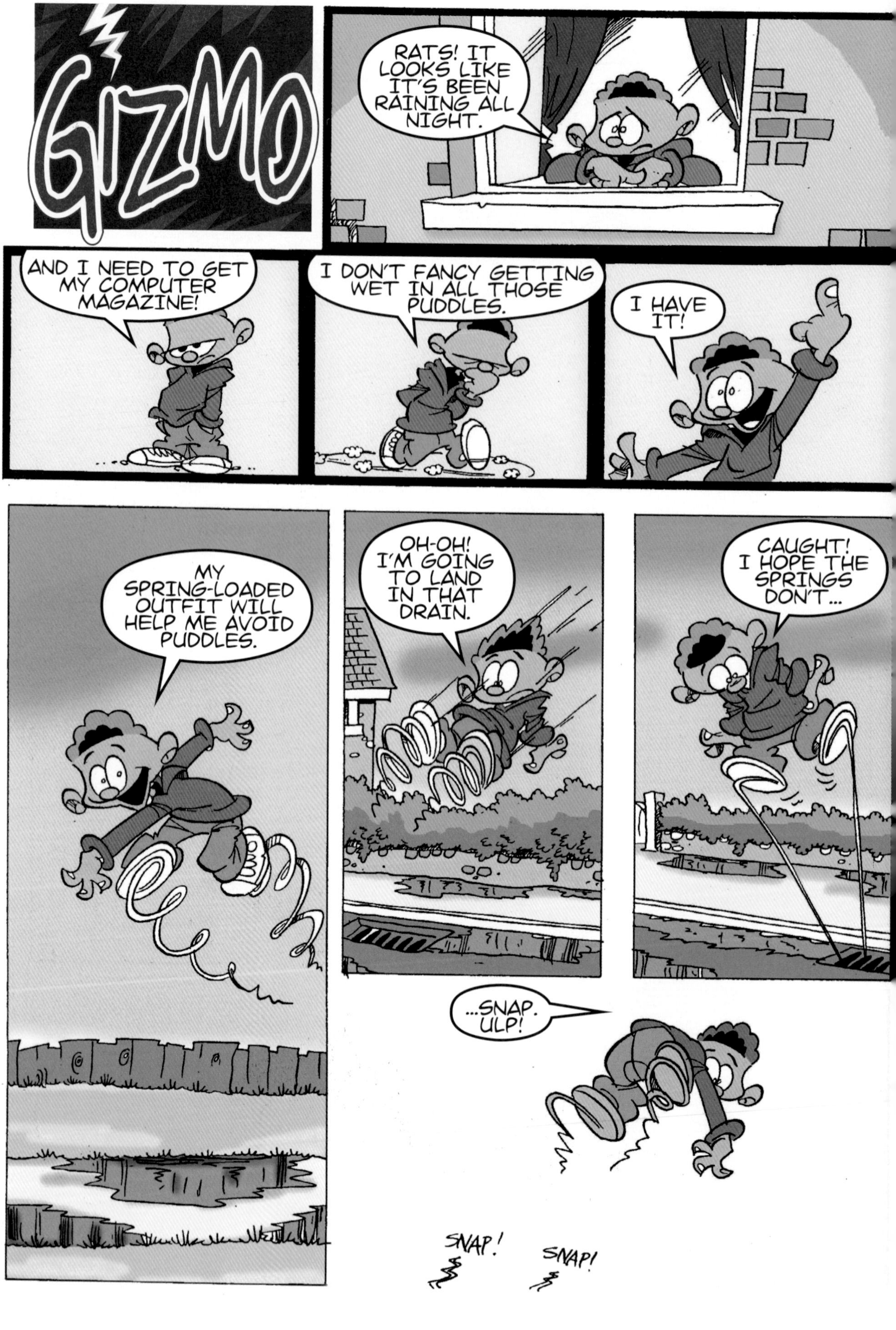
GIZMO
RATS! IT LOOKS LIKE IT'S BEEN RAINING ALL NIGHT.
AND I NEED TO GET MY COMPUTER MAGAZINE!
I DON'T FANCY GETTING WET IN ALL THOSE PUDDLES.
I HAVE IT!
MY SPRING-LOADED OUTFIT WILL HELP ME AVOID PUDDLES.
OH-OH! I'M GOING TO LAND IN THAT DRAIN.
CAUGHT! I HOPE THE SPRINGS DON'T...
...SNAP. ULP!
SNAP!
SNAP!

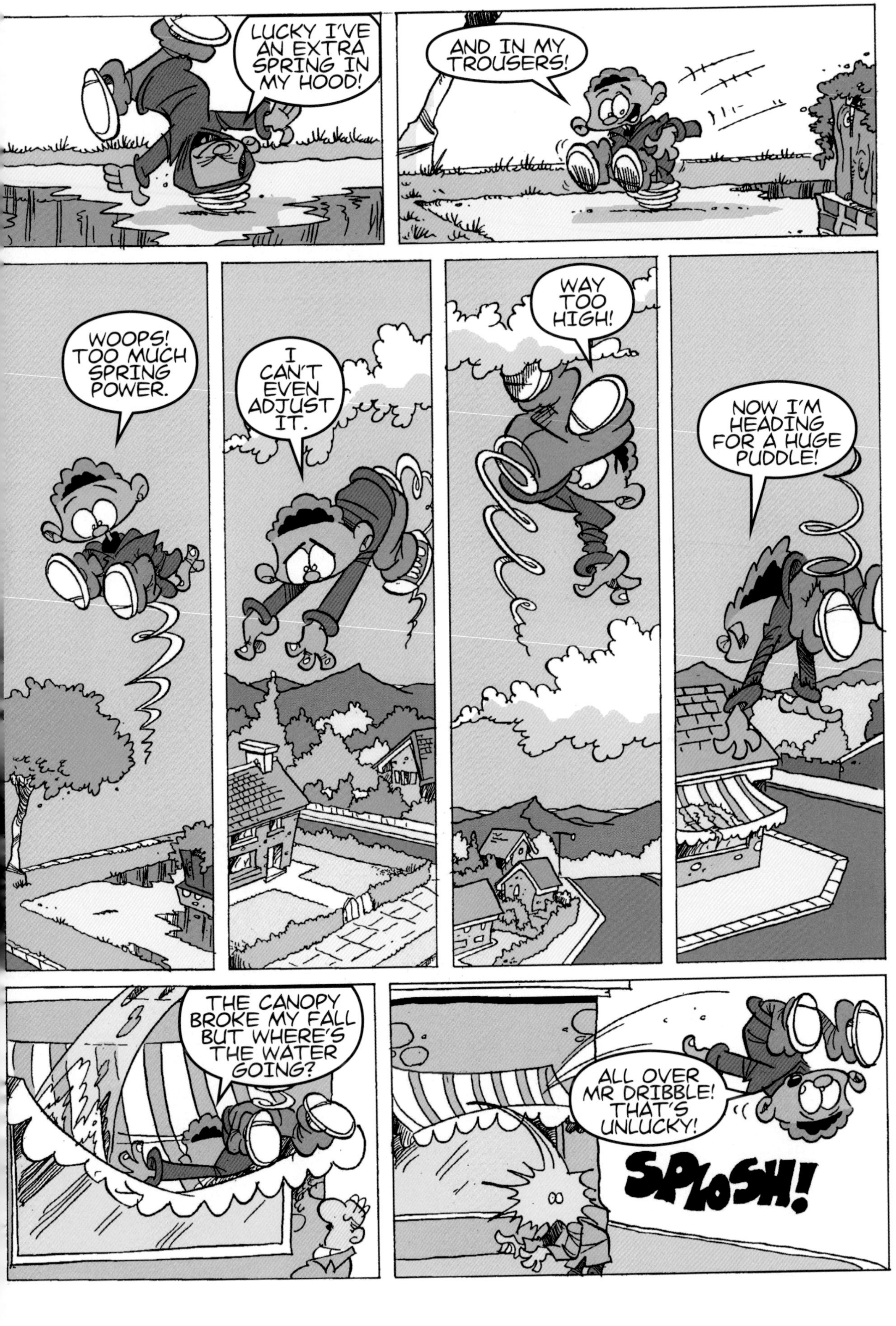

LUCKY I'VE AN EXTRA SPRING IN MY HOOD!
AND IN MY TROUSERS!
WOOPS! TOO MUCH SPRING POWER.
I CAN'T EVEN ADJUST IT.
WAY TOO HIGH!
NOW I'M HEADING FOR A HUGE PUDDLE!
THE CANOPY BROKE MY FALL BUT WHERE'S THE WATER GOING?
ALL OVER MR DRIBBLE! THAT'S UNLUCKY!
SPLOSH!

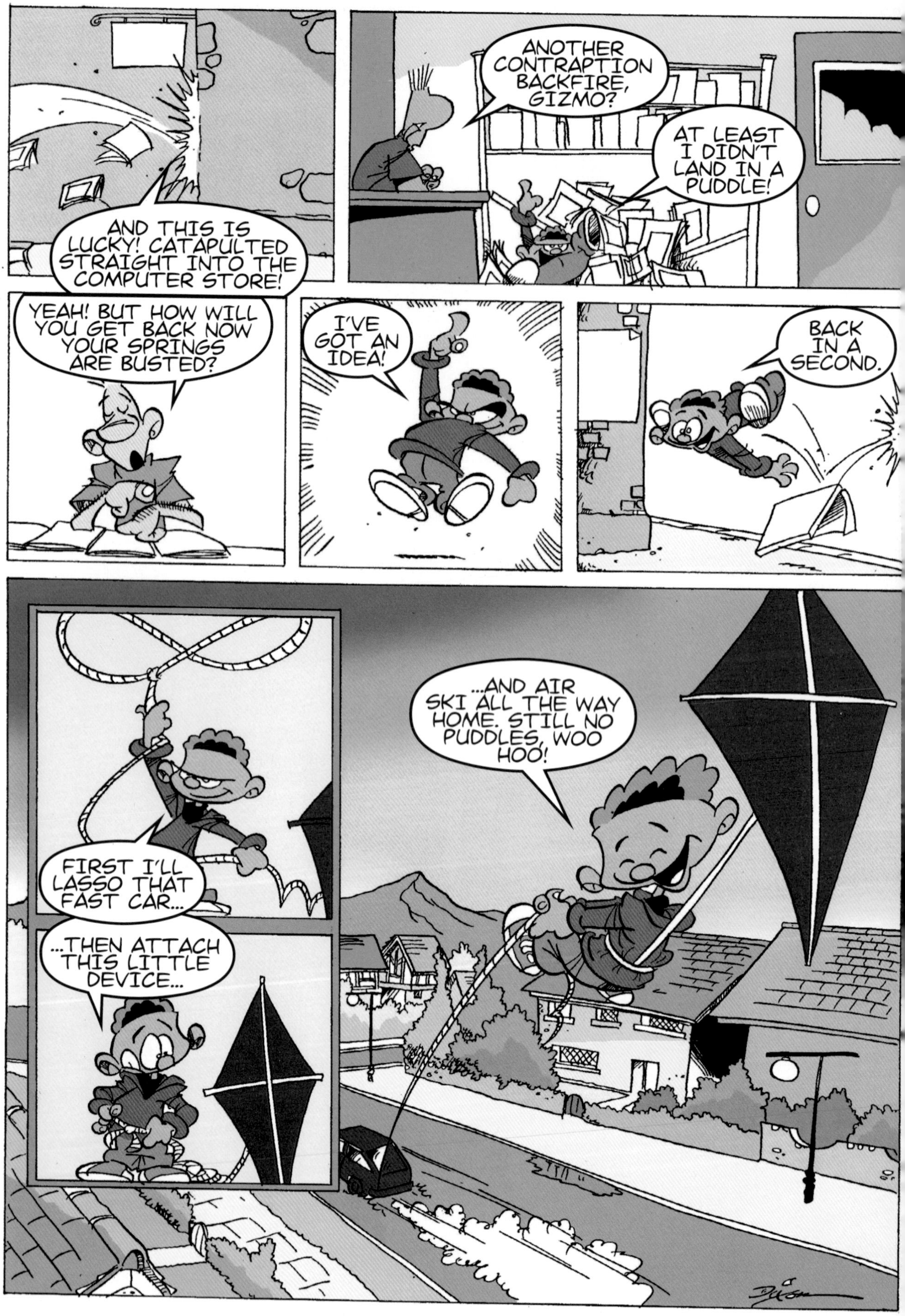
AND THIS IS LUCKY! CATAPULTED STRAIGHT INTO THE COMPUTER STORE!
ANOTHER CONTRAPTION BACKFIRE, GIZMO?
AT LEAST I DIDN'T LAND IN A PUDDLE!
YEAH! BUT HOW WILL YOU GET BACK NOW YOUR SPRINGS ARE BUSTED?
I'VE GOT AN IDEA!
BACK IN A SECOND.
FIRST I'LL LASSO THAT FAST CAR...
...THEN ATTACH THIS LITTLE DEVICE...
...AND AIR SKI ALL THE WAY HOME. STILL NO PUDDLES, WOO HOO!

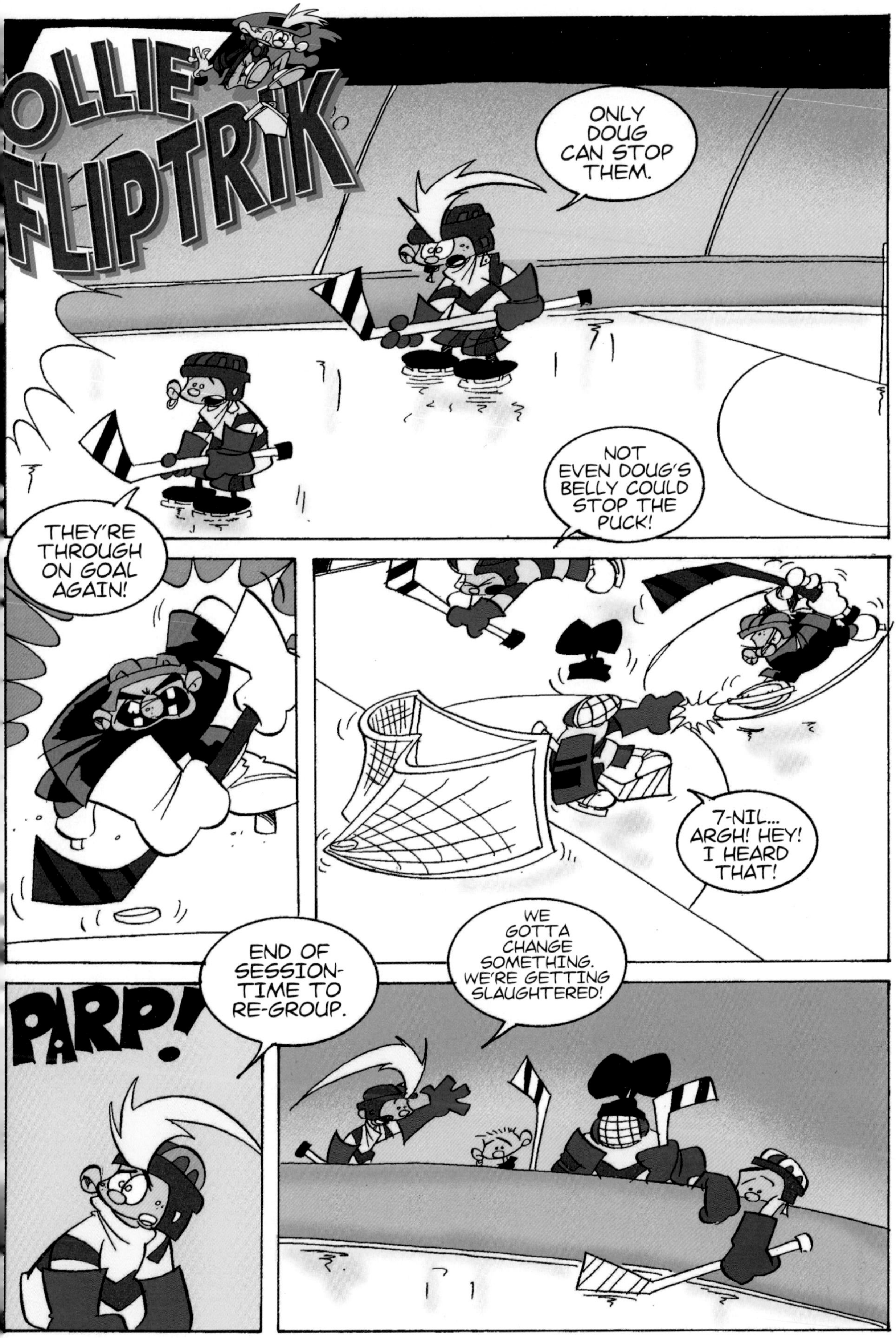
OLLIE FLIPTRIK
ONLY DOUG CAN STOP THEM.
NOT EVEN DOUG'S BELLY COULD STOP THE PUCK!
THEY'RE THROUGH ON GOAL AGAIN!
7-NIL... ARGH! HEY! I HEARD THAT!
PARP!
END OF SESSION- TIME TO RE-GROUP.
WE GOTTA CHANGE SOMETHING. WE'RE GETTING SLAUGHTERED!

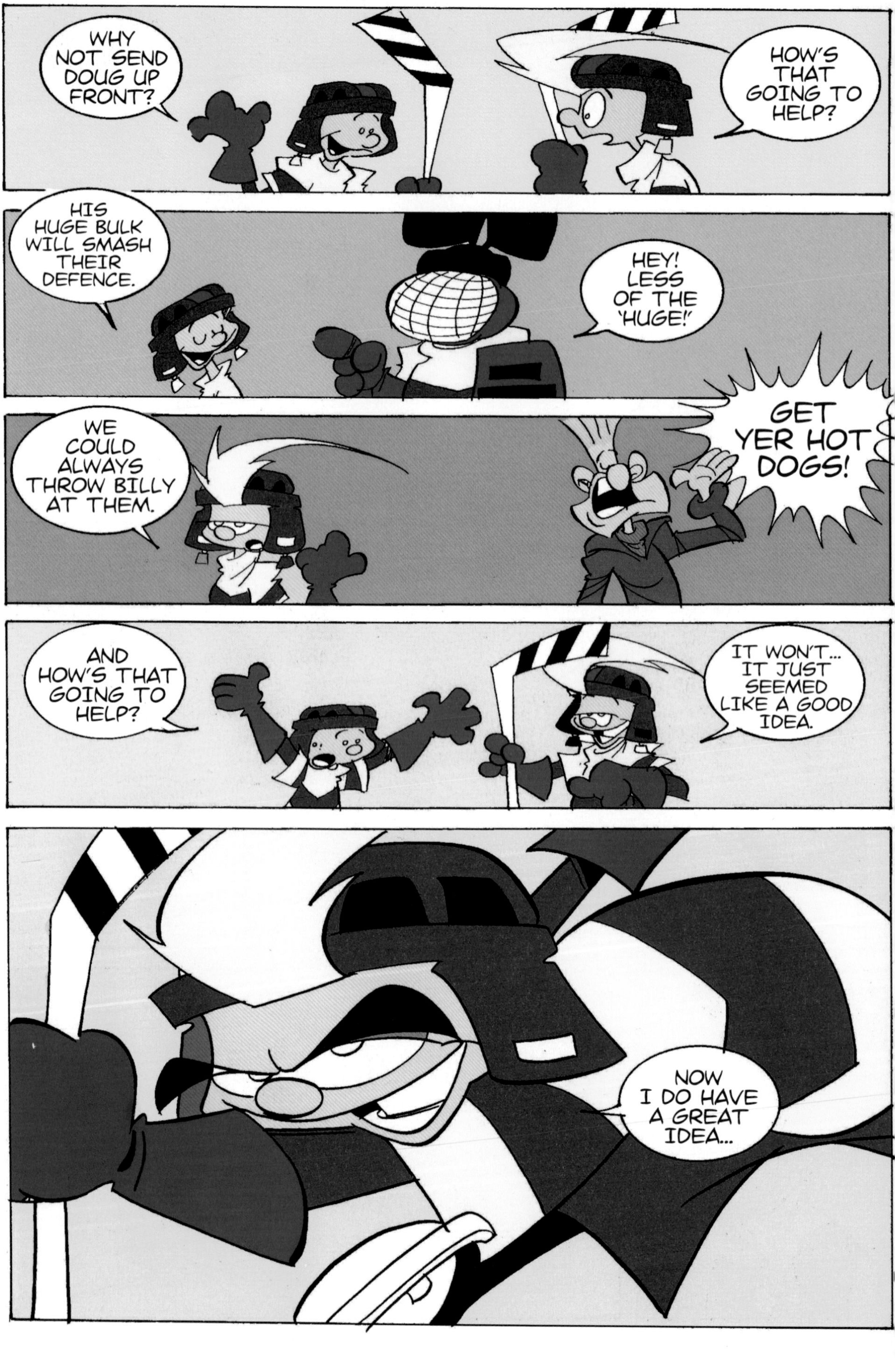
WHY NOT SEND DOUG UP FRONT?
HOW'S THAT GOING TO HELP?
HIS HUGE BULK WILL SMASH THEIR DEFENCE.
HEY! LESS OF THE 'HUGE!'
WE COULD ALWAYS THROW BILLY AT THEM.
GET YER HOT DOGS!
AND HOW'S THAT GOING TO HELP?
IT WON'T... IT JUST SEEMED LIKE A GOOD IDEA.
NOW I DO HAVE A GREAT IDEA...

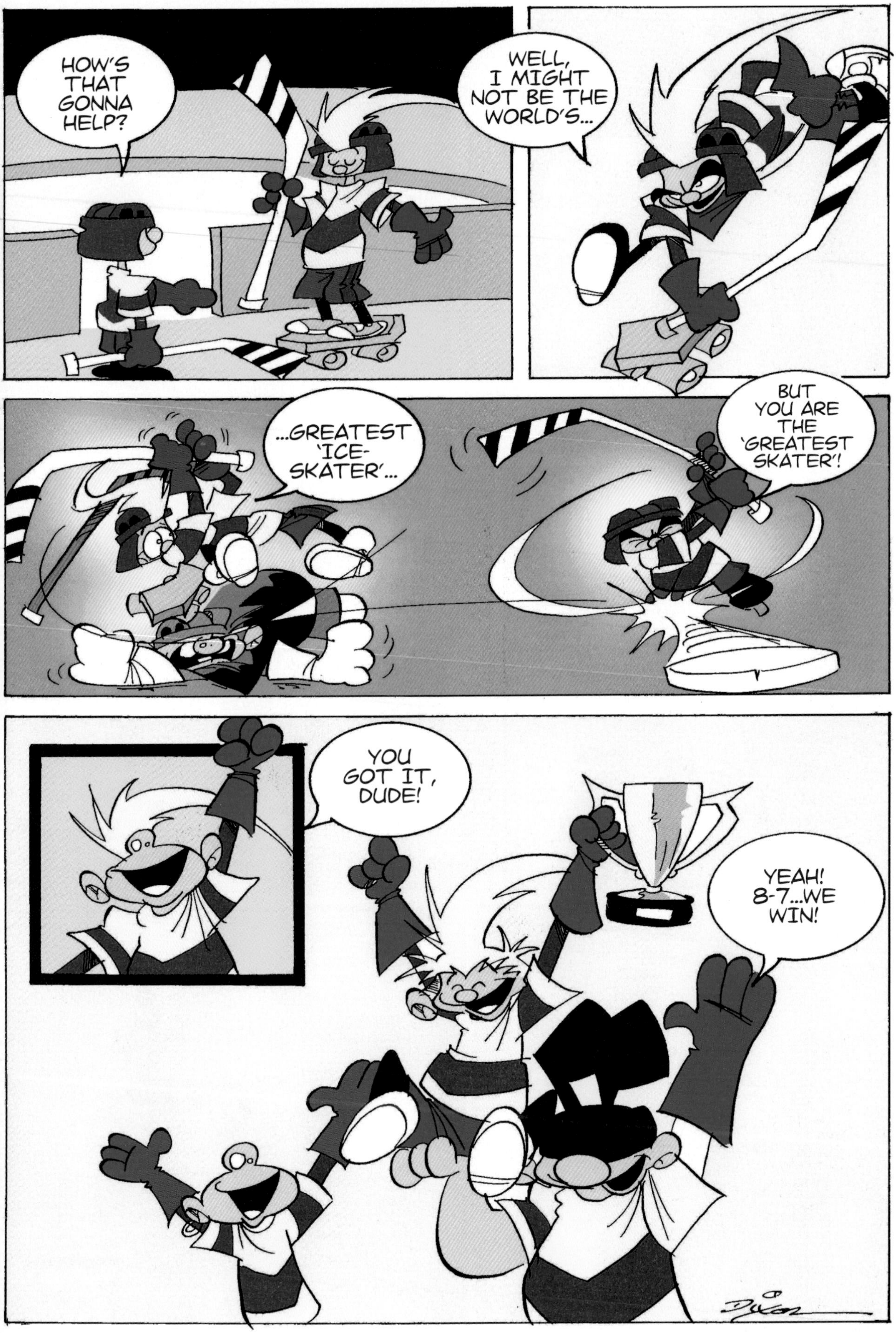
HOW'S THAT GONNA HELP?
WELL, I MIGHT NOT BE THE WORLD'S...
...GREATEST 'ICE-SKATER'...
BUT YOU ARE THE 'GREATEST SKATER'!
YOU GOT IT, DUDE!
YEAH! 8-7...WE WIN!

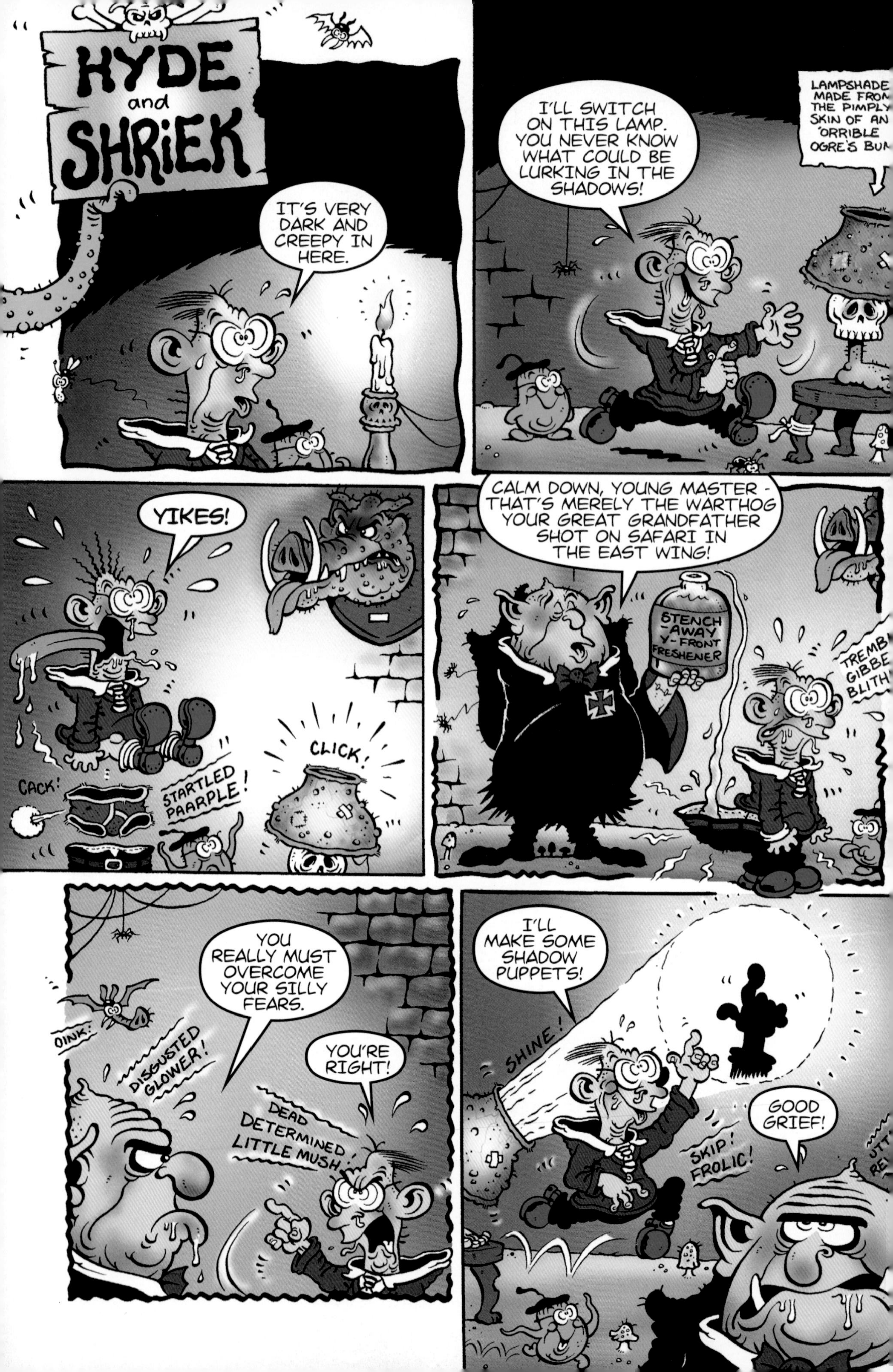
HYDE and SHRiEK
IT'S VERY DARK AND CREEPY IN HERE.
I'LL SWITCH ON THIS LAMP. YOU NEVER KNOW WHAT COULD BE LURKING IN THE SHADOWS!
LAMPSHADE MADE FROM THE PIMPLY SKIN OF AN 'ORRIBLE OGRE'S BUM
YIKES!
CACK!
STARTLED PAARPLE!
CLICK!
CALM DOWN, YOUNG MASTER - THAT'S MERELY THE WARTHOG YOUR GREAT GRANDFATHER SHOT ON SAFARI IN THE EAST WING!
STENCH -AWAY Y-FRONT FRESHENER
YOU REALLY MUST OVERCOME YOUR SILLY FEARS.
OINK!
DISGUSTED GLOWER!
YOU'RE RIGHT!
DEAD DETERMINED LITTLE MUSH!
I'LL MAKE SOME SHADOW PUPPETS!
SHINE!
SKIP! FROLIC!
GOOD GRIEF!

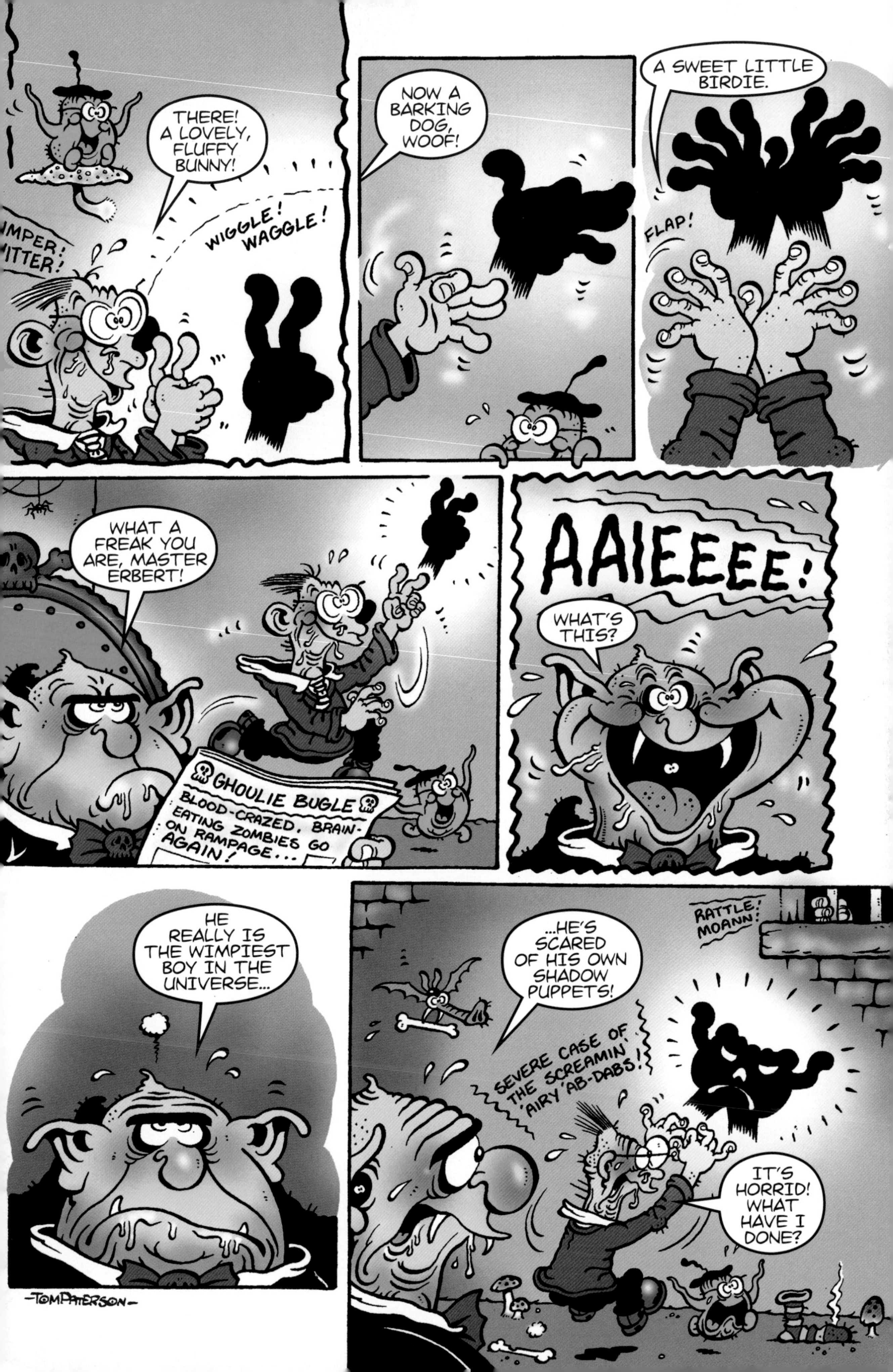
THERE! A LOVELY, FLUFFY BUNNY!
IMPER!
ITTER!
WIGGLE! WAGGLE!
NOW A BARKING DOG, WOOF!
A SWEET LITTLE BIRDIE.
FLAP!
WHAT A FREAK YOU ARE, MASTER ERBERT!
GHOULIE BUGLE
BLOOD-CRAZED, BRAIN-EATING ZOMBIES GO ON RAMPAGE... AGAIN!
AAIEEEEE!
WHAT'S THIS?
HE REALLY IS THE WIMPIEST BOY IN THE UNIVERSE...
-TOM PATERSON-
...HE'S SCARED OF HIS OWN SHADOW PUPPETS!
RATTLE! MOANN!
SEVERE CASE OF THE SCREAMIN' 'AIRY 'AB-DABS!
IT'S HORRID! WHAT HAVE I DONE?

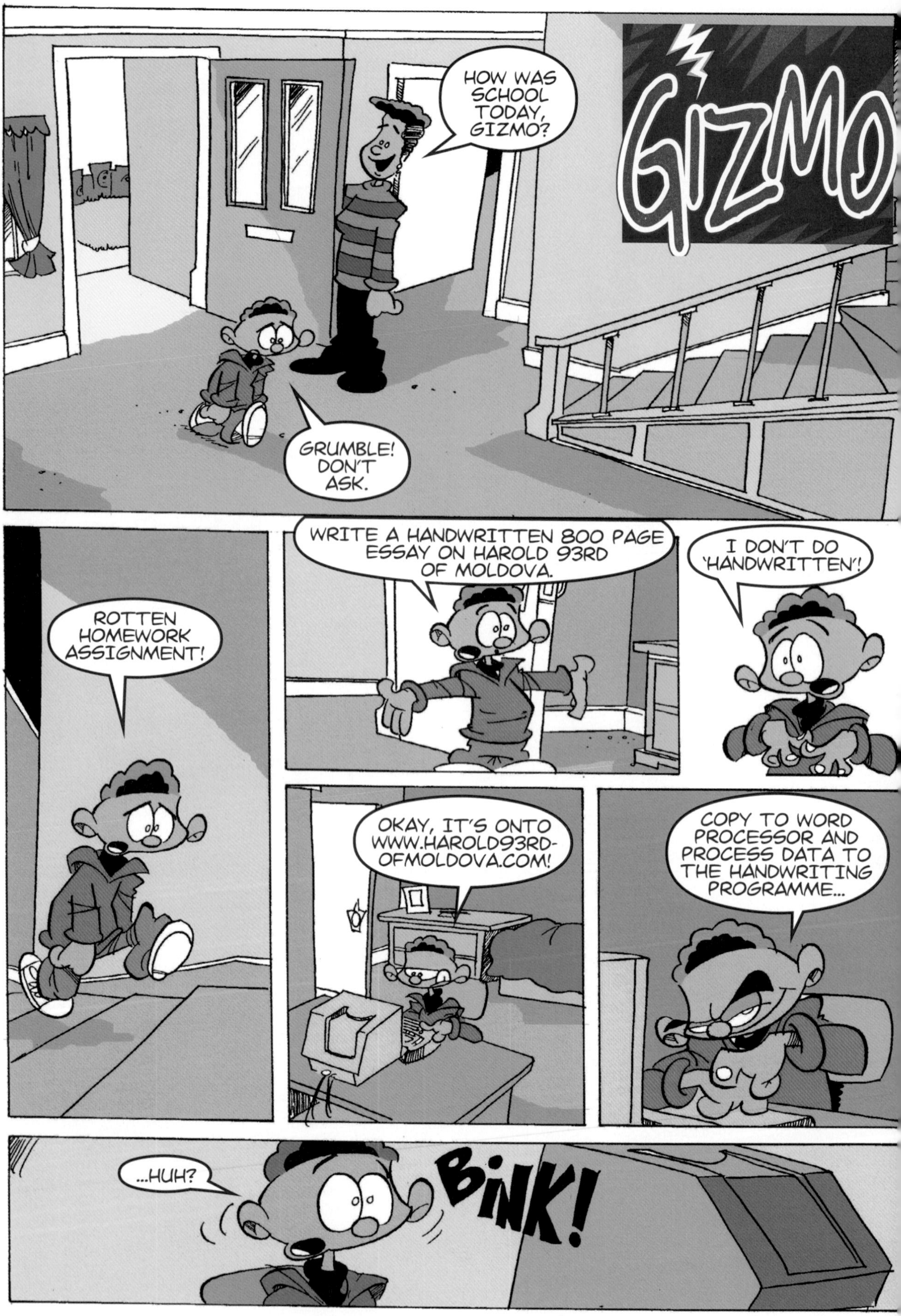
GIZMO
HOW WAS SCHOOL TODAY, GIZMO?
GRUMBLE! DON'T ASK.
ROTTEN HOMEWORK ASSIGNMENT!
WRITE A HANDWRITTEN 800 PAGE ESSAY ON HAROLD 93RD OF MOLDOVA.
I DON'T DO 'HANDWRITTEN'!
OKAY, IT'S ONTO WWW.HAROLD93RD-OFMOLDOVA.COM!
COPY TO WORD PROCESSOR AND PROCESS DATA TO THE HANDWRITING PROGRAMME...
...HUH?
BINK!

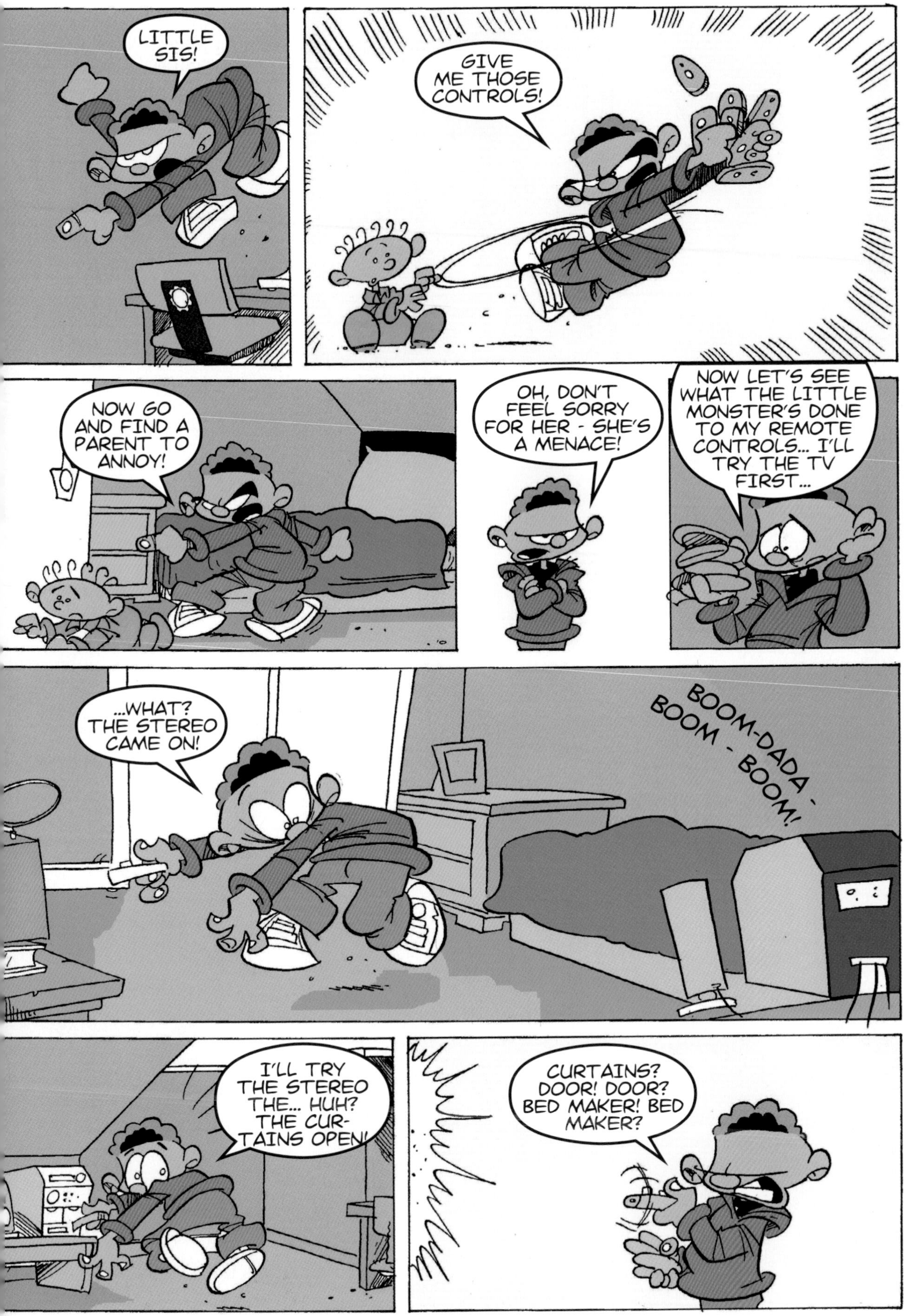
LITTLE SIS!
GIVE ME THOSE CONTROLS!
NOW GO AND FIND A PARENT TO ANNOY!
OH, DON'T FEEL SORRY FOR HER - SHE'S A MENACE!
NOW LET'S SEE WHAT THE LITTLE MONSTER'S DONE TO MY REMOTE CONTROLS... I'LL TRY THE TV FIRST...
...WHAT? THE STEREO CAME ON!
BOOM-DADA-BOOM - BOOM!
I'LL TRY THE STEREO THE... HUH? THE CUR-TAINS OPEN!
CURTAINS? DOOR! DOOR? BED MAKER! BED MAKER?

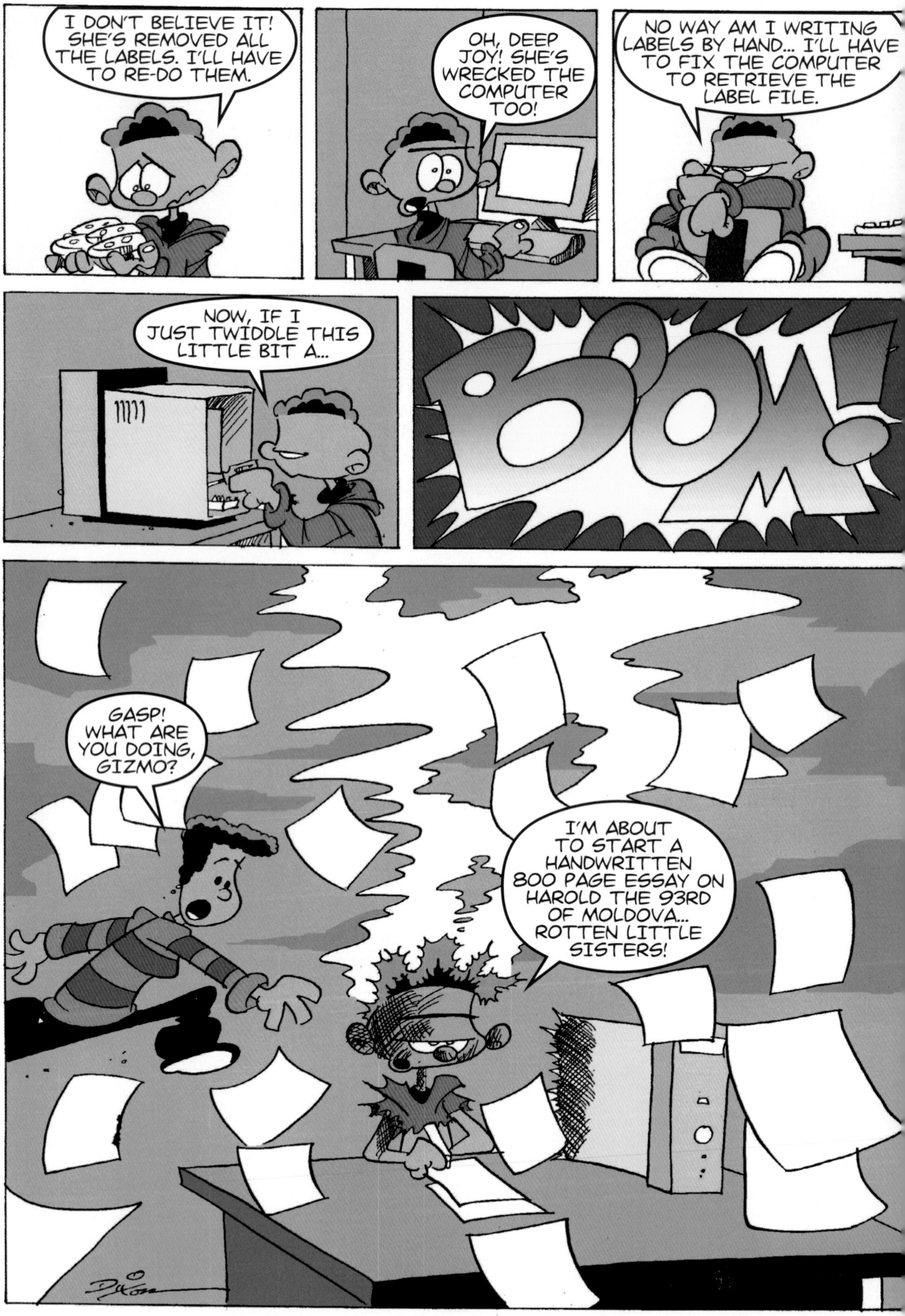
I DON'T BELIEVE IT! SHE'S REMOVED ALL THE LABELS. I'LL HAVE TO RE-DO THEM.
OH, DEEP JOY! SHE'S WRECKED THE COMPUTER TOO!
NO WAY AM I WRITING LABELS BY HAND... I'LL HAVE TO FIX THE COMPUTER TO RETRIEVE THE LABEL FILE.
NOW, IF I JUST TWIDDLE THIS LITTLE BIT A...
BOOM!
GASP! WHAT ARE YOU DOING, GIZMO?
I'M ABOUT TO START A HANDWRITTEN 800 PAGE ESSAY ON HAROLD THE 93RD OF MOLDOVA... ROTTEN LITTLE SISTERS!

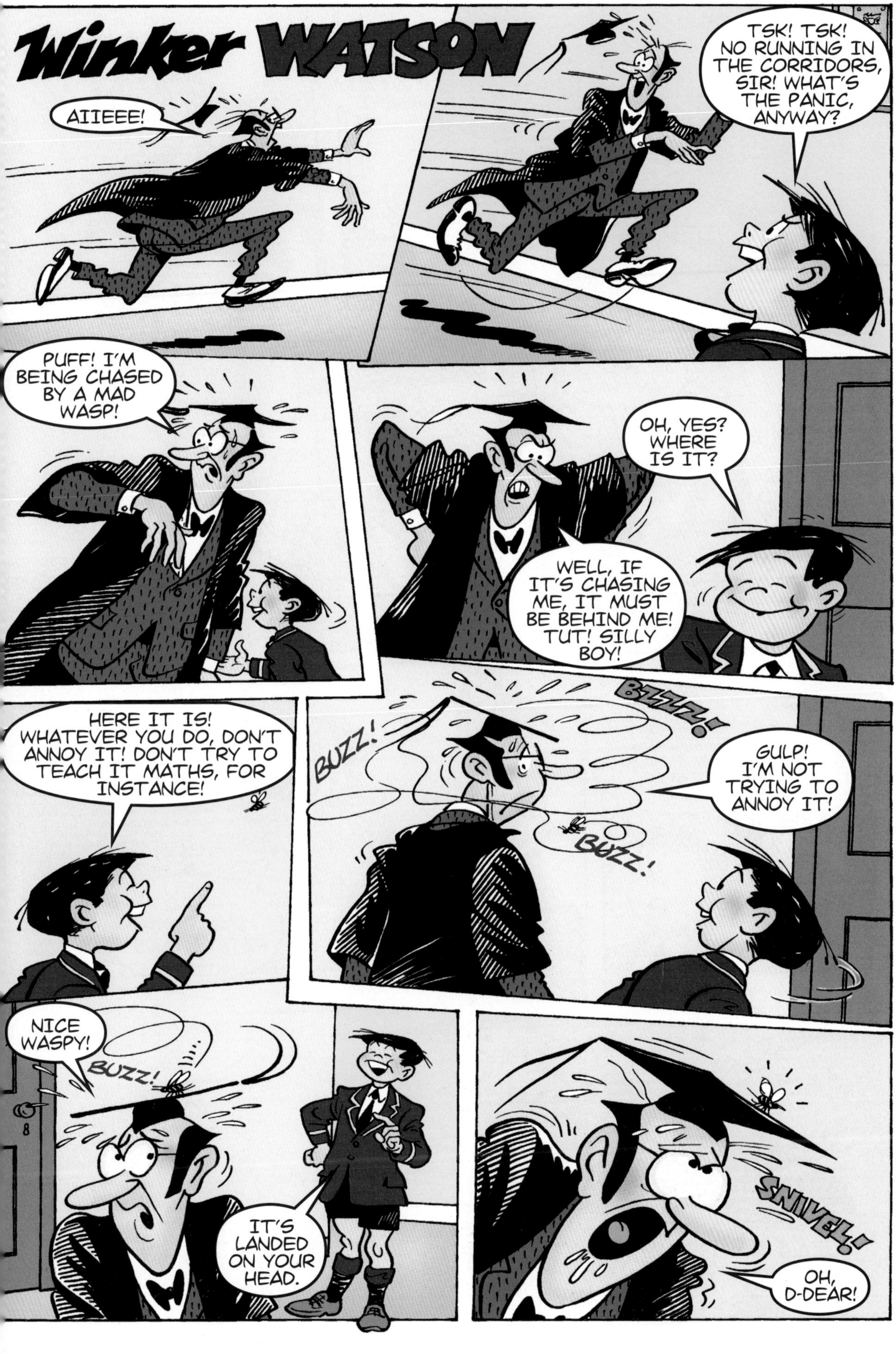
Winker WATSON
AIIEEE!
TSK! TSK! NO RUNNING IN THE CORRIDORS, SIR! WHAT'S THE PANIC, ANYWAY?
PUFF! I'M BEING CHASED BY A MAD WASP!
OH, YES? WHERE IS IT?
WELL, IF IT'S CHASING ME, IT MUST BE BEHIND ME! TUT! SILLY BOY!
HERE IT IS! WHATEVER YOU DO, DON'T ANNOY IT! DON'T TRY TO TEACH IT MATHS, FOR INSTANCE!
BUZZ!
BZZZZ!
GULP! I'M NOT TRYING TO ANNOY IT!
BUZZ!
NICE WASPY!
BUZZ!
IT'S LANDED ON YOUR HEAD.
SNIVEL!
OH, D-DEAR!

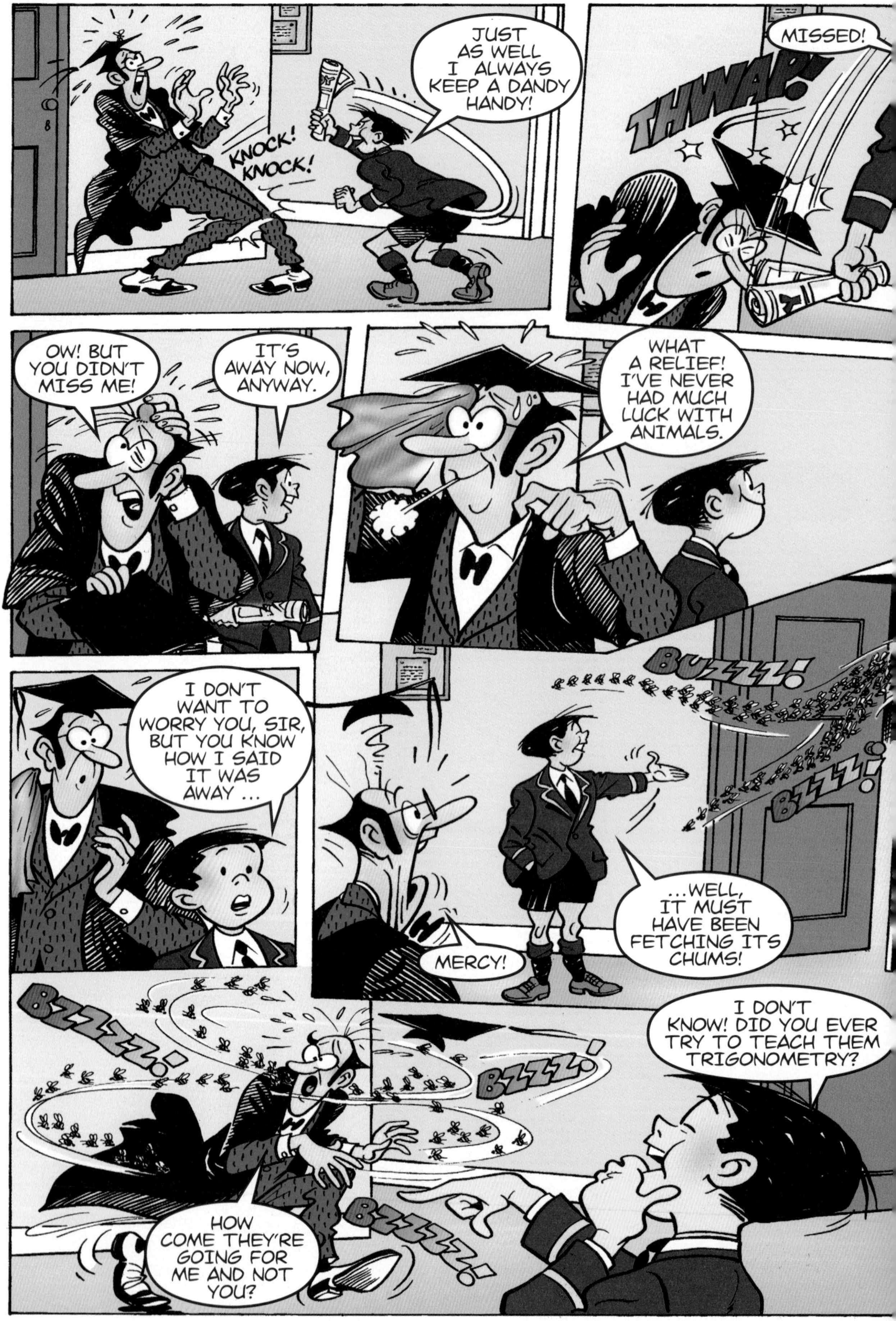
KNOCK!
KNOCK!
JUST AS WELL I ALWAYS KEEP A DANDY HANDY!
MISSED!
THWAP!
OW! BUT YOU DIDN'T MISS ME!
IT'S AWAY NOW, ANYWAY.
WHAT A RELIEF! I'VE NEVER HAD MUCH LUCK WITH ANIMALS.
I DON'T WANT TO WORRY YOU, SIR, BUT YOU KNOW HOW I SAID IT WAS AWAY ...
BUZZZZ!
BZZZ!
MERCY!
...WELL, IT MUST HAVE BEEN FETCHING ITS CHUMS!
BZZZZ!
BZZZ!
BZZZZZ!
HOW COME THEY'RE GOING FOR ME AND NOT YOU?
I DON'T KNOW! DID YOU EVER TRY TO TEACH THEM TRIGONOMETRY?

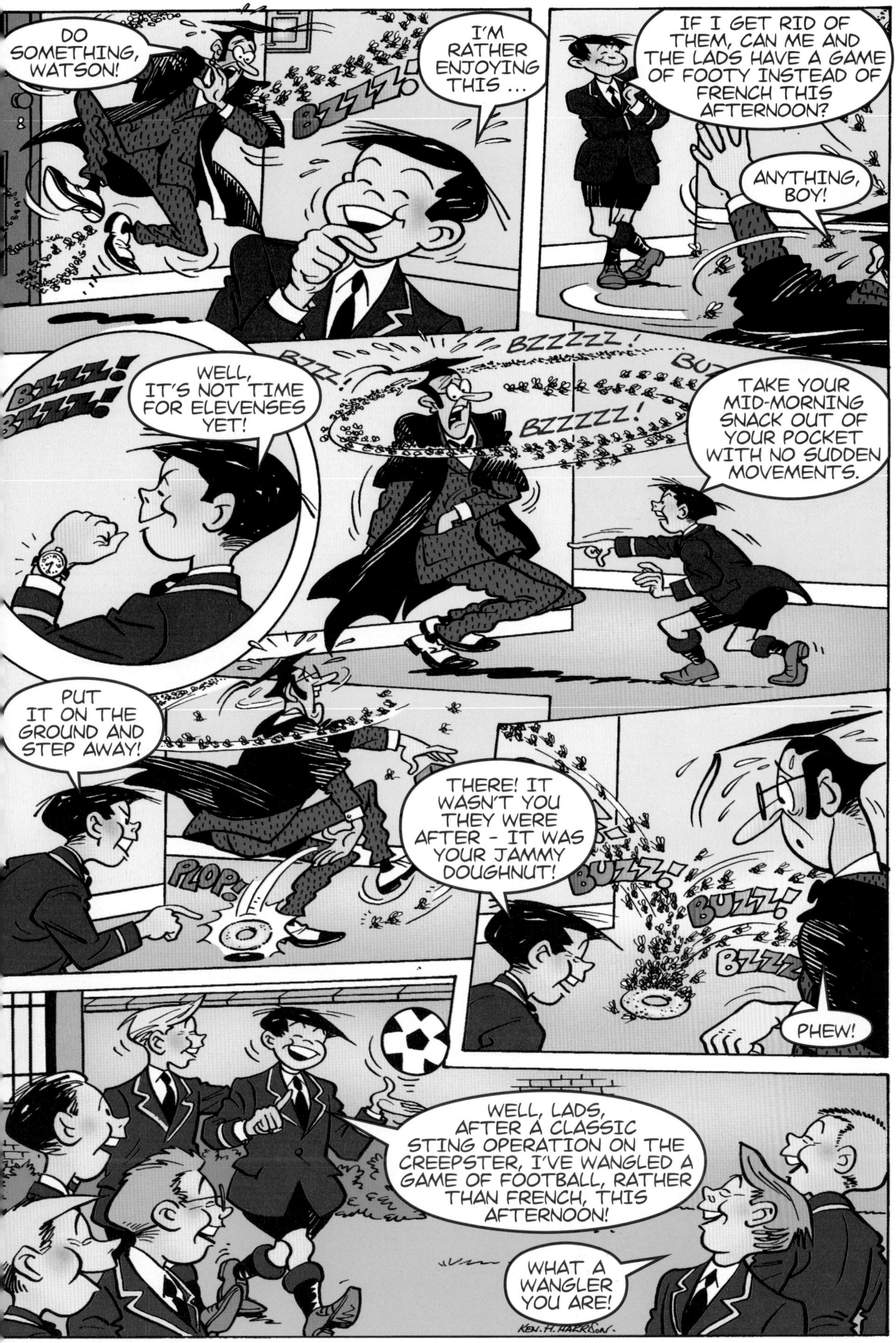
DO SOMETHING, WATSON!
BZZZZ!
I'M RATHER ENJOYING THIS ...
IF I GET RID OF THEM, CAN ME AND THE LADS HAVE A GAME OF FOOTY INSTEAD OF FRENCH THIS AFTERNOON?
ANYTHING, BOY!
BZZZ! BZZZ!
WELL, IT'S NOT TIME FOR ELEVENSES YET!
BZZZZZZ!
BZZZZZ!
TAKE YOUR MID-MORNING SNACK OUT OF YOUR POCKET WITH NO SUDDEN MOVEMENTS.
PUT IT ON THE GROUND AND STEP AWAY!
PLOP!
THERE! IT WASN'T YOU THEY WERE AFTER - IT WAS YOUR JAMMY DOUGHNUT!
BUZZ!
BUZZ!
PHEW!
WELL, LADS, AFTER A CLASSIC STING OPERATION ON THE CREEPSTER, I'VE WANGLED A GAME OF FOOTBALL, RATHER THAN FRENCH, THIS AFTERNOON!
WHAT A WANGLER YOU ARE!
KEN. H. HARRISON.

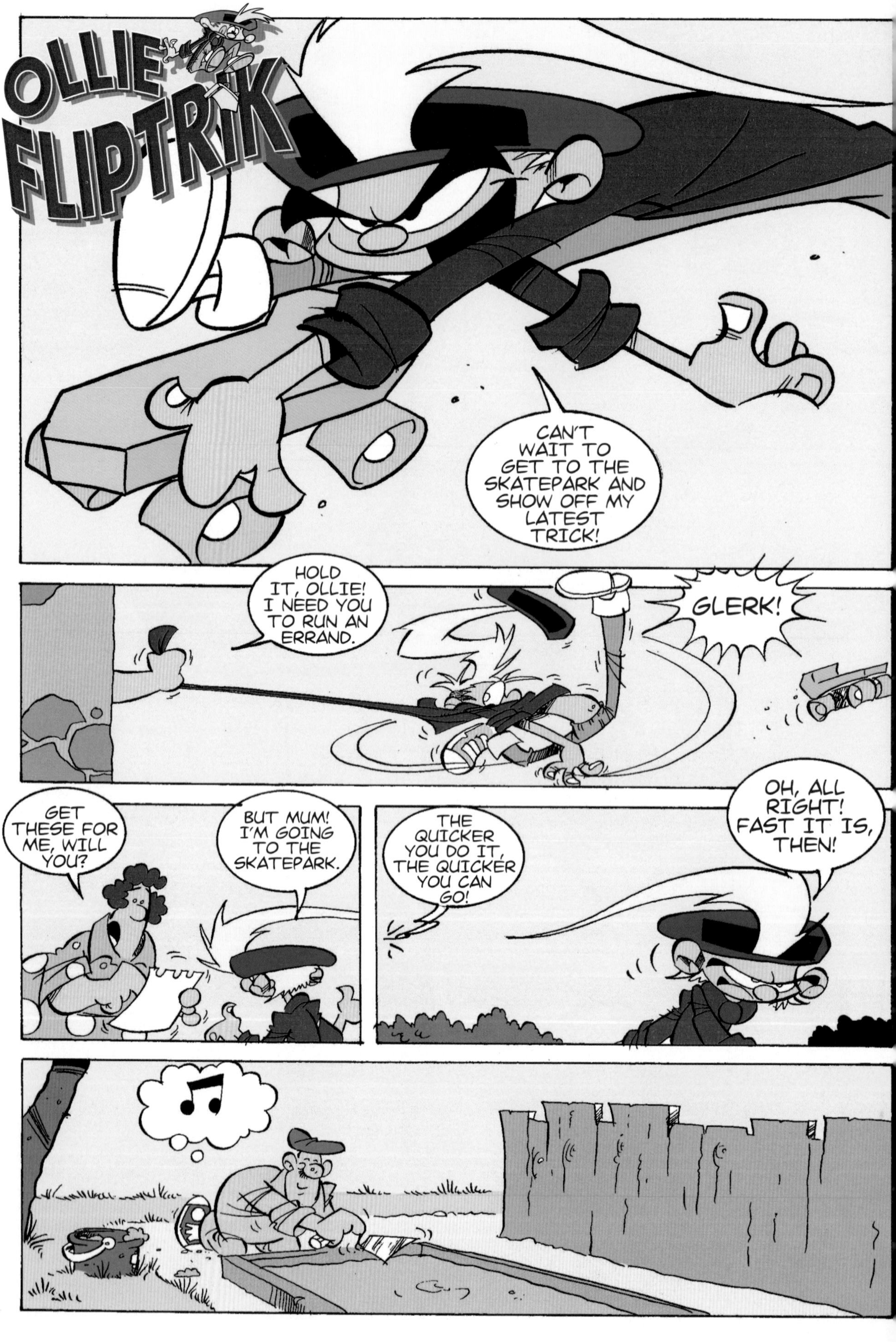
OLLIE FLIPTRIK
CAN'T WAIT TO GET TO THE SKATEPARK AND SHOW OFF MY LATEST TRICK!
HOLD IT, OLLIE! I NEED YOU TO RUN AN ERRAND.
GLERK!
GET THESE FOR ME, WILL YOU?
BUT MUM! I'M GOING TO THE SKATEPARK.
THE QUICKER YOU DO IT, THE QUICKER YOU CAN GO!
OH, ALL RIGHT! FAST IT IS, THEN!

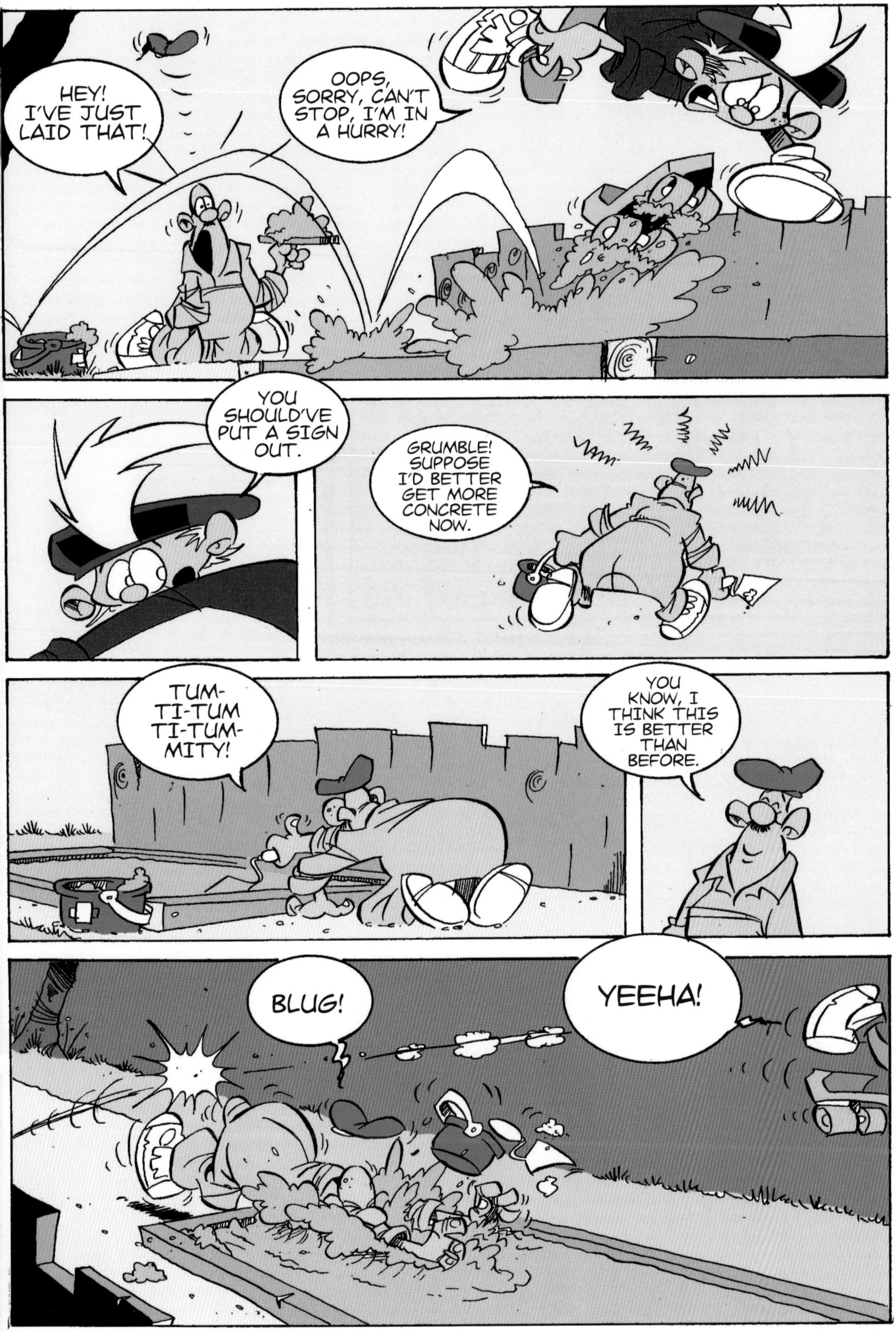
HEY! I'VE JUST LAID THAT!
OOPS, SORRY, CAN'T STOP, I'M IN A HURRY!
YOU SHOULD'VE PUT A SIGN OUT.
GRUMBLE! SUPPOSE I'D BETTER GET MORE CONCRETE NOW.
TUM-TI-TUM TI-TUMMITY!
YOU KNOW, I THINK THIS IS BETTER THAN BEFORE.
BLUG!
YEEHA!

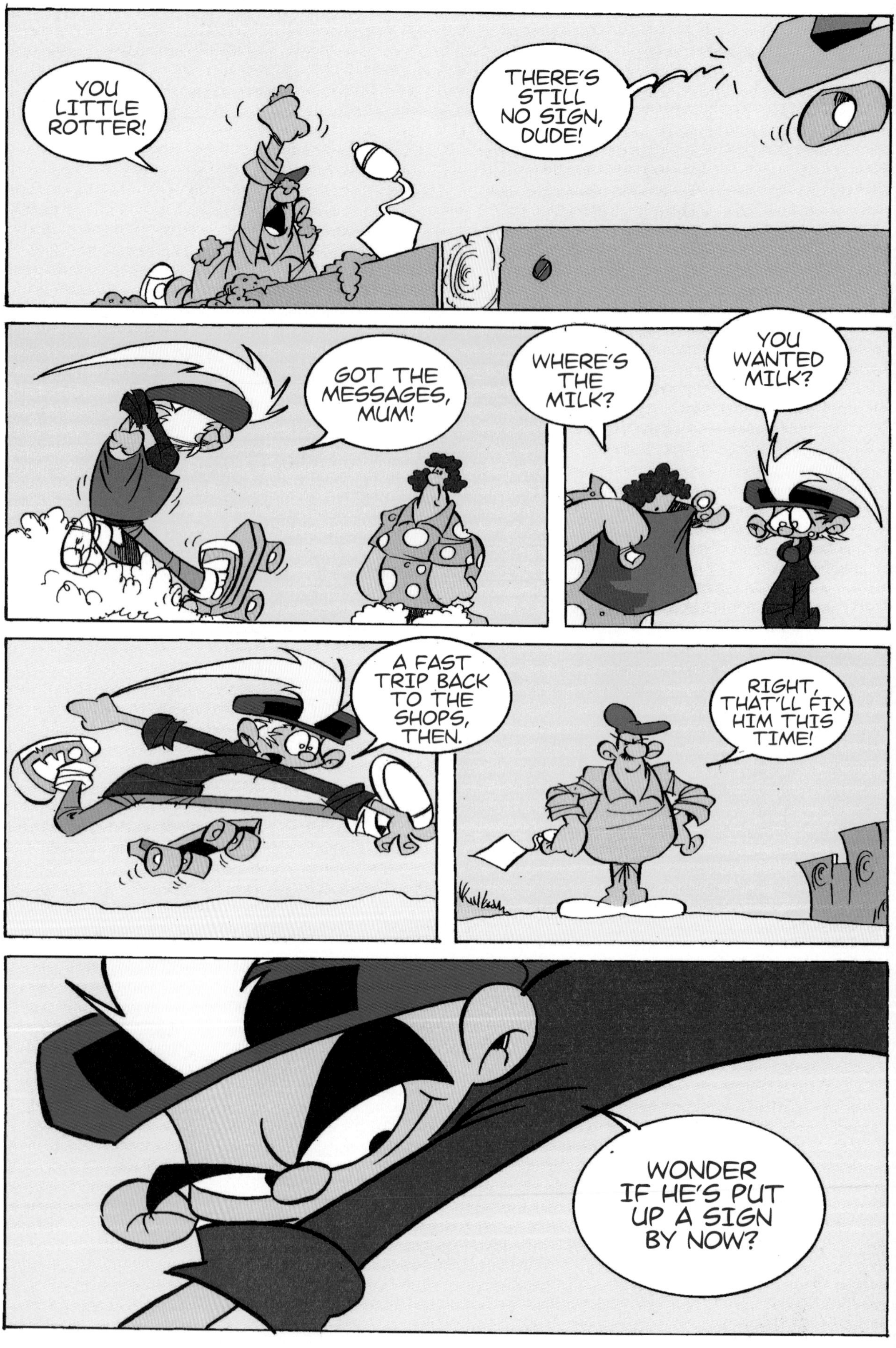
YOU LITTLE ROTTER!
THERE'S STILL NO SIGN, DUDE!
GOT THE MESSAGES, MUM!
WHERE'S THE MILK?
YOU WANTED MILK?
A FAST TRIP BACK TO THE SHOPS, THEN.
RIGHT, THAT'LL FIX HIM THIS TIME!
WONDER IF HE'S PUT UP A SIGN BY NOW?

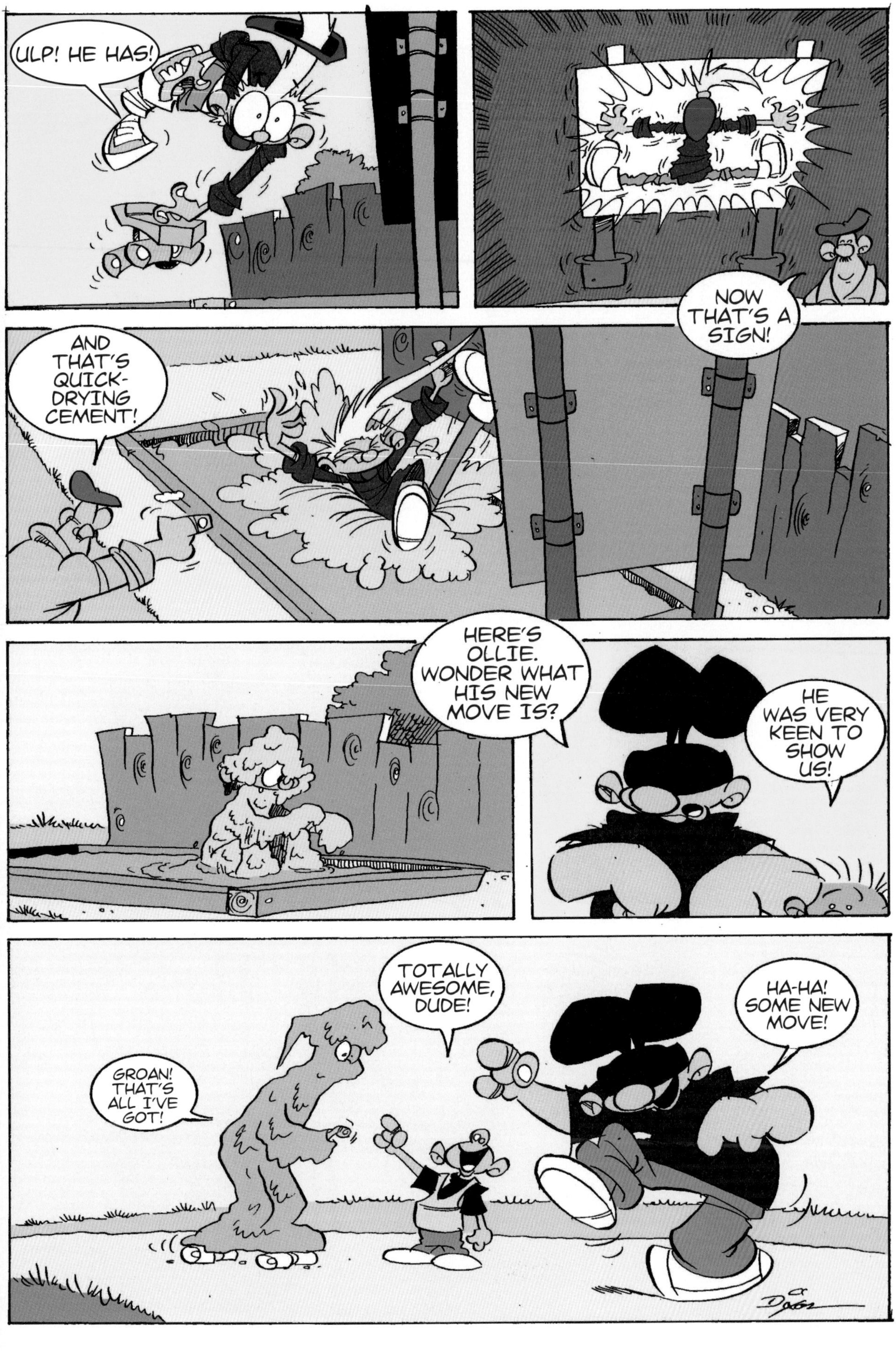
ULP! HE HAS!
NOW THAT'S A SIGN!
AND THAT'S QUICK-DRYING CEMENT!
HERE'S OLLIE. WONDER WHAT HIS NEW MOVE IS?
HE WAS VERY KEEN TO SHOW US!
GROAN! THAT'S ALL I'VE GOT!
TOTALLY AWESOME, DUDE!
HA-HA! SOME NEW MOVE!

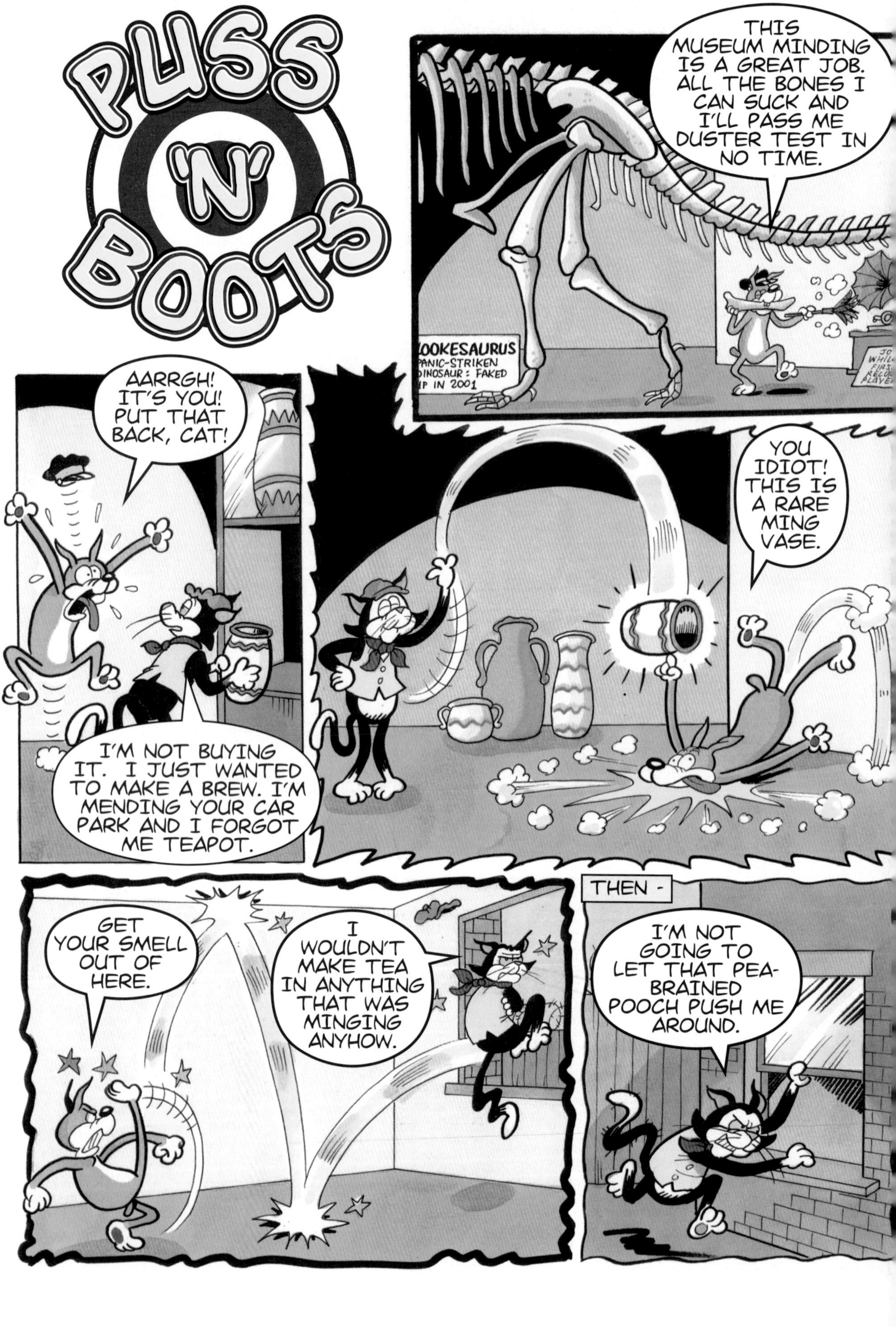
PUSS 'N' BOOTS
THIS MUSEUM MINDING IS A GREAT JOB. ALL THE BONES I CAN SUCK AND I'LL PASS ME DUSTER TEST IN NO TIME.
PANIC-STRIKEN DINOSAUR: FAKED UP IN 2001
AARRGH! IT'S YOU! PUT THAT BACK, CAT!
I'M NOT BUYING IT. I JUST WANTED TO MAKE A BREW. I'M MENDING YOUR CAR PARK AND I FORGOT ME TEAPOT.
YOU IDIOT! THIS IS A RARE MING VASE.
GET YOUR SMELL OUT OF HERE.
I WOULDN'T MAKE TEA IN ANYTHING THAT WAS MINGING ANYHOW.
THEN -
I'M NOT GOING TO LET THAT PEA-BRAINED POOCH PUSH ME AROUND.

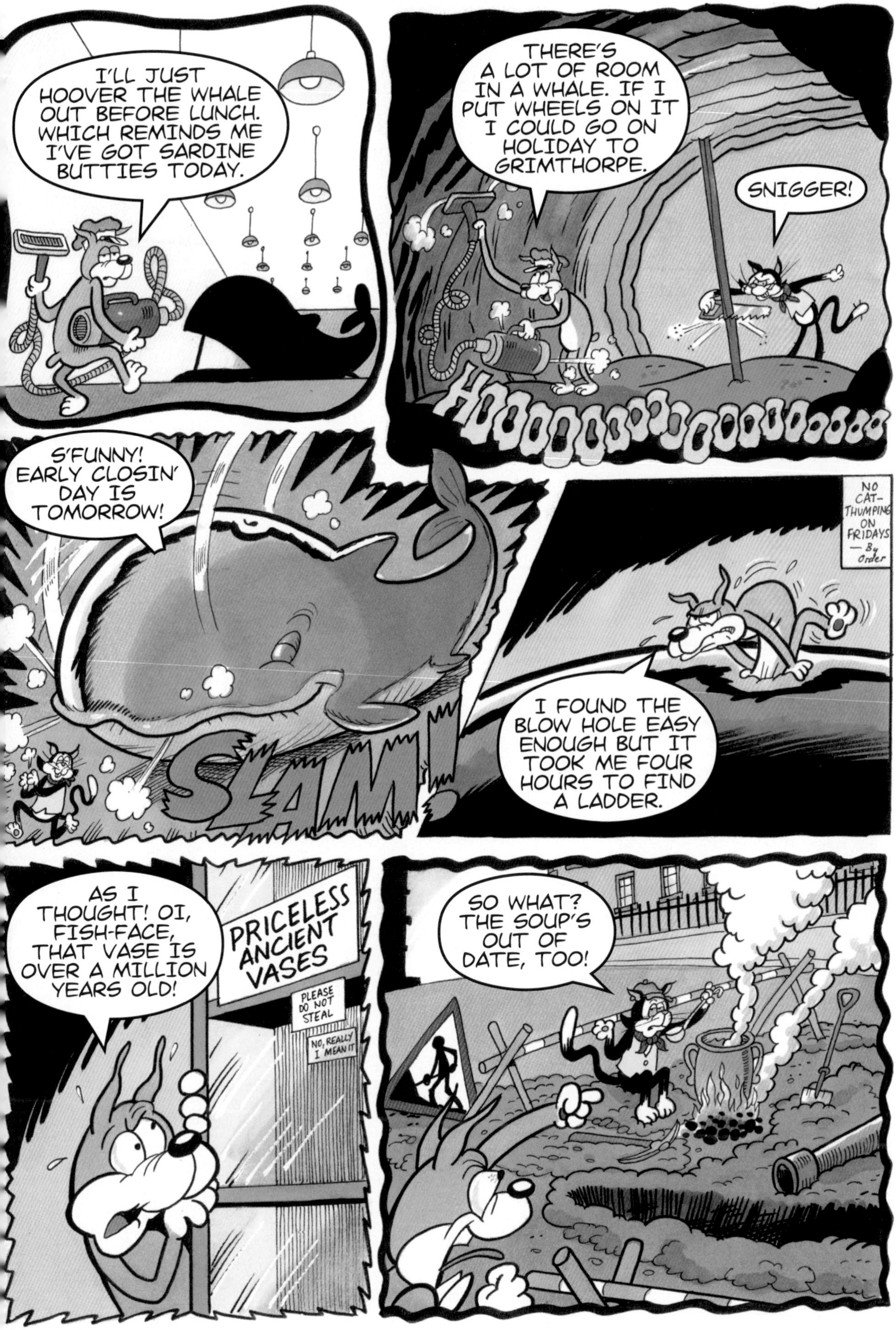
I'LL JUST HOOVER THE WHALE OUT BEFORE LUNCH. WHICH REMINDS ME I'VE GOT SARDINE BUTTIES TODAY.
THERE'S A LOT OF ROOM IN A WHALE. IF I PUT WHEELS ON IT I COULD GO ON HOLIDAY TO GRIMTHORPE.
SNIGGER!
HOOOOOOOOOOOOOOOO
S'FUNNY! EARLY CLOSIN' DAY IS TOMORROW!
SLAM!
NO CAT-THUMPING ON FRIDAYS — By Order
I FOUND THE BLOW HOLE EASY ENOUGH BUT IT TOOK ME FOUR HOURS TO FIND A LADDER.
AS I THOUGHT! OI, FISH-FACE, THAT VASE IS OVER A MILLION YEARS OLD!
PRICELESS ANCIENT VASES
PLEASE DO NOT STEAL
NO, REALLY I MEAN IT
SO WHAT? THE SOUP'S OUT OF DATE, TOO!

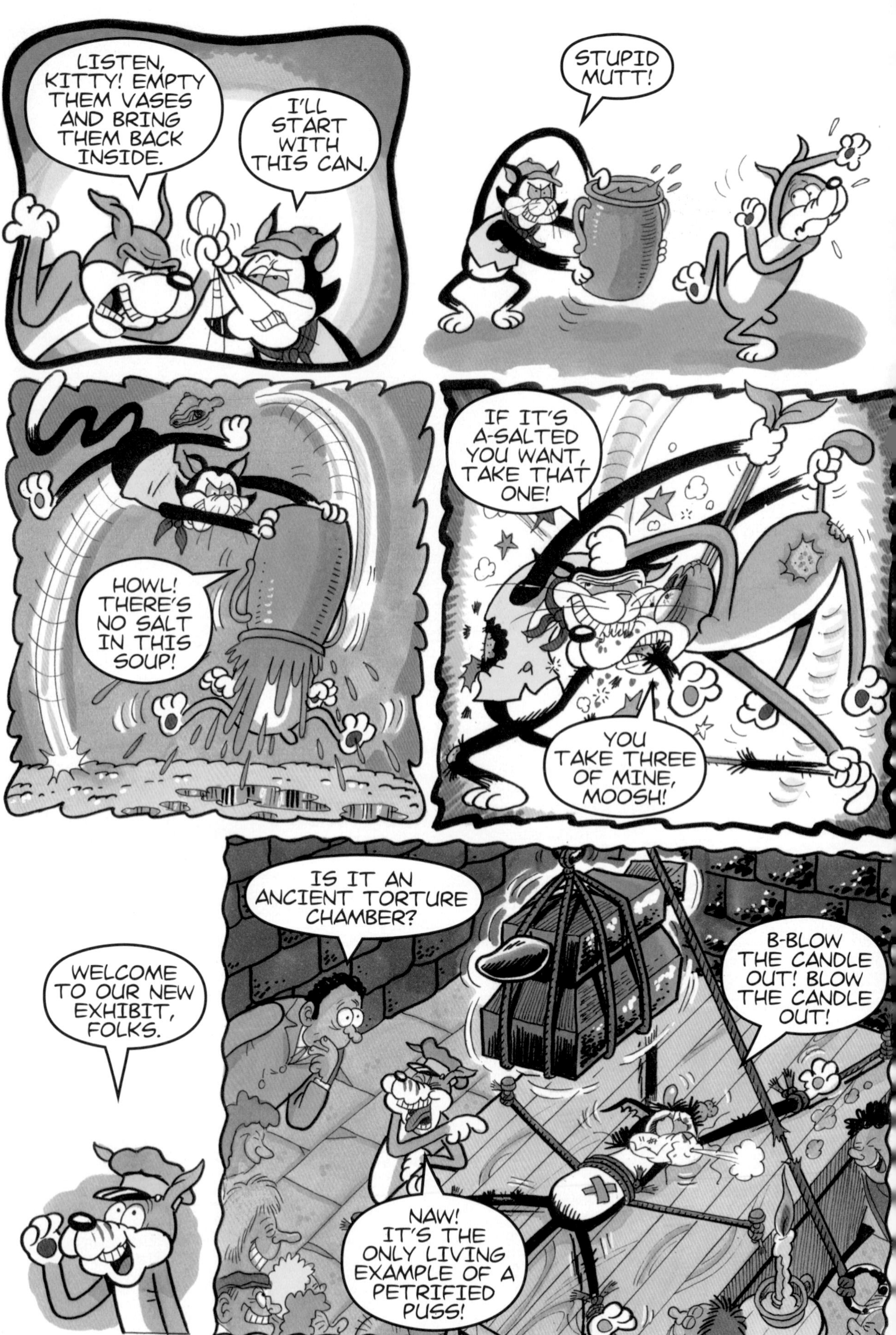
LISTEN, KITTY! EMPTY THEM VASES AND BRING THEM BACK INSIDE.
I'LL START WITH THIS CAN.
STUPID MUTT!
HOWL! THERE'S NO SALT IN THIS SOUP!
IF IT'S A-SALTED YOU WANT, TAKE THAT ONE!
YOU TAKE THREE OF MINE, MOOSH!
WELCOME TO OUR NEW EXHIBIT, FOLKS.
IS IT AN ANCIENT TORTURE CHAMBER?
B-BLOW THE CANDLE OUT! BLOW THE CANDLE OUT!
NAW! IT'S THE ONLY LIVING EXAMPLE OF A PETRIFIED PUSS!

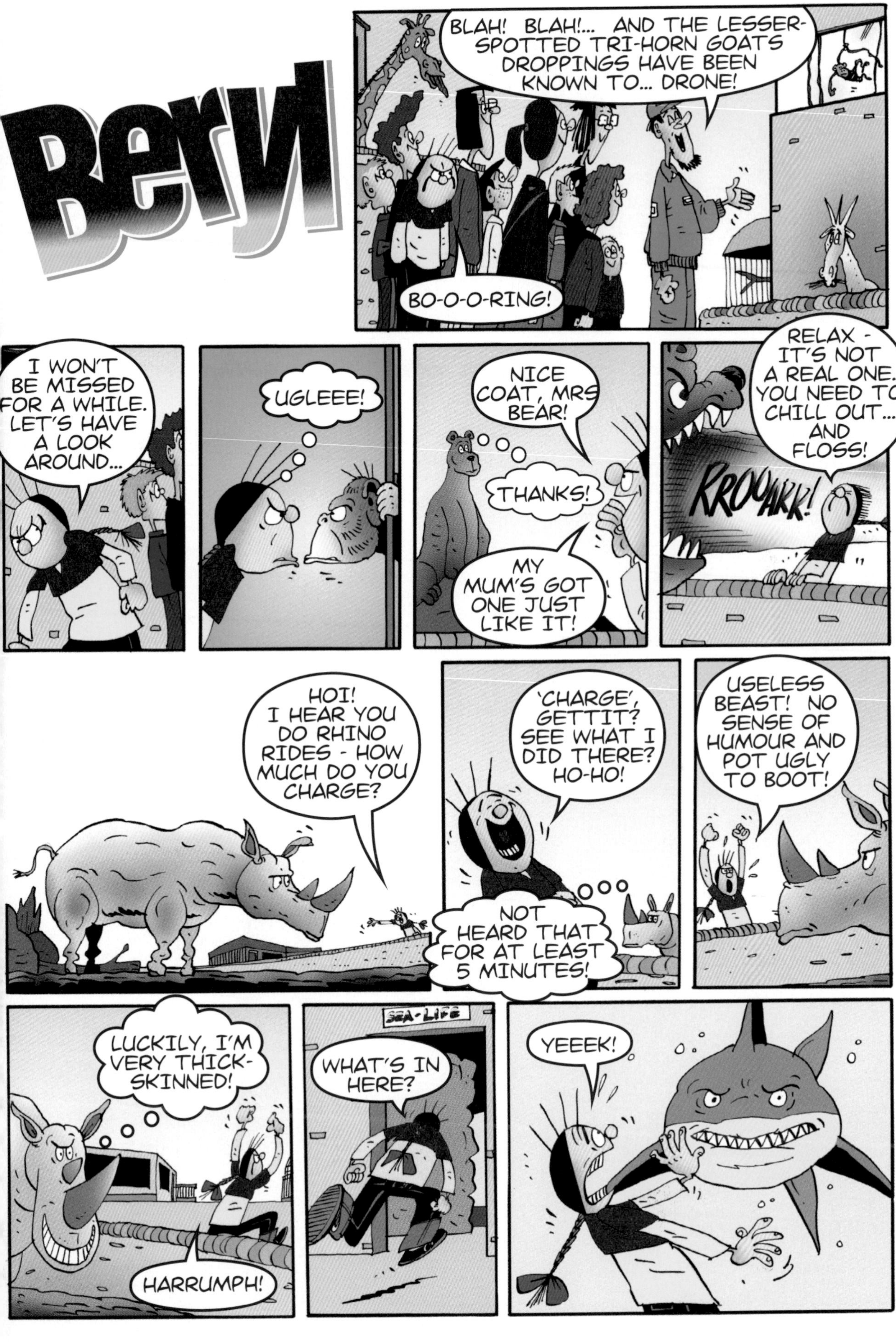
Beryl
BLAH! BLAH!... AND THE LESSER-SPOTTED TRI-HORN GOATS DROPPINGS HAVE BEEN KNOWN TO... DRONE!
BO-O-O-RING!
I WON'T BE MISSED FOR A WHILE. LET'S HAVE A LOOK AROUND...
UGLEEE!
NICE COAT, MRS BEAR!
THANKS!
MY MUM'S GOT ONE JUST LIKE IT!
KROOAKK!
RELAX - IT'S NOT A REAL ONE. YOU NEED TO CHILL OUT... AND FLOSS!
HOI! I HEAR YOU DO RHINO RIDES - HOW MUCH DO YOU CHARGE?
'CHARGE', GETTIT? SEE WHAT I DID THERE? HO-HO!
NOT HEARD THAT FOR AT LEAST 5 MINUTES!
USELESS BEAST! NO SENSE OF HUMOUR AND POT UGLY TO BOOT!
LUCKILY, I'M VERY THICK-SKINNED!
HARRUMPH!
SEA-LIFE
WHAT'S IN HERE?
YEEEK!

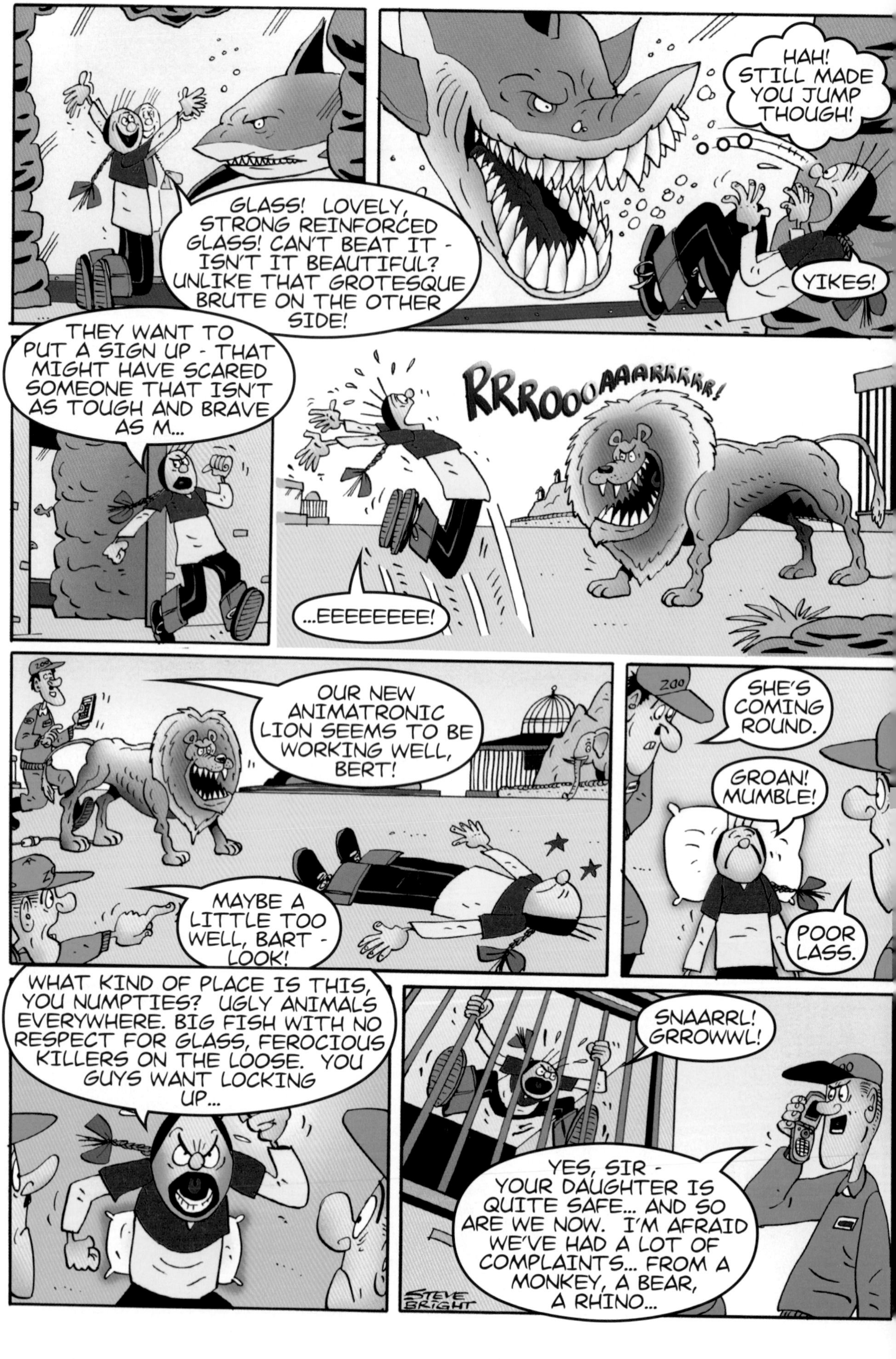
GLASS! LOVELY, STRONG REINFORCED GLASS! CAN'T BEAT IT - ISN'T IT BEAUTIFUL? UNLIKE THAT GROTESQUE BRUTE ON THE OTHER SIDE!
HAH! STILL MADE YOU JUMP THOUGH!
YIKES!
THEY WANT TO PUT A SIGN UP - THAT MIGHT HAVE SCARED SOMEONE THAT ISN'T AS TOUGH AND BRAVE AS M...
RRROOOAAARRRRR!
...EEEEEEEE!
ZOO
OUR NEW ANIMATRONIC LION SEEMS TO BE WORKING WELL, BERT!
MAYBE A LITTLE TOO WELL, BART - LOOK!
ZOO
SHE'S COMING ROUND.
GROAN! MUMBLE!
POOR LASS.
WHAT KIND OF PLACE IS THIS, YOU NUMPTIES? UGLY ANIMALS EVERYWHERE. BIG FISH WITH NO RESPECT FOR GLASS, FEROCIOUS KILLERS ON THE LOOSE. YOU GUYS WANT LOCKING UP...
SNAARRL! GRROWWL!
YES, SIR - YOUR DAUGHTER IS QUITE SAFE... AND SO ARE WE NOW. I'M AFRAID WE'VE HAD A LOT OF COMPLAINTS... FROM A MONKEY, A BEAR, A RHINO...
STEVE BRIGHT

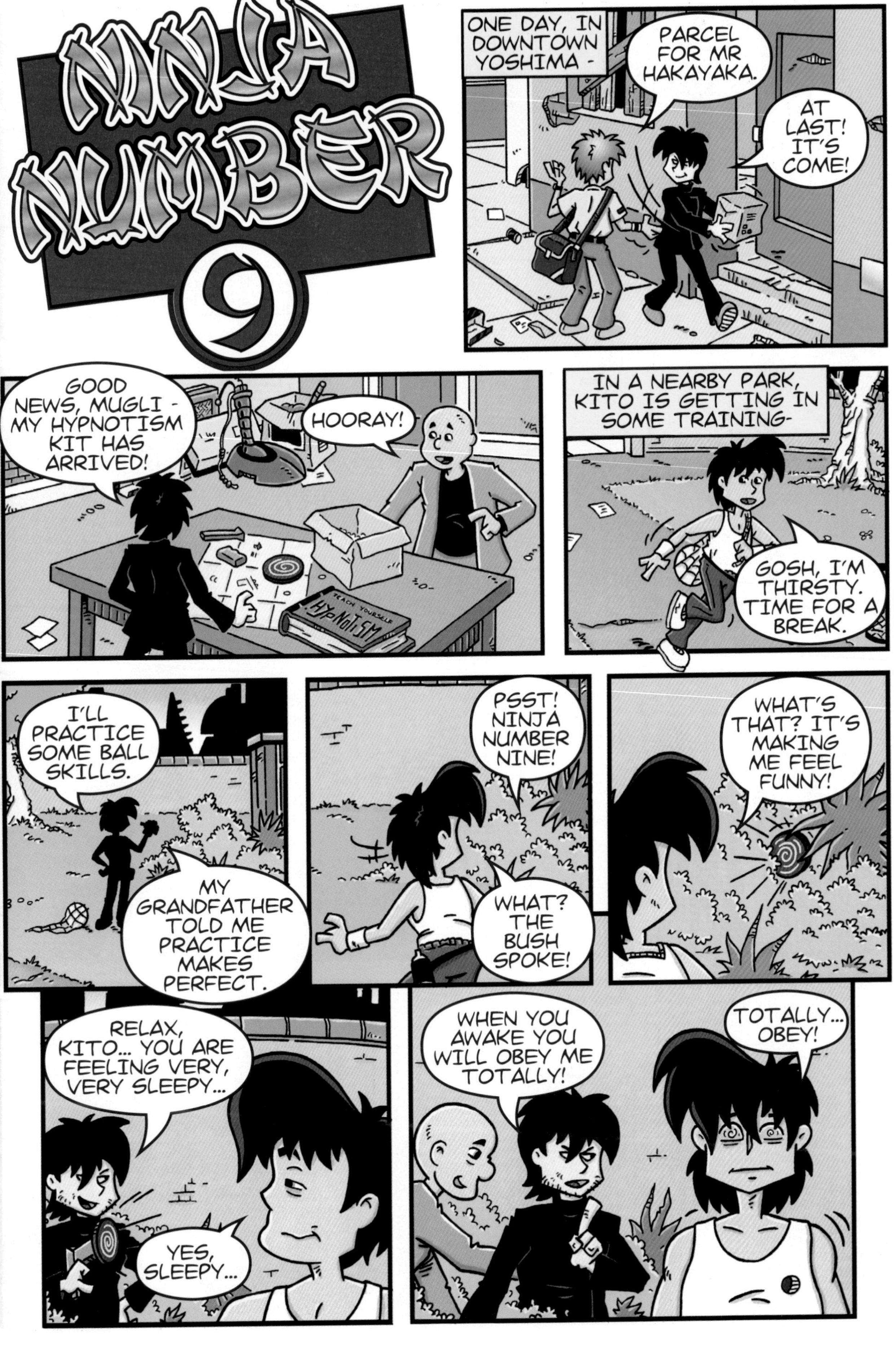
NINJA NUMBER 9
ONE DAY, IN DOWNTOWN YOSHIMA -
PARCEL FOR MR HAKAYAKA.
AT LAST! IT'S COME!
GOOD NEWS, MUGLI - MY HYPNOTISM KIT HAS ARRIVED!
HOORAY!
TEACH YOURSELF HYPNOTISM
IN A NEARBY PARK, KITO IS GETTING IN SOME TRAINING-
GOSH, I'M THIRSTY. TIME FOR A BREAK.
I'LL PRACTICE SOME BALL SKILLS.
MY GRANDFATHER TOLD ME PRACTICE MAKES PERFECT.
PSST! NINJA NUMBER NINE!
WHAT? THE BUSH SPOKE!
WHAT'S THAT? IT'S MAKING ME FEEL FUNNY!
RELAX, KITO... YOU ARE FEELING VERY, VERY SLEEPY...
YES, SLEEPY...
WHEN YOU AWAKE YOU WILL OBEY ME TOTALLY!
TOTALLY... OBEY!

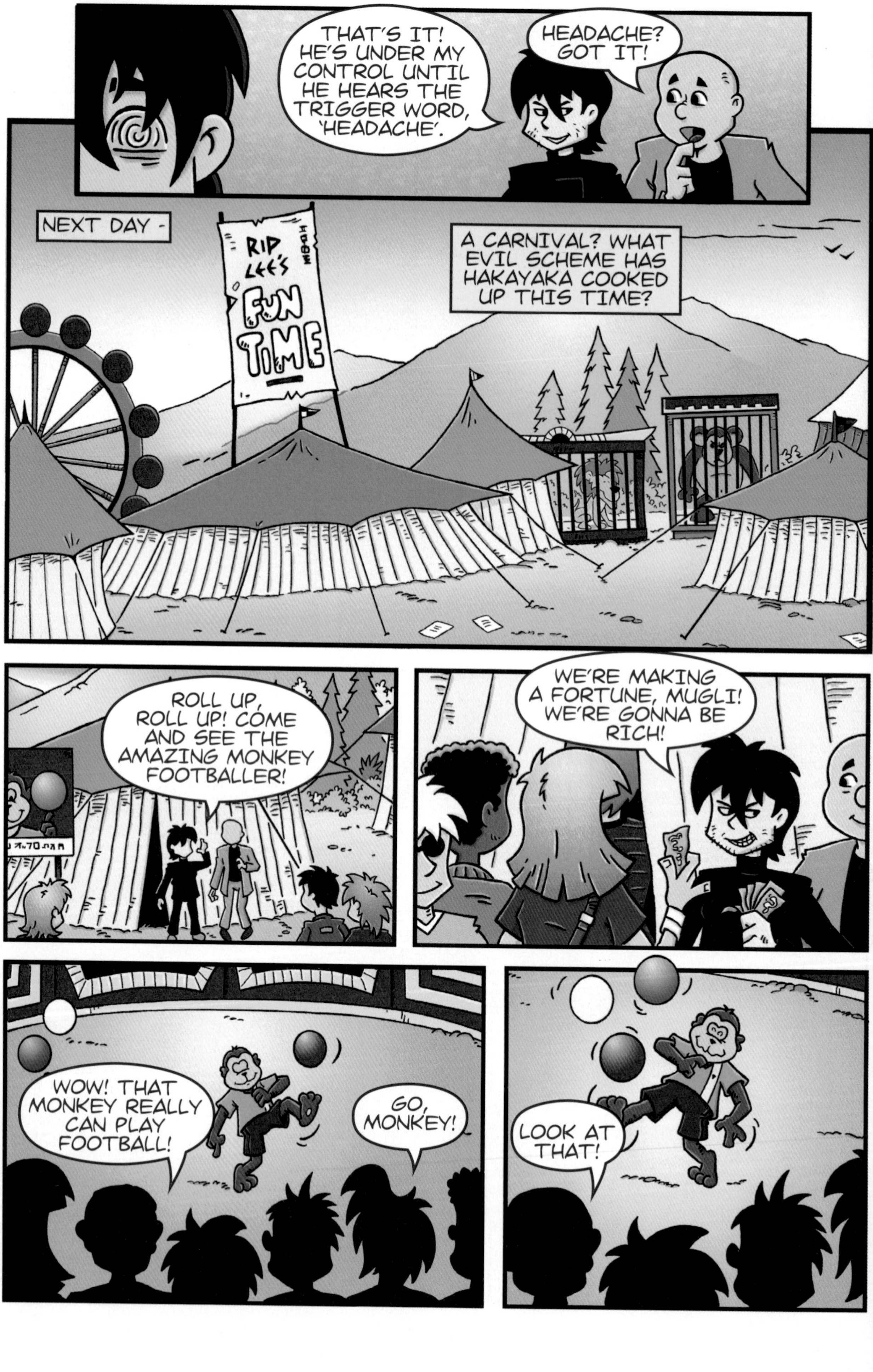
THAT'S IT! HE'S UNDER MY CONTROL UNTIL HE HEARS THE TRIGGER WORD, 'HEADACHE'.
HEADACHE? GOT IT!
NEXT DAY -
RIP LEE'S FUN TIME
A CARNIVAL? WHAT EVIL SCHEME HAS HAKAYAKA COOKED UP THIS TIME?
ROLL UP, ROLL UP! COME AND SEE THE AMAZING MONKEY FOOTBALLER!
WE'RE MAKING A FORTUNE, MUGLI! WE'RE GONNA BE RICH!
WOW! THAT MONKEY REALLY CAN PLAY FOOTBALL!
GO, MONKEY!
LOOK AT THAT!

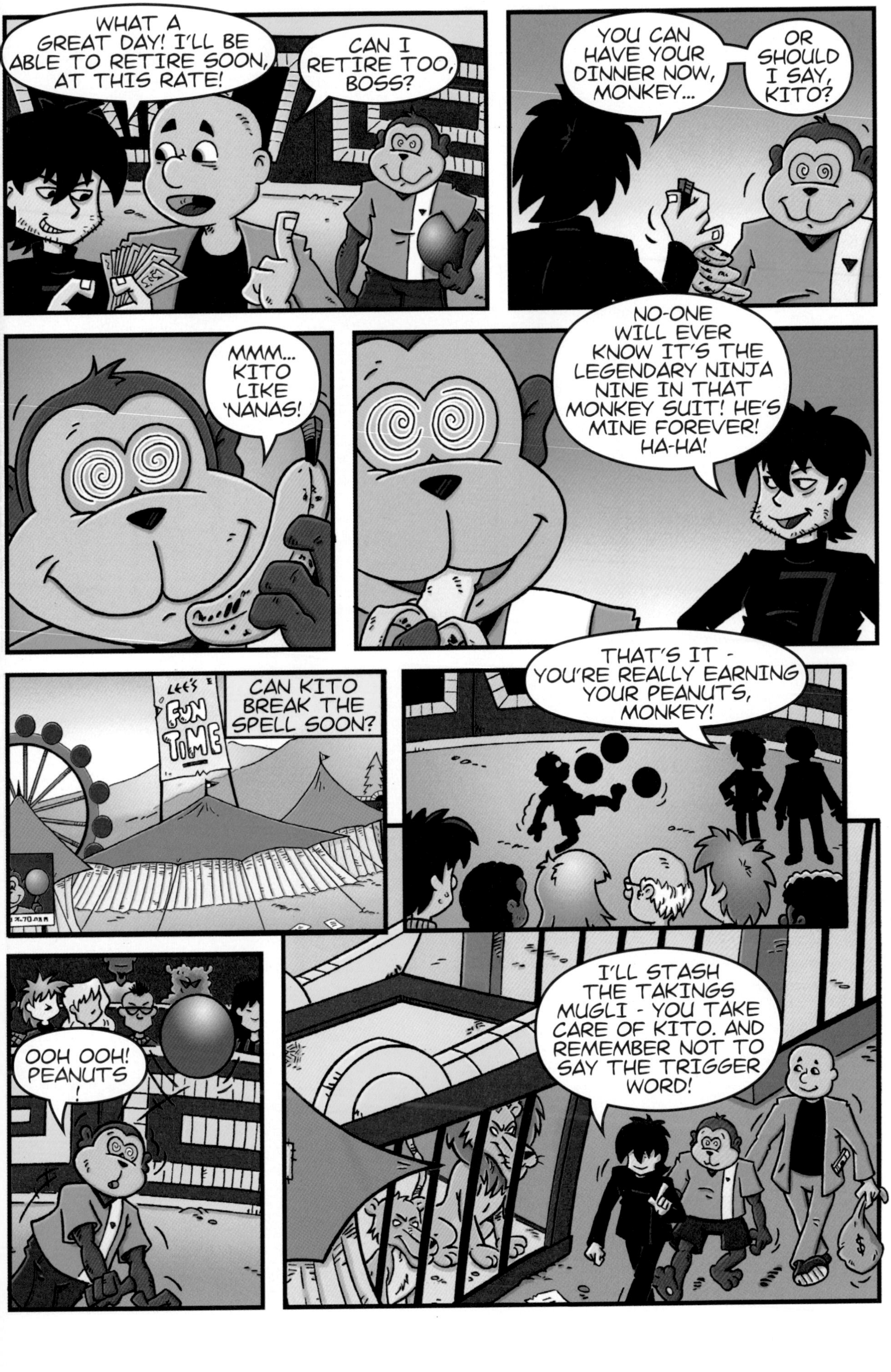

WHAT A GREAT DAY! I'LL BE ABLE TO RETIRE SOON, AT THIS RATE!
CAN I RETIRE TOO, BOSS?
YOU CAN HAVE YOUR DINNER NOW, MONKEY...
OR SHOULD I SAY, KITO?
MMM... KITO LIKE 'NANAS!
NO-ONE WILL EVER KNOW IT'S THE LEGENDARY NINJA NINE IN THAT MONKEY SUIT! HE'S MINE FOREVER! HA-HA!
LEE'S FUN TIME
CAN KITO BREAK THE SPELL SOON?
THAT'S IT - YOU'RE REALLY EARNING YOUR PEANUTS, MONKEY!
OOH OOH! PEANUTS!
I'LL STASH THE TAKINGS MUGLI - YOU TAKE CARE OF KITO. AND REMEMBER NOT TO SAY THE TRIGGER WORD!

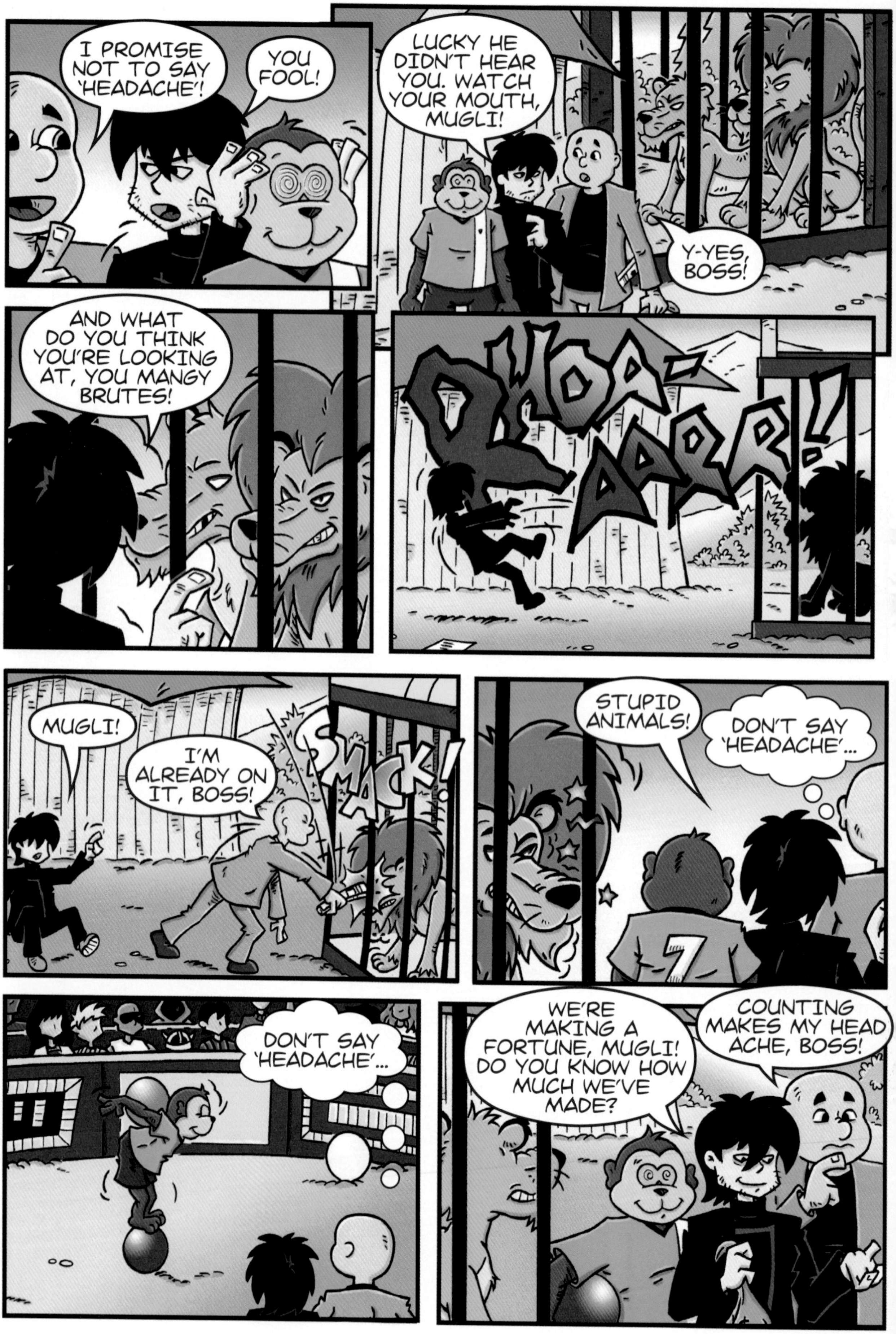
I PROMISE NOT TO SAY 'HEADACHE'!
YOU FOOL!
LUCKY HE DIDN'T HEAR YOU. WATCH YOUR MOUTH, MUGLI!
Y-YES, BOSS!
AND WHAT DO YOU THINK YOU'RE LOOKING AT, YOU MANGY BRUTES!
OHOA-AARR!!
MUGLI!
I'M ALREADY ON IT, BOSS!
SMACK!
STUPID ANIMALS!
DON'T SAY 'HEADACHE'...
DON'T SAY 'HEADACHE'...
WE'RE MAKING A FORTUNE, MUGLI! DO YOU KNOW HOW MUCH WE'VE MADE?
COUNTING MAKES MY HEAD ACHE, BOSS!

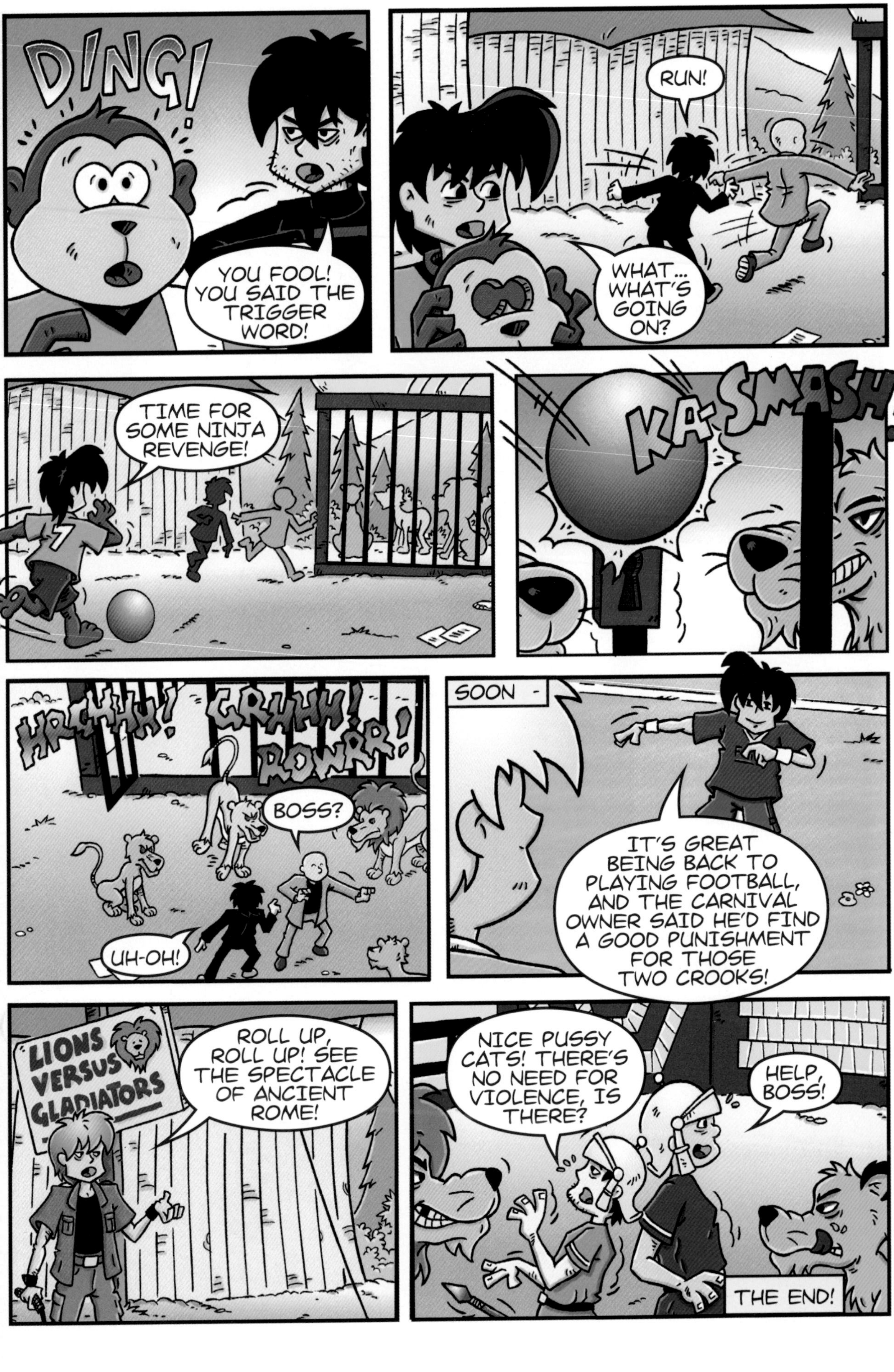
DING!
YOU FOOL! YOU SAID THE TRIGGER WORD!
RUN!
WHAT... WHAT'S GOING ON?
TIME FOR SOME NINJA REVENGE!
KA-SMASH!
HRGHHH! GRHHH! ROWRR!
BOSS?
UH-OH!
SOON -
IT'S GREAT BEING BACK TO PLAYING FOOTBALL, AND THE CARNIVAL OWNER SAID HE'D FIND A GOOD PUNISHMENT FOR THOSE TWO CROOKS!
LIONS VERSUS GLADIATORS
ROLL UP, ROLL UP! SEE THE SPECTACLE OF ANCIENT ROME!
NICE PUSSY CATS! THERE'S NO NEED FOR VIOLENCE, IS THERE?
HELP, BOSS!
THE END!

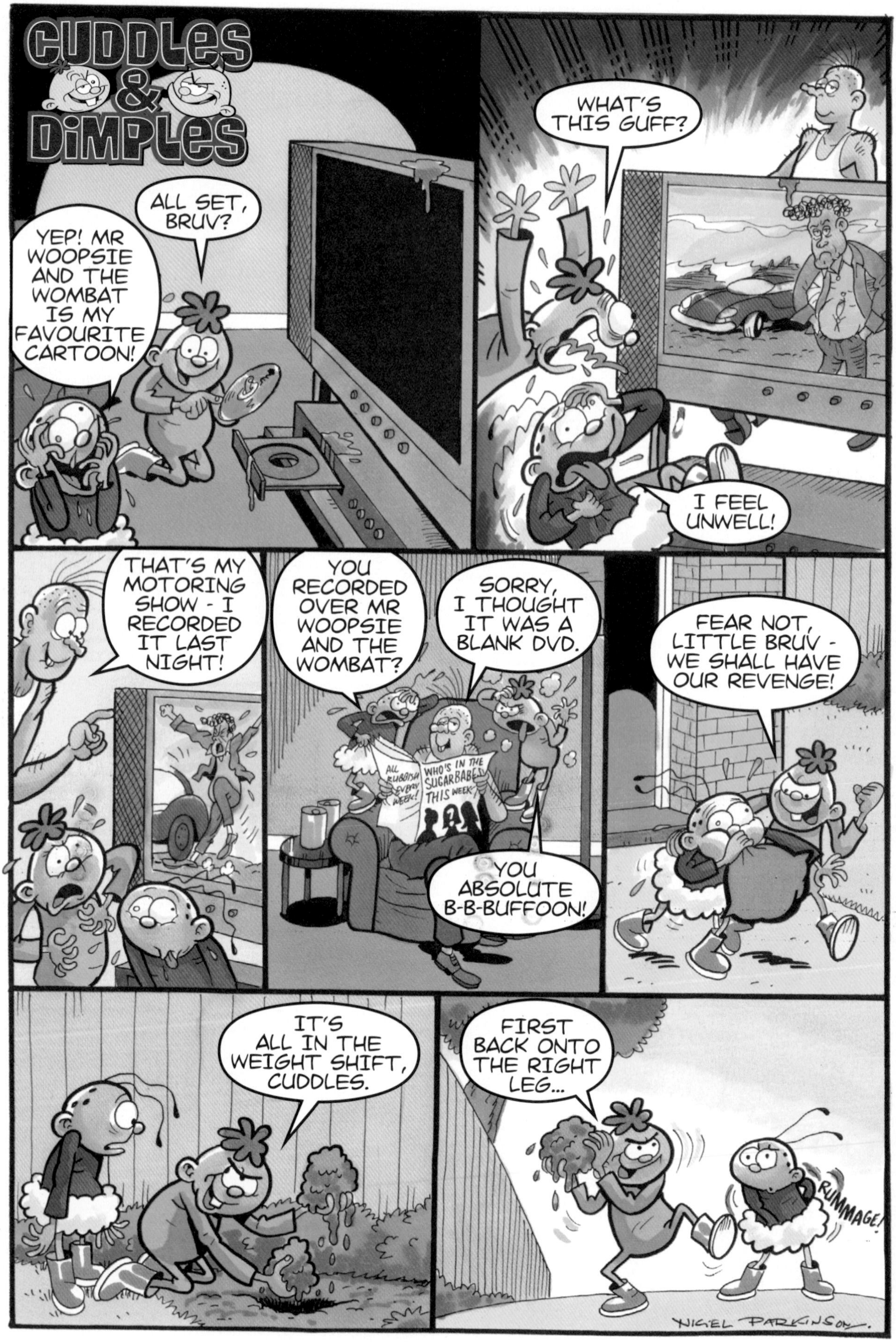
CUDDLES & DIMPLES
ALL SET, BRUV?
YEP! MR WOOPSIE AND THE WOMBAT IS MY FAVOURITE CARTOON!
WHAT'S THIS GUFF?
I FEEL UNWELL!
THAT'S MY MOTORING SHOW - I RECORDED IT LAST NIGHT!
YOU RECORDED OVER MR WOOPSIE AND THE WOMBAT?
SORRY, I THOUGHT IT WAS A BLANK DVD.
ALL RUBBISH EVERY WEEK!
WHO'S IN THE SUGARBABES THIS WEEK
YOU ABSOLUTE B-B-BUFFOON!
FEAR NOT, LITTLE BRUV - WE SHALL HAVE OUR REVENGE!
IT'S ALL IN THE WEIGHT SHIFT, CUDDLES.
FIRST BACK ONTO THE RIGHT LEG...
RUMMAGE!
NIGEL PARKINSON.

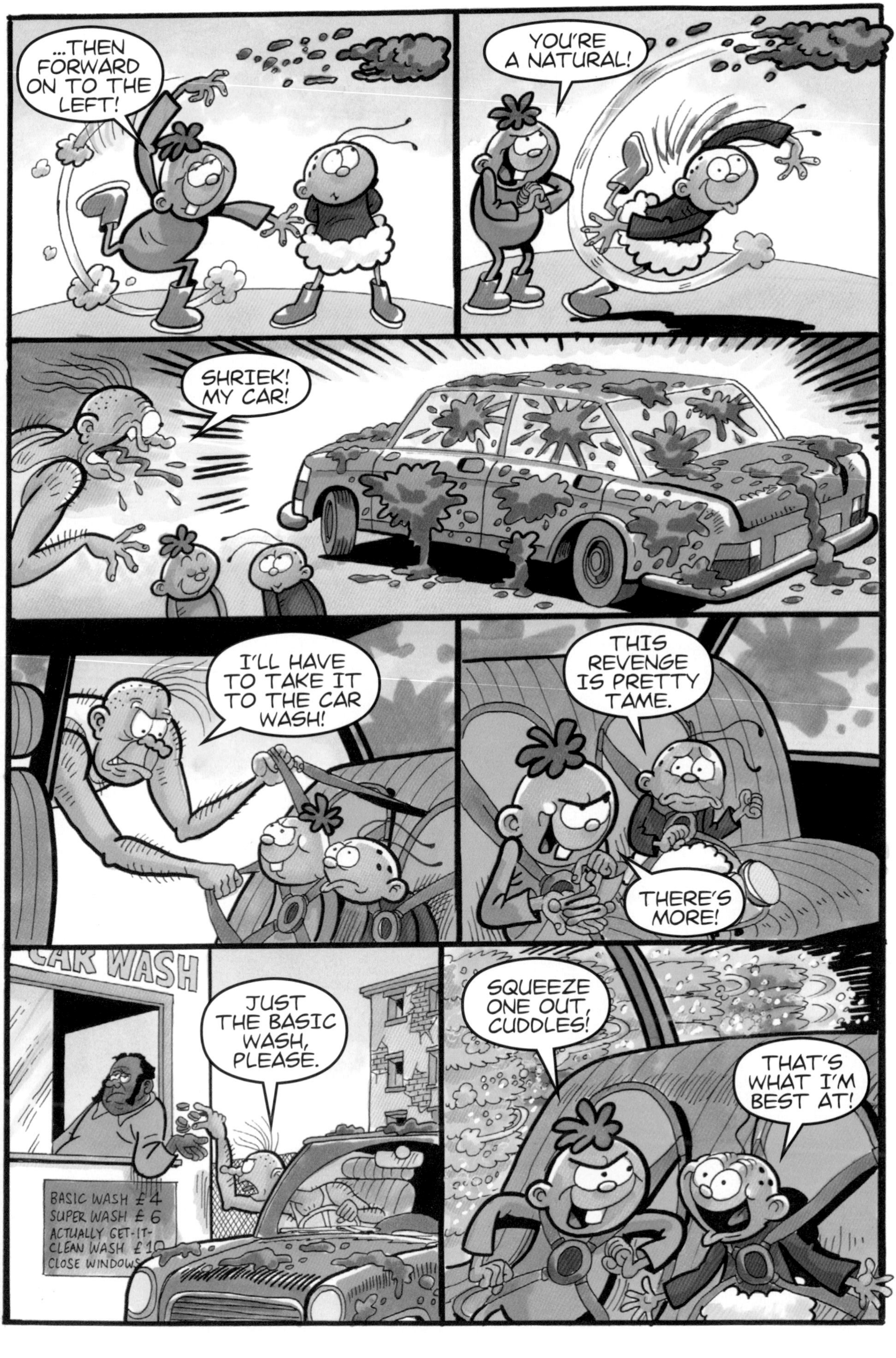

...THEN FORWARD ON TO THE LEFT!
YOU'RE A NATURAL!
SHRIEK! MY CAR!
I'LL HAVE TO TAKE IT TO THE CAR WASH!
THIS REVENGE IS PRETTY TAME.
THERE'S MORE!
CAR WASH
BASIC WASH £4
SUPER WASH £6
ACTUALLY GET-IT-CLEAN WASH £10
CLOSE WINDOWS
JUST THE BASIC WASH, PLEASE.
SQUEEZE ONE OUT, CUDDLES!
THAT'S WHAT I'M BEST AT!

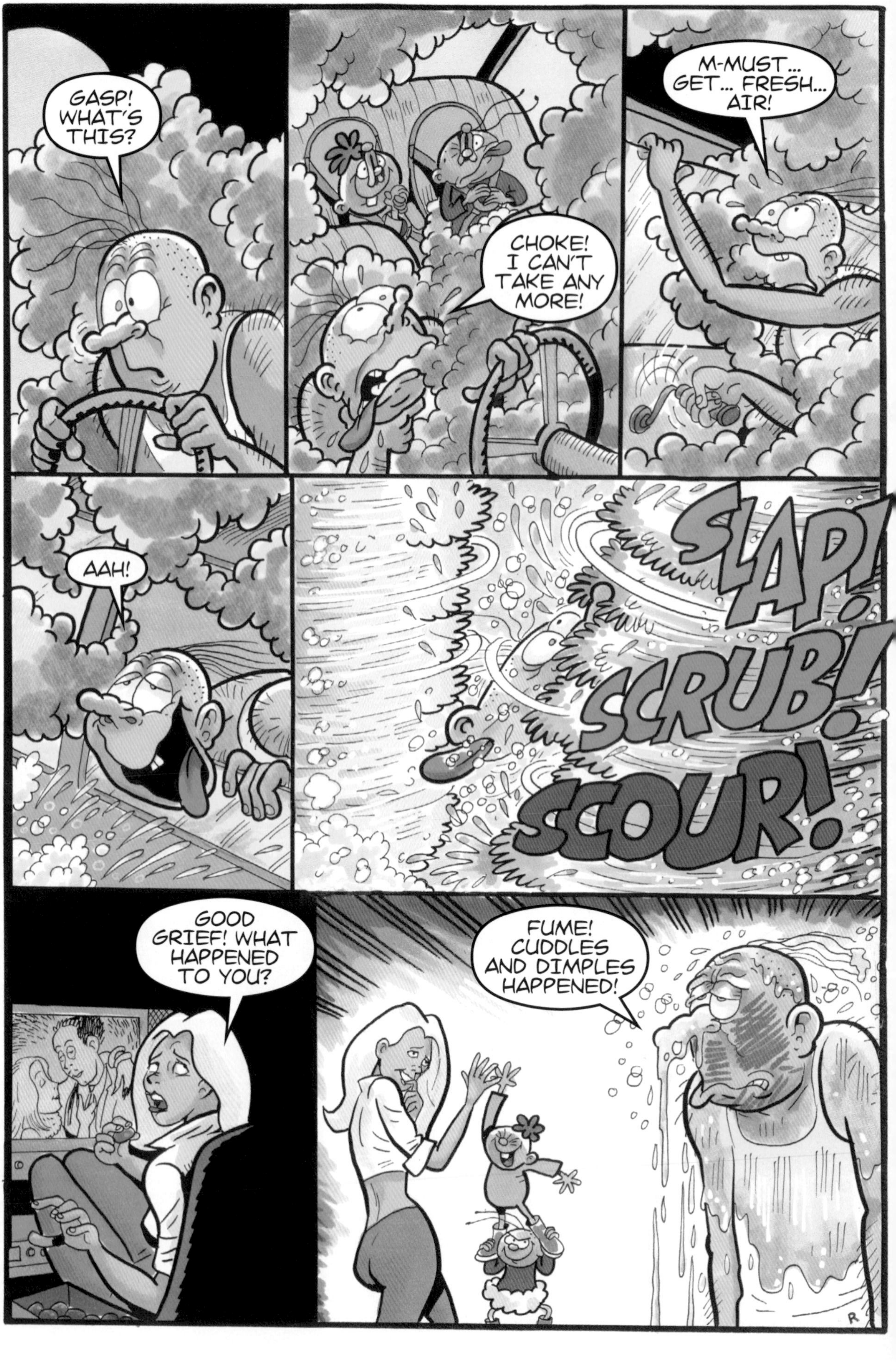
GASP! WHAT'S THIS?
CHOKE! I CAN'T TAKE ANY MORE!
M-MUST... GET... FRESH... AIR!
AAH!
SLAP!
SCRUB!
SCOUR!
GOOD GRIEF! WHAT HAPPENED TO YOU?
FUME! CUDDLES AND DIMPLES HAPPENED!

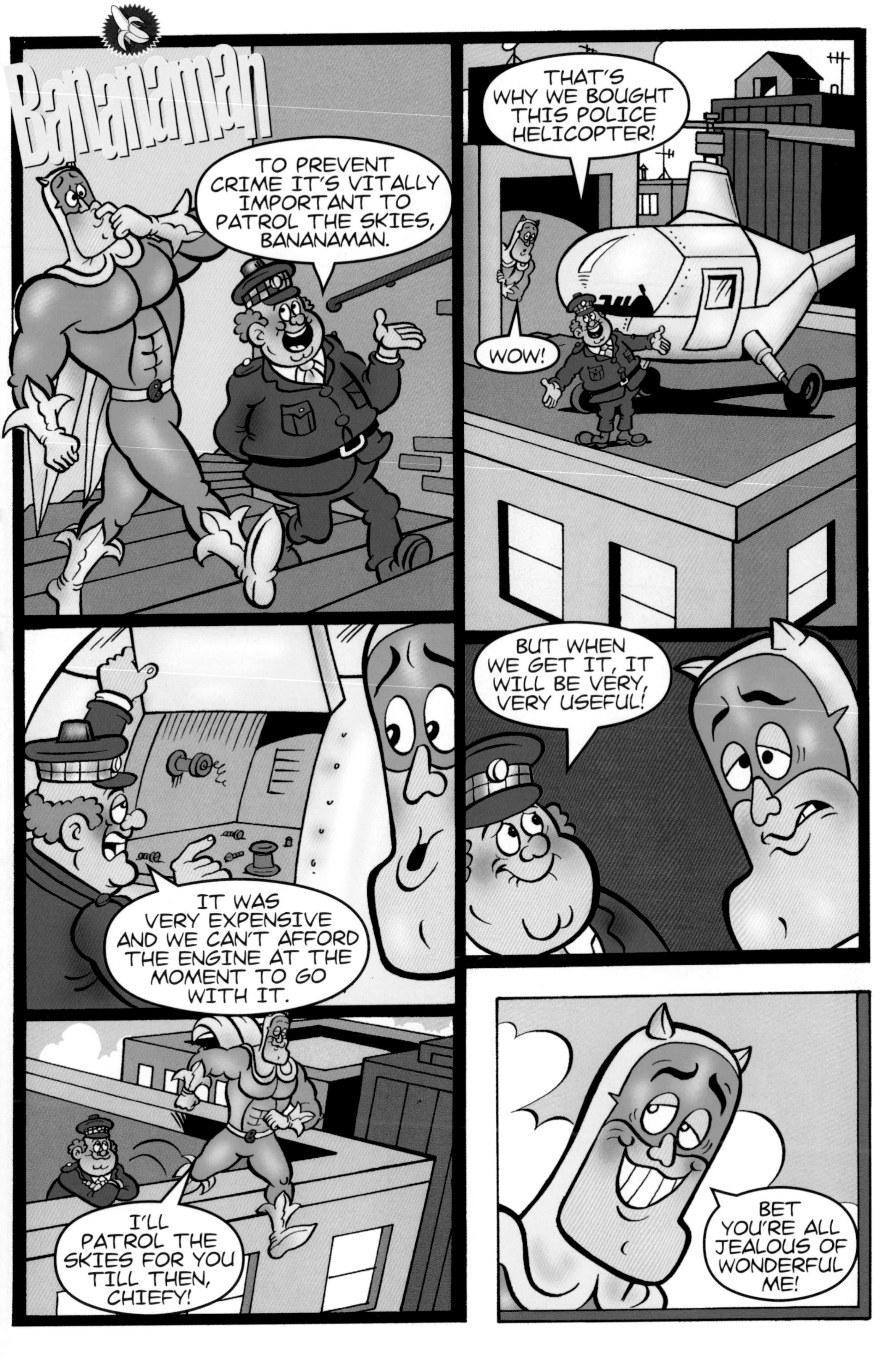
Bananaman
TO PREVENT CRIME IT'S VITALLY IMPORTANT TO PATROL THE SKIES, BANANAMAN.
THAT'S WHY WE BOUGHT THIS POLICE HELICOPTER!
WOW!
IT WAS VERY EXPENSIVE AND WE CAN'T AFFORD THE ENGINE AT THE MOMENT TO GO WITH IT.
BUT WHEN WE GET IT, IT WILL BE VERY, VERY USEFUL!
I'LL PATROL THE SKIES FOR YOU TILL THEN, CHIEFY!
BET YOU'RE ALL JEALOUS OF WONDERFUL ME!

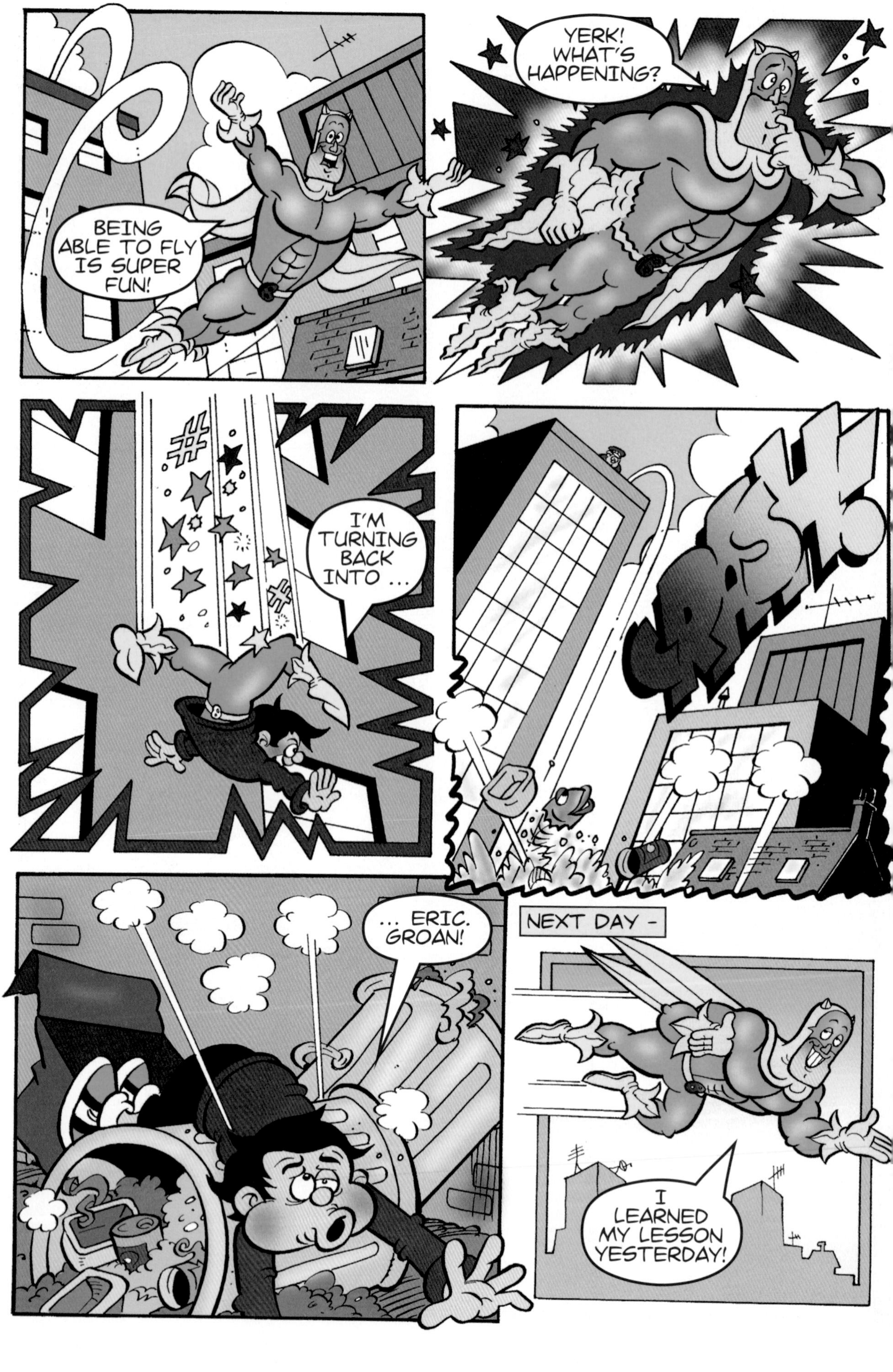
BEING ABLE TO FLY IS SUPER FUN!
YERK! WHAT'S HAPPENING?
I'M TURNING BACK INTO ...
CRASH!
... ERIC. GROAN!
NEXT DAY -
I LEARNED MY LESSON YESTERDAY!

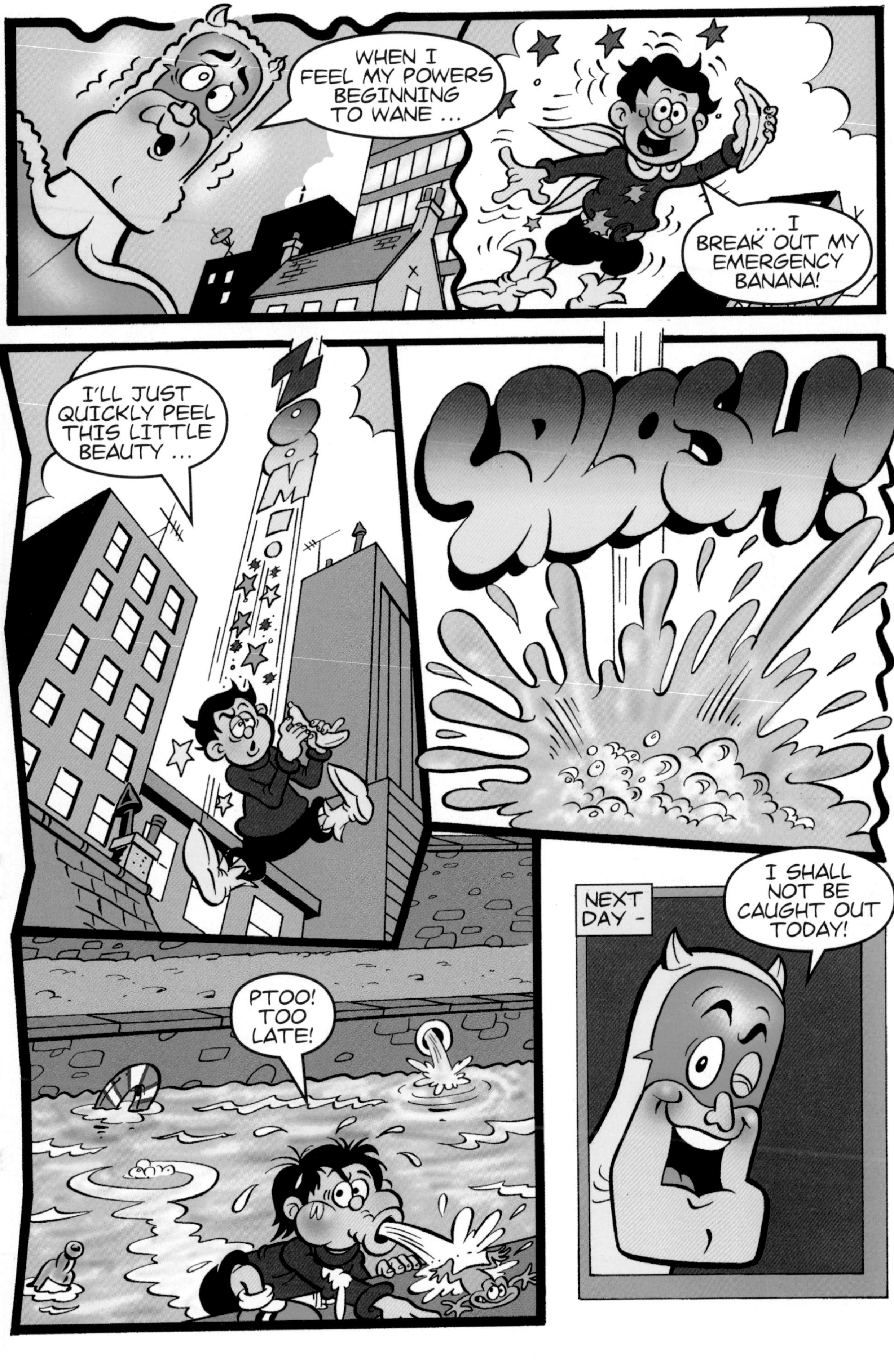
WHEN I FEEL MY POWERS BEGINNING TO WANE ...
... I BREAK OUT MY EMERGENCY BANANA!
I'LL JUST QUICKLY PEEL THIS LITTLE BEAUTY ...
ZOOM
SPLOSH!
PTOO! TOO LATE!
NEXT DAY -
I SHALL NOT BE CAUGHT OUT TODAY!

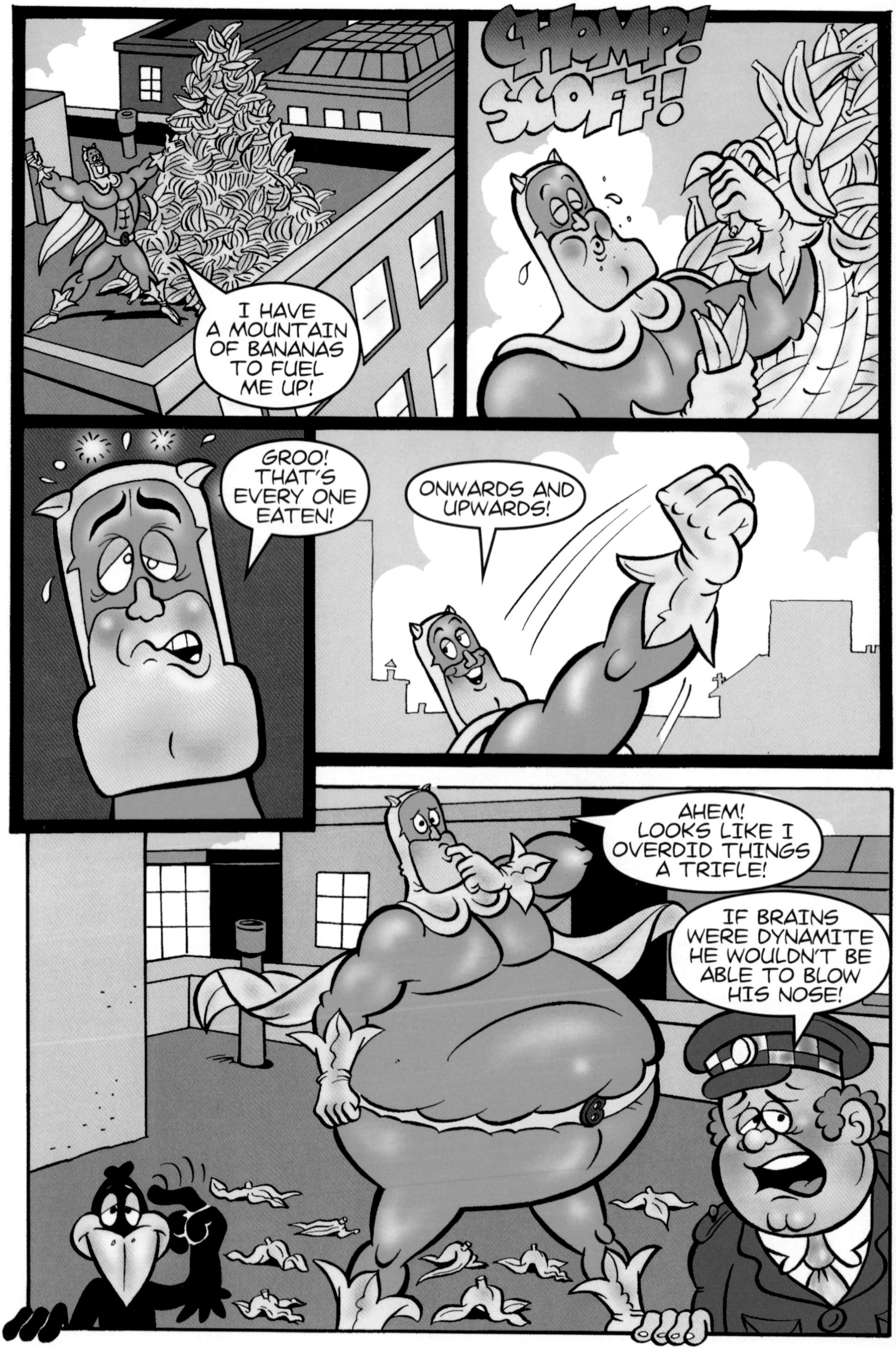
I HAVE A MOUNTAIN OF BANANAS TO FUEL ME UP!
CHOMP! SCOFF!
GROO! THAT'S EVERY ONE EATEN!
ONWARDS AND UPWARDS!
AHEM! LOOKS LIKE I OVERDID THINGS A TRIFLE!
IF BRAINS WERE DYNAMITE HE WOULDN'T BE ABLE TO BLOW HIS NOSE!

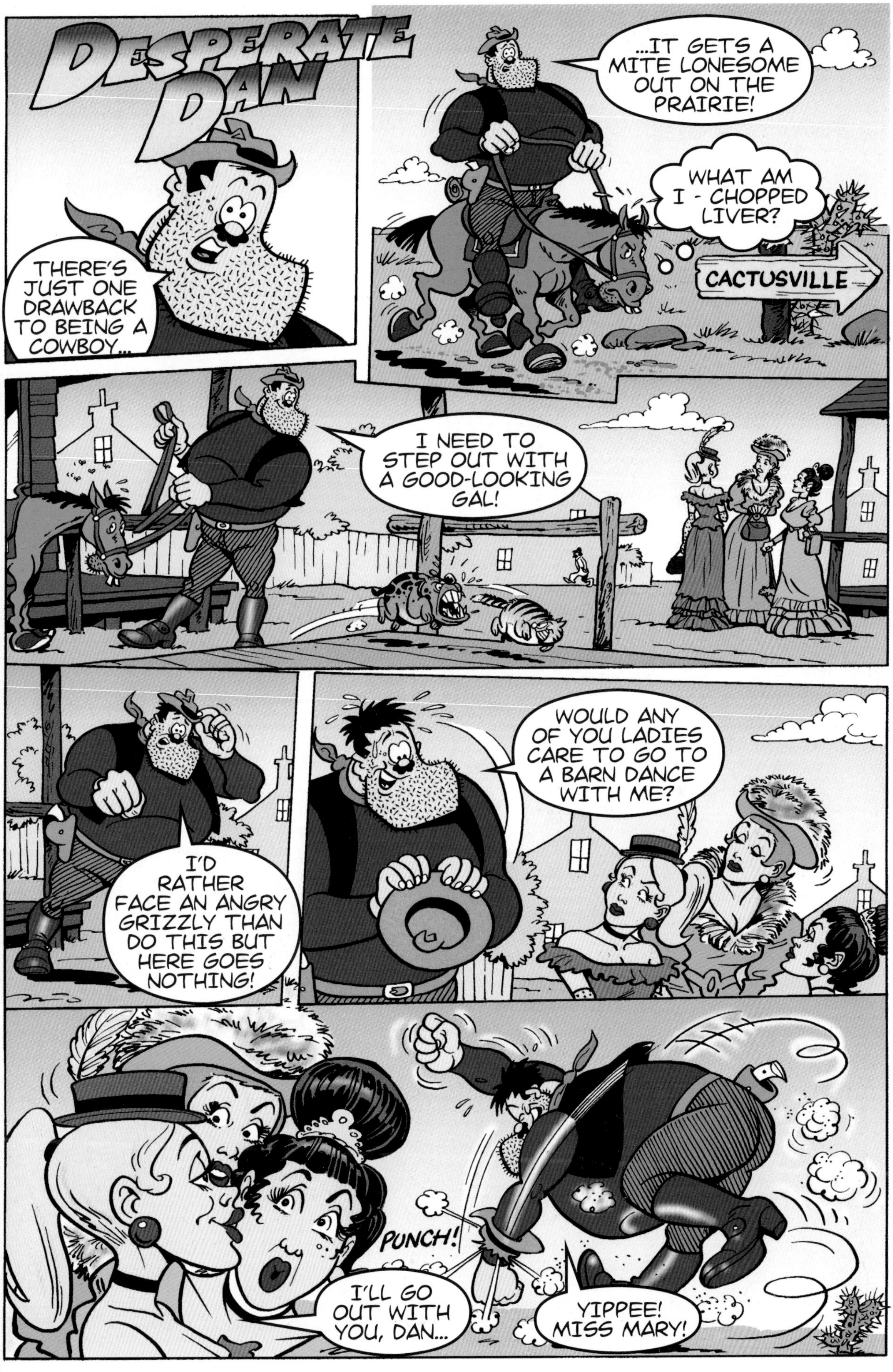
DESPERATE DAN
THERE'S JUST ONE DRAWBACK TO BEING A COWBOY...
...IT GETS A MITE LONESOME OUT ON THE PRAIRIE!
WHAT AM I - CHOPPED LIVER?
CACTUSVILLE
I NEED TO STEP OUT WITH A GOOD-LOOKING GAL!
I'D RATHER FACE AN ANGRY GRIZZLY THAN DO THIS BUT HERE GOES NOTHING!
WOULD ANY OF YOU LADIES CARE TO GO TO A BARN DANCE WITH ME?
PUNCH!
I'LL GO OUT WITH YOU, DAN...
YIPPEE! MISS MARY!

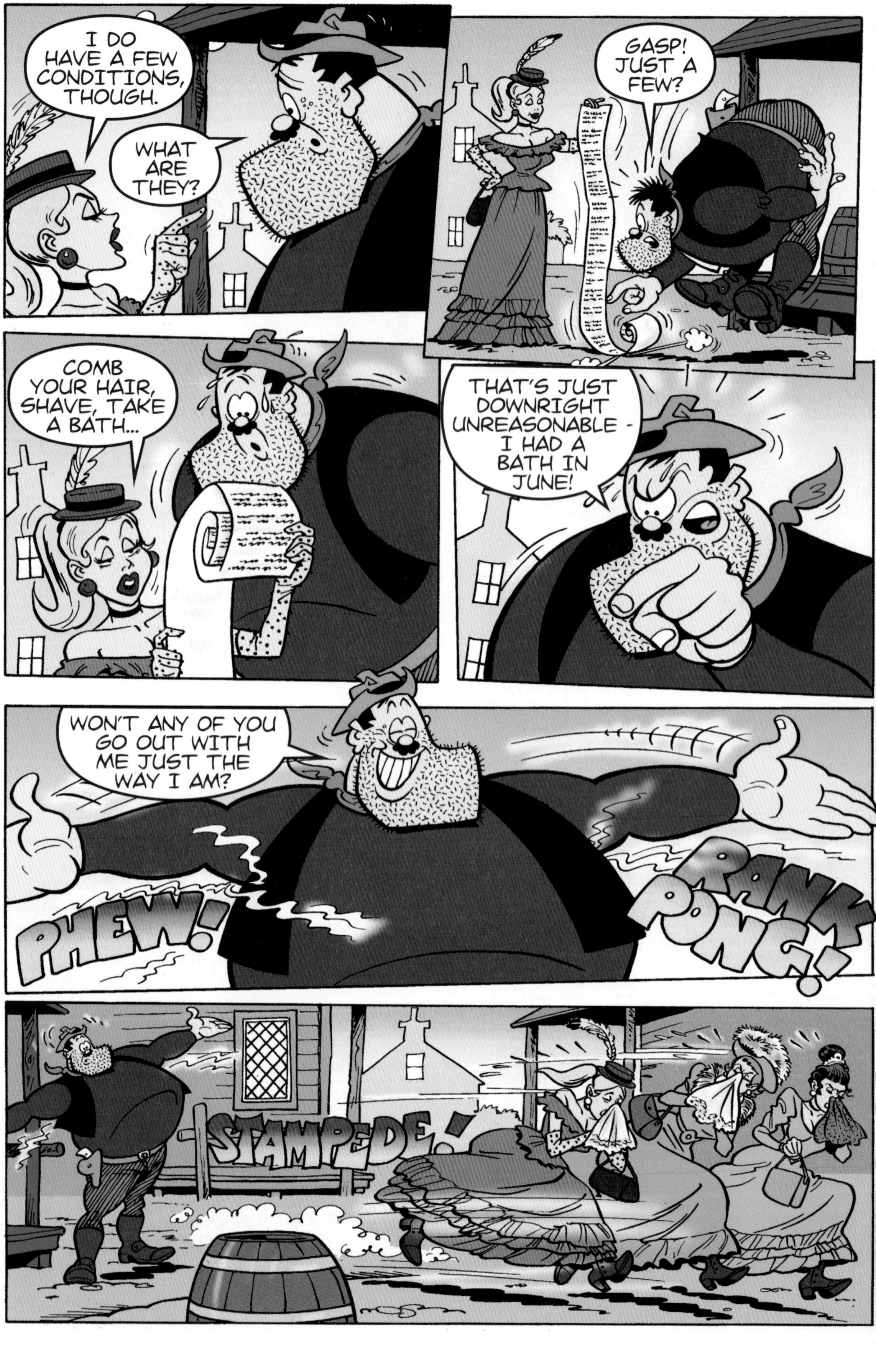
I DO HAVE A FEW CONDITIONS, THOUGH.
WHAT ARE THEY?
GASP! JUST A FEW?
COMB YOUR HAIR, SHAVE, TAKE A BATH...
THAT'S JUST DOWNRIGHT UNREASONABLE - I HAD A BATH IN JUNE!
WON'T ANY OF YOU GO OUT WITH ME JUST THE WAY I AM?
PHEW!
RANK
PONG!
STAMPEDE!

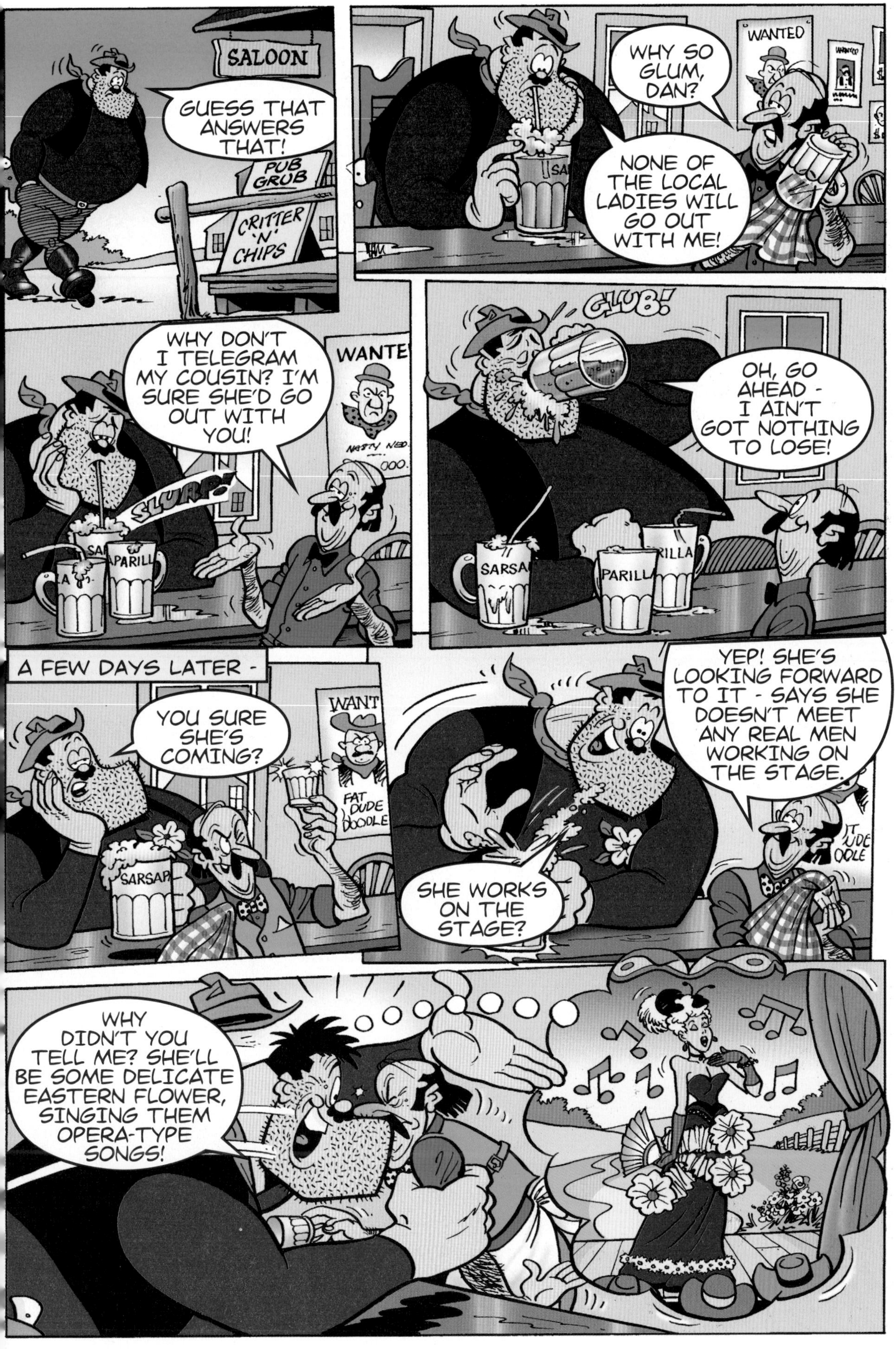
SALOON
GUESS THAT ANSWERS THAT!
PUB GRUB
CRITTER 'N' CHIPS
WANTED
WHY SO GLUM, DAN?
NONE OF THE LOCAL LADIES WILL GO OUT WITH ME!
WHY DON'T I TELEGRAM MY COUSIN? I'M SURE SHE'D GO OUT WITH YOU!
WANTE
NASTY NED
SLURP!
GLUB!
OH, GO AHEAD - I AIN'T GOT NOTHING TO LOSE!
SARSA
PARILLA
A FEW DAYS LATER -
YOU SURE SHE'S COMING?
WANT
FAT DUDE DOODLE
SARSAP
YEP! SHE'S LOOKING FORWARD TO IT - SAYS SHE DOESN'T MEET ANY REAL MEN WORKING ON THE STAGE.
SHE WORKS ON THE STAGE?
WHY DIDN'T YOU TELL ME? SHE'LL BE SOME DELICATE EASTERN FLOWER, SINGING THEM OPERA-TYPE SONGS!

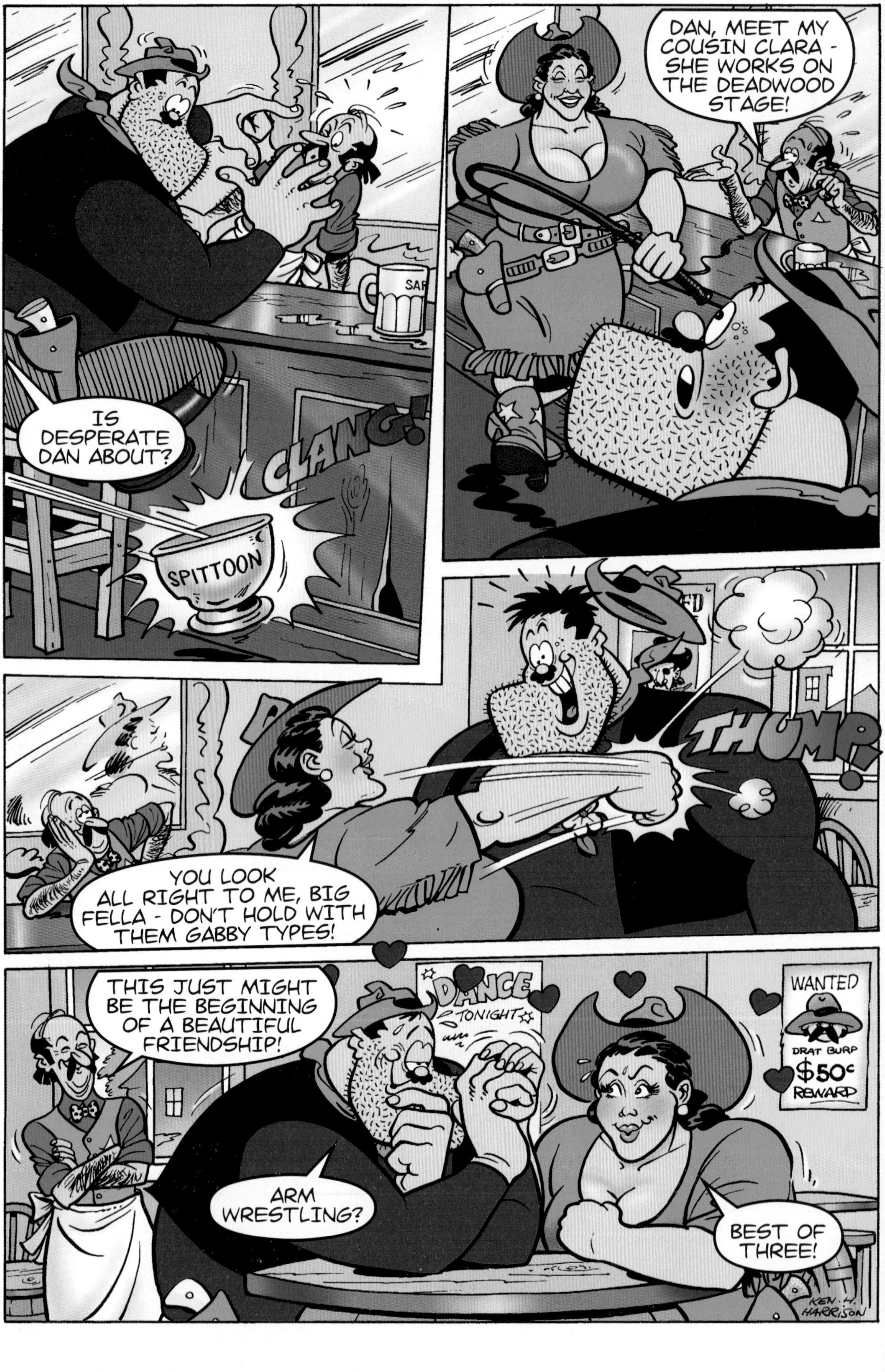
IS DESPERATE DAN ABOUT?
CLANG!
SPITTOON
SAR
DAN, MEET MY COUSIN CLARA - SHE WORKS ON THE DEADWOOD STAGE!
THUMP!
YOU LOOK ALL RIGHT TO ME, BIG FELLA - DON'T HOLD WITH THEM GABBY TYPES!
THIS JUST MIGHT BE THE BEGINNING OF A BEAUTIFUL FRIENDSHIP!
DANCE TONIGHT
WANTED
DRAT BURP
$50c
REWARD
ARM WRESTLING?
BEST OF THREE!
KEN H. HARRISON

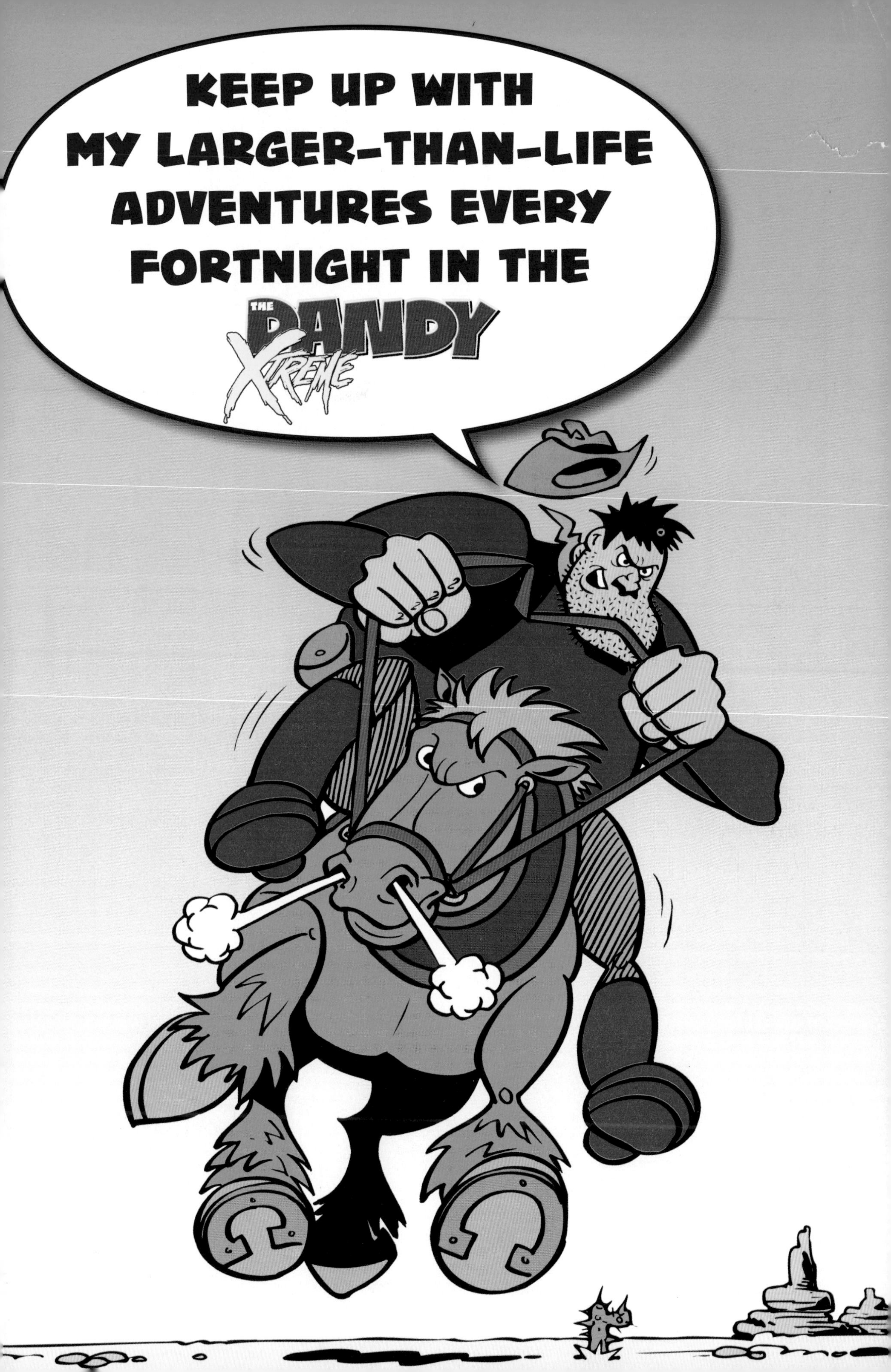
KEEP UP WITH MY LARGER-THAN-LIFE ADVENTURES EVERY FORTNIGHT IN THE
THE DANDY XTREME

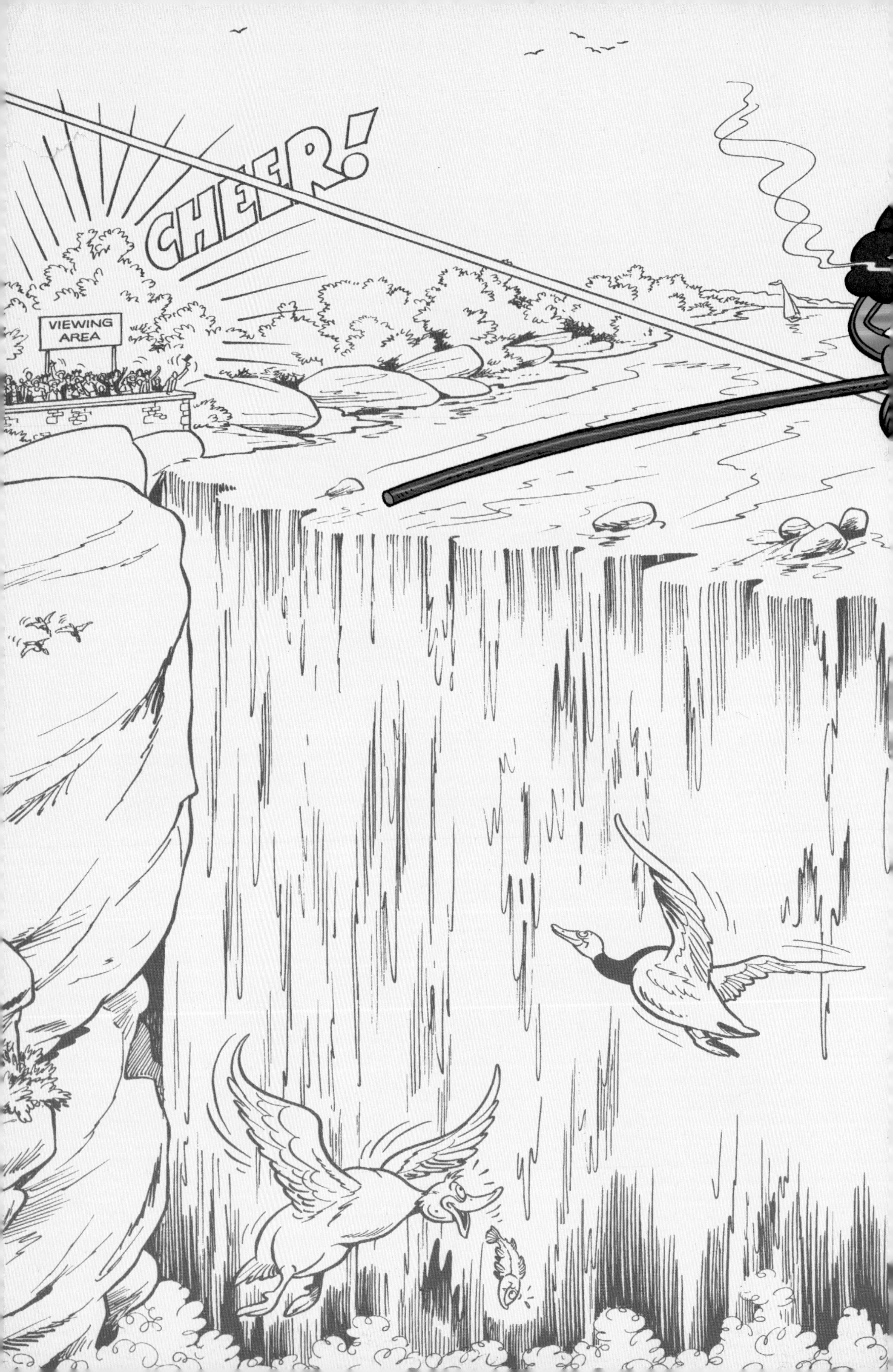
CHEER!
VIEWING AREA